Breaking Negative
Relationship Patterns

Breaking Negative Relationship Patterns

A Schema Therapy Self-help and Support Book

Bruce A. Stevens and
Eckhard Roediger

WILEY Blackwell

This edition first published 2017
© 2017 John Wiley & Sons, Ltd

Registered Office
John Wiley & Sons, Ltd, The Atrium, Southern Gate, Chichester, West Sussex, PO19 8SQ, UK

Editorial Offices
350 Main Street, Malden, MA 02148-5020, USA
9600 Garsington Road, Oxford, OX4 2DQ, UK
The Atrium, Southern Gate, Chichester, West Sussex, PO19 8SQ, UK

For details of our global editorial offices, for customer services, and for information about
how to apply for permission to reuse the copyright material in this book please see our
website at www.wiley.com/wiley-blackwell.

The right of Bruce A. Stevens and Eckhard Roediger to be identified as the authors of this
work has been asserted in accordance with the UK Copyright, Designs and Patents Act 1988.

Library of Congress Cataloging-in-Publication data applied for

ISBN Hardback: 9781119162773
ISBN Paperback: 9781119162827

A catalogue record for this book is available from the British Library.

Cover image: Design Pics/Darren Greenwood/Gettyimages

Set in 10/12.5pt Galliard by SPi Global, Pondicherry, India

10 9 8 7 6 5 4 3 2 1

For the next generation—my students and those who have attended my professional workshops.
—Bruce A. Stevens

For all people striving for a better life with the ones they love. From my personal experience, after more than 30 years I say: Yes, we can!
—Eckhard Roediger

Contents

About the Authors

Professor Bruce A. Stevens (Ph.D., Boston University, 1987) is an endorsed clinical and forensic psychologist. He occupies the Wicking Chair of Ageing and Practical Theology at Charles Sturt University, Canberra, and is director of the Centre for Ageing and Pastoral Studies in the School of Theology. He started the Canberra Clinical and Forensic Psychology practice in Canberra in the early 1990s. He is with Shayleen and he has three daughters and a son (a clinical psychologist, one completing training in clinical psychology, a nurse training as a sex therapist, and a lawyer). He has written six books, the most recent with Chiara Simone-DiFrancesco and Eckhard Roediger, *Schema Therapy with Couples: A Practitioner's Guide to Healing Relationships* (Wiley-Blackwell, 2015).

Dr. Eckhard Roediger (M.D., Frankfurt, Germany, 1986) is a neurologist, psychiatrist, and psychotherapist. He trained in psychodynamic and cognitive behavior therapy. He was the director of the psychosomatic department of a clinic in Berlin until 2007, and has since worked in private practice and as director of the Schema Therapy Training Center in Frankfurt. He has been married to Andrea for more than 27 years and is the father of three children. As well as being a schema therapy trainer and supervisor and the author or co-author of numerous German books, book chapters, and articles on schema therapy (www.schematherapie-roediger.de), he has been the secretary of the International Society of Schema Therapy (ISST) since 2008; he is currently the ISST president.

Introduction

A New Start?

Why did you start reading this book? Are you just curious about how relationships work? Are you thinking in terms of preparing yourself while you're starting a new relationship? This is probably a good idea since there are already existing marital preparation courses based on concepts like schema therapy. But maybe you're unhappy about your relationship and are looking for some ideas to improve it. These are all good reasons to be open to fresh ideas and to develop new skills in relationships.

Research indicates that 80% of those in troubled relationships tend to separate within four or five years, without external intervention. John Gottman, the world's leading relationships researcher, found this with more than 600 couples in his "Love Lab" in Seattle. Indeed, crisis brings risk, but also a chance for improvement and growth. And there are many crises over the course of any lasting relationship.

So you're not alone but in very good company! We appreciate that you're willing to do something to improve your relationship. This means paying into your relationship account. And maybe once you get started your partner will become curious and possibly involved. Improvement usually starts with the willingness of one of you. Be assured, anything you do will have some impact on your relationship. So just go ahead and start making improvements from your side. This book will give you a lot of practical advice. It doesn't explain the whole world of relationships, but it will give you an idea why you find yourself again and again in the same life-traps, and it shows you a way out. Isn't that a good point to start?

Breaking Negative Relationship Patterns: A Schema Therapy Self-help and Support Book, First Edition. Bruce A. Stevens and Eckhard Roediger.
© 2017 John Wiley & Sons, Ltd. Published 2017 by John Wiley & Sons, Ltd.

Introductions

Allow us, the authors of this book, to introduce ourselves (since you're trusting us by reading our book). Bruce Stevens is a clinical psychologist who has specialized in couples therapy for over 25 years. He's a research professor at an Australian university. Eckhard Roediger is a neurologist, psychiatrist, and psychotherapist with two decades of clinical experience. He's the current president of the ISST, the International Society of Schema Therapists. Both of us are advanced trainers in schema therapy and established authors.

Candidate Therapies?

If you were in a supermarket of various therapies, what would you take to the checkout? You would want the therapy you choose to make a profound difference, so it should meet the following criteria:

1. *Explain.* The therapy will need to explain why we do what we do (including our thoughts, feelings, and behavior). A good therapy will point to the underlying causes of psychological problems.
2. *Childhood origins.* It will find the childhood origins of adult difficulties. These are the experiences that have taught us to behave in certain ways.
3. *Proven effective.* Therapists working from this perspective will potentially work more effectively. This will be proven by evidence from gold-standard clinical trials.
4. *Practical.* Such a therapy must have principles that are easy to put into practice. Interventions need to make sense, "feel relevant," and, most importantly, be able to effect change.
5. *Range of effectiveness.* Ideally, this therapy will be able to deal with issues that are simple and straightforward, but also make a difference to the most chronic and difficult of personal problems. It will have been road-tested with the personality disordered, who present the greatest challenge for therapists.
6. *Integration.* This therapy should be integrative and draw on what works from other therapies, such as mindfulness techniques, which are now widely popular.

A big ask? You might be surprised that any among the hundreds of psychological and relational therapies could meet such criteria. Happily, there's good news. Potentially, three therapies could qualify. The best evidence of effectiveness with couples is from *emotionally focused therapy for couples.* This works well for most couple issues, but wasn't designed to address difficult character problems. However, two therapies have a proven record of effectiveness with the most entrenched and difficult of personal problems. They are *schema therapy* and *dialectical behavior therapy*, but proof of effectiveness has been mostly with individuals. Besides that, John Gottman and David Schnarch are two authors who have influenced us. We have adapted schema therapy to helping couples.

We're two of the three authors who wrote the first schema therapy book on couple relationships to guide therapists. *Breaking Negative Relationship Patterns* is the first schema therapy self-help book for couples.

It's up to You

You probably want everything that this book has to offer. In that case, you'll have to engage with the exercises. It's not enough to skim-read the text, hope that a few principles will sink in and then leave the book on the shelf. You must become practically involved in the many different kinds of exercises for reflection, experience, and behavioral change. There are 90+ exercises. Choose what interests you. Some are demanding and even complex, but all are useful for getting the most out of this book. Some are adaptations of interventions routinely used by therapists who do schema therapy.

The exercises in this book generally fall into three categories:

1. *Reflection.* You'll be encouraged to use a journal as you read this book. This can be a locked file on a computer. Start this with a story of your life. Think of it as a psychological autobiography. You can do writing in association with visualization and changing life scripts in later chapters.
2. *Experiential exercises.* The focus will be on trying to experience something in a different way. For example, *Stuart* wanted to decide whether to become a volunteer to serve overseas. He had a journal and wrote from a place of "indecision," and then later wrote a response. He also imaginatively wrote what his deceased father might say. While this may seem artificial, it was helpful to take different perspectives, clarify the issues he faced, and try to understand what was best for him.
3. *Behavior change.* You'll be encouraged to try different activities. Think of these as scientific experiments. You may be asked to predict the outcome; for example, "My spouse will become angry and put me down

if I ask for what I need." This is rated in percentage terms (such as "95% likely") and later compared with what really happened. And then you might reflect on the meaning and implication for your deeply held beliefs. This will eventually lead to behavior pattern breaking, which is described later in the book. But even if you don't fully carry out what you had intended, it's still a successful experiment if you manage to break through your avoidance of the issue.

All the exercises are "self-help". Initially, you'll be the focus, not your partner. Usually, we prefer that our partner change first, but the greatest impact we have is on ourselves. This will enable you to make some immediate changes. You might feel better about yourself—which is a good place to begin what may be a long journey. And if you change your behavior that will have an impact on your partner.

But there's a bitter pill right from the start: We don't support the idea that your partner is in charge of soothing your wounds. If you don't accept yourself, it's not likely that anybody else will like you, either. Self-acceptance and self-compassion cannot be delegated to somebody else, perhaps by saying: "I hate me, but if you like me I feel better!" As in the approach of David Schnarch, our model is based on the idea of strengthening what we call the "Healthy Adult" mode within ourselves. This makes us more independent from our partners and gives each partner room to move and to grow. Healthy relationships are built on two healthy adults and not on dependency of any kind, no matter how good it might feel in the beginning. What starts as a romance might end up as a prison. This book can help you to better take care of yourself as the basis for a flourishing relationship.

To do: Are you prepared to make a contract with yourself? We suggest making a commitment to work on a practical exercise of your choice, as suggested in this book, each day for the next 90 days. We know we're asking a lot, but that commitment will honor the importance of your relationship (actually, your happiness) and make sure that you'll make substantial progress.

A healthy and well-balanced intimate relationship is based on two people being emotionally grounded and balanced in themselves. Love songs usually say something different, like "I can't live without you" or "I'll die for you." Both are a bit too much of a good thing, because needing your partner for your emotional balance and promising too much will both burden your relationship. You can *lean* in a relationship at times, but not always. To mention an important message from the very beginning: It is essential to balance your attachment need with a good deal of autonomy and assertiveness. Standing on two legs provides a good balance in a relationship. Leaning too much on the attachment leg might feel good in the beginning, but over the course of time will probably lead to enmeshment and result in a boring relationship. Especially in the sexual sphere. Usually, autonomy and some secrets make partners more attractive, while knowing "everything" about each other tends to blunt sexual attraction. So a good balance between your autonomy and assertiveness legs is what will lead to a healthy relationship. You're standing better on two legs!

There's nothing to stop you doing the exercises in this book on your own, but it's even better if your partner gets involved as well. But even if your partner isn't interested right now, we predict that the changes that you can bring to your relationship will make a difference, maybe interest your partner and even transform the relationship. Dare to hope!

Reflect: There are options to deeply engage with the material on a first or later reading, but naturally you should select what you think will be most helpful. If you become distressed at any point doing an exercise, *please stop immediately.* If you lack a sense of emotional safety, don't resume the exercise, and use caution with any later exercises.

Warning: If you and your partner have chronic relationship problems and are not currently seeing a relationship therapist together, then we advise you to take that important step. Some difficulties are hard to resolve—so better get some help! See a mental health professional, preferably someone informed about schema therapy. But don't forget to use the book as well.

Exercise: Imagine that family and friends have gathered for your 80th birthday. Think about: What place will you eventually live in? Who will be with you? Who will visit you? What would you like to hear from them? What would you like recognized about how you have lived your life? What small changes, beginning now, could possibly lead to a full and satisfying life? What would you regret in the distant future—say, at your 80th birthday—if you do not make some changes now? Write about this in your journal. This exercise can bring you in touch with your core values and gives you a compass for making your way through your life.

Reading and engaging with the concepts of schema therapy in this book may be the first step to making what you can now only imagine to be a lasting reality.

Option: You might consider a skim-read of this book to get an overview. Or begin with a look at Heathy Adult mode. That is fine, but don't leave it there or you'll get very little of lasting benefit.

Have you made a contract with yourself? Why not write it out, sign, and date it! Will your romantic partner also sign? Our part of the deal has been to find or create exercises that will work for you. Hold us to it.

An Overview

There's an overall plan in this book about how we introduce schema therapy and apply it to couple relationships. The initial focus is on the *schemas* that are unique to this therapy. This will give you a developmental perspective on couple problems, and it's natural to focus on your psychological history. Then we introduce the idea of *modes*, which is how schema therapy is currently practiced. The steps to dealing with dysfunctional modes are *being mode aware*, then *mode management*, and finally *mode change*. This is followed by a chapter on strengthening the Healthy Adult mode. The specific topics of couple communication and affairs are raised, and we don't avoid writing a bit on sexual relationships, too. Finally, the topic of emotional learning is more fully explored.

To Read Further

- For the pattern of mode aware, mode management, and mode change see the group schema therapy (Farrell, Reiss, and Shaw, 2014).
- John Gottman has written many books, but his book with Silver (1999), *The Seven Principles for Making a Marriage Work*, is the easiest to read.
- Gitta Jacob and her colleagues (2015) have written a schema therapy self-help book for individuals, which we highly recommend.
- For emotionally focused therapy for couples see Susan Johnson (2004).
- David Schnarch has written *Passionate Marriage* (1998) and *Intimacy and Desire* (2009).
- Behavioral pattern breaking is described by van Vreeswijk, Broersen, Bloo, and Haeyen (2012).
- Jeffrey Young's original self-help book, *Reinventing Your Life*, is still helpful but a bit dated; it's based on the schema model but didn't include the newer concept of modes (Young and Klosko, 1993).
- We contributed to the first book to guide therapists in applying schema therapy to couples (DiFrancesco, Roediger, and Stevens, 2015).

References

DiFrancesco, C., Roediger, E., & Stevens, B. (2015). *Schema therapy for couples: A practitioner's guide to healing relationships*. Malden, MA: Wiley-Blackwell.

Farrell, J., Reiss, N., & Shaw, I. (2014). *The schema therapy clinician's guide: A complete resource for building and delivering individual, group and integrated schema mode treatment programs*. Malden, MA: Wiley-Blackwell.

Gottman, J., & Silver, N. (1999). *The seven principles for making a marriage work.* New York, NY: Three Rivers Press.

Jacob, G., van Genderen, H., & Seebauer, L. (2015). *Breaking negative thought patterns: A schema therapy self-help and support book.* Malden, MA: Wiley-Blackwell.

Johnson, S. M. (2004). *The practice of emotionally focused couple therapy: Creating connection* (2nd ed.). New York, NY: Brunner-Routledge.

Schnarch, D. (1998). *Passionate marriage: Keeping love and intimacy alive in committed relationships.* New York, NY: Owl.

Schnarch, D. (2009). *Intimacy and desire—awaken the passion in your relationship.* New York, NY: Beaufort Books.

van Vreeswijk, M., Broersen, J., Bloo, J., & Haeyen, S. (2012). Techniques within schema therapy. In M. van Vreeswijk, J. Broersen, & M. Nadort (Eds.), *The Wiley-Blackwell handbook of schema therapy: Theory, research and practice* (pp. 186–195). Oxford, UK: Wiley-Blackwell.

Young, J. E., & Klosko, J. S. (1993). *Reinventing your life.* New York, NY: Plume.

1

Schema Therapy
Toward a Science of Relationships

There are many "flat earth" theories of relationships. They're limited and prescientific, and what doesn't fit falls off the edge!

Think about how the various approaches are classified. Ask what is the focus—and what is ignored. This selective mapping is characteristic of almost all therapies: One may closely follow thoughts and forget about feelings, while for another the goal is opening up the emotional depths, and a few put behavior under the spotlight. But, speaking generally, the most important reality-that-doesn't-fit is the influence of personality disorder on intimate relationships.

Personality Disorder

Ask any experienced therapist what is the greatest challenge in helping a couple and you'll soon hear about problems in personality. Usually, this dimension is central to volatile relationships and disordered thinking. This includes the emotional instability of the borderline, the withdrawal of the schizoid, the self-focus of the narcissist, and the "moral insanity" of the psychopath. In this book, we keep returning to the "hard cases" because such challenges will always make or break committed relationships.

Character problems usually last a lifetime. This is another way of describing personality disorder, with the result that relationship difficulties are inevitable:

> *Larry* was a spendthrift. He was very impulsive, and soon there was conflict with Amanda, his wife. She attended church and wanted to give regularly. But, as she expressed it, "Larry buys things without any thought for our commitments. Bills are left unpaid. This is not a responsible way to live."

Breaking Negative Relationship Patterns: A Schema Therapy Self-help and Support Book, First Edition. Bruce A. Stevens and Eckhard Roediger.
© 2017 John Wiley & Sons, Ltd. Published 2017 by John Wiley & Sons, Ltd.

The novels of Jane Austen are helpful in thinking about the importance of character. Look at any of her popular books, such as *Pride and Prejudice*, *Sense and Sensibility*, or *Mansfield Park*. Romance, yes, but it's soon tested by character.

Reflect: Think for a moment about a previous romantic relationship that failed. Make a list of the problem areas. Tick any item that describes a lack of character. Are you reminded of Mr. Willoughby or Colonel Brandon in *Sense and Sensibility?*

Also: Watch a film based on a novel by Jane Austen and discuss the role of character with a friend. How does lack of character result in unhappiness in their relationships? Follow this carefully: It's true in Austen's novels but also in life.

Theoretical note: You may find it puzzling that we begin this book with such an emphasis on the dynamics of personality. The reality is that personality problems are usually ignored in self-help literature. But unless you become aware of your personality traits, understand them as reactions to childhood experiences, and start working on them, they will influence and undermine all your attempts to improve your relationship. It's like building sand castles: They might look nice for a moment, but the tide will wash them away and you'll find yourself repetitively in the same life-trap. So first start working with what is most enduring about your own personality.

Research indicates that features of personality disorder are very common in the general population. Only 23% of people are relatively free of them. Indeed, over 70% have some degree of personality disturbance. This is why it's essential to take dysfunctional aspects of personality into any comprehensive theory of change. And it also explains why a "strong" therapy, such as schema therapy, is so necessary—and why this book is potentially so different.

First, we outline schema therapy and its clinical perspective with schemas, and then we look at the legacy we all carry from childhood. We then look at the complexity of couple dynamics seen in modes and suggest powerful ways to change entrenched patterns of dysfunction. Finally, we look more deeply at emotional learning.

Schema Therapy: Mapping the Bad Lands

Schema therapy offers a comprehensive map. The central idea is to identify how we're vulnerable to patterns (schemas) created in childhood and adolescence. Schema therapy doesn't just describe but provides a powerful therapy leading to lasting change—even with the most unstable and difficult of problems. Schema therapy deals with problems largely ignored by mainstream cognitive therapy: the processing of troublesome memories, difficulties coming from childhood, uncontrolled emotional reactions, and recurrent problems in intimate relationships. Indeed, it combines the depth and developmental theory of longer-term treatments with the active, change-oriented approach of short-term therapies.

When you learn to recognize your reactions and understand their origins, things will begin to make sense. This is a good starting point for self-compassion and self-acceptance. And you can share this understanding with your partner, too! Better yet, you'll find in schema therapy practical tools that can intercept habitually negative interactions and open the door to new ways of relating. Few therapies can offer schema therapy's proven potential for change.

Theoretical note: Where does schema therapy fit? In what part of the therapy "library" is this book? Schema therapy grew out of cognitive therapy. The cognitive approaches, with a focus on thoughts, have the advantage of conceptual clarity and ease of understanding. Aaron Beck initiated the "cognitive revolution" and developed the extensively researched cognitive behavioral therapy for the treatment of depression. This approach was then applied to the whole range of psychological disorders. While cognitive behavior therapy proved effective with a range of human problems, it wasn't as helpful with the personality disordered. This recognition of its limits led to the development of "stronger" therapies, including schema therapy.

Schema therapy is highly integrative. Indeed, Young outlined parallels and differences with major therapies, including Beck's "reformulated" model, psychoanalytic theory, Bowlby's attachment theory (especially internal working models), and emotion-focused therapy. There has also been an influence from gestalt, transactional analysis, and psychodrama. Schema therapy, in contrast to most cognitive therapies, has a greater emotional focus and willingness to explore the childhood and adolescent origins of psychological problems. There's a shift from current problems to whole-of-life patterns. Additionally, there are a breadth, applicability, and ease of understanding that encourage a broader application. While dialectical behavior therapy was developed to treat borderline personality disorder, schema therapy works with almost all kinds of personality disorders.

Schemas in Focus

While Beck referred to schemas, he used the term to describe clusters of negative beliefs. Jesse Wright noted that people typically have a mix of different kinds of schemas, including those that are positive and adaptive.

Even people with severe symptoms or profound despair have adaptive schemas that can help them cope.

Jeffrey Young thought that dysfunctional schemas develop as a result of toxic childhood experiences. They reflect the emotional wounds lasting from unfulfilled but important needs of the child and are a way of coping with negative experiences, such as family quarrels, rejection, hostility, or aggression from parents, teachers, or peers, as well as inadequate parental care and support.

Reflect: Can you identify a negative childhood experience? How did you cope at that time? Do you think that this has influenced how you react to similar stresses today?

Schemas reveal underlying assumptions. This is more than negative thoughts ("Things will never work out well"). It's more than rules ("Don't get angry with your father"). At the schema level, core beliefs are unconditional ("I am worthless"). Schemas are like short video clips storing complex memories, including intense emotions and bodily reactions. They affect the whole person. Once they're activated, you travel back through a time tunnel and find yourself in the old life-traps of your childhood. You look at your current world through childlike glasses.

Schemas are the basis of how we see ourselves and others. They're also foundational to how we act. Schemas are a meeting point of thoughts, emotions, attitudes, and behavioral tendencies, all of which may have different neural pathways in the brain but which meet in a schema when activated.

Young identified a comprehensive set of early maladaptive schemas, defined as "self-defeating emotional and cognitive patterns that begin early in our development and repeat throughout life." They provide a blueprint for styles of thinking, emotional responses, and characteristic behavioral tendencies in the child's and later the adult's world. A more severe schema can be distinguished by how readily it's activated, its high emotional intensity, and lasting distress. While there may have been survival benefits in childhood and perhaps it was the best or only possible solution at the time, by adulthood schemas tend to be inaccurate, maladaptive, and limiting. They become strongly held, often outside conscious awareness. Repeated negative experiences lead to schema coping being more "worn and rigid."

Amanda was often left by her single mother on her own in their apartment. She was always frightened as a child. She has tended to be clingy in relationships, and no reassurance from romantic partners is ever enough. So, sooner or later, they all left her and she finds herself alone again.

If a current situation is similar to a defining childhood experience, it triggers or *activates* a schema in the present. This idea of schema activation is fundamental to understanding Young's contribution and the development of a therapy based on modes (which are activated schemas). If a schema is activated, the past intrudes into our present awareness.

> *Sally* has nagging worries about her weight. She went to a fashion show and reacted to the stick-thin models. She said to her friend that she felt "bloated, like a beached whale" and was determined to go on another fad diet. Ken, her husband, was exasperated by what he called her "diet merry-go-round."

In this case, an event (going to the fashion show) triggered an emotional reaction in Sally. She was flooded by feelings of being defective. This also led to a somewhat questionable plan of action. This is an example of schema activation and automatic coping.

Reflect: It's important to grasp the idea of activation. A schema can be compared to a landmine. If there's a tendency toward suspicion from a schema, then with activation distrust becomes overwhelming. It's as if someone stood on the landmine, which exploded. This is why many problems only emerge in a relationship: As long as the mine is buried in the sand and no one steps on it, you're not aware of the problem. But once you have one ...

Identifying and Understanding Schemas

The following list of individual schemas has been revised over the past two decades. We have also included brief summaries, which are drawn largely from Young and Arntz. The schemas are grouped in five categories (called "domains"): disconnection and rejection; impaired autonomy and performance; impaired limits; other-directedness; and over-vigilance and inhibition.

First domain: Disconnection and rejection

This domain shows attachment difficulties. There's a link between a lack of safety and reliability in interpersonal relationships. An individual who scores highly on these schemas cannot rely on others. What is missing is any expectation of reliability, support, empathy, and respect. He[1] may come from a family in which he was treated in a cold, rejecting manner. Emotional support may have been lacking, perhaps even basic care in extreme cases. Caregivers were unpredictable, uninterested, or abusive.

1. **Abandonment (instability):** She expects to lose those with whom she has an emotional attachment. Important others are seen as unreliable and unpredictable in their ability or willingness to offer nurturing. All intimate relationships will eventually end. She believes that her partner will leave or die.
2. **Mistrust-Abuse:** He's convinced that others will eventually take advantage of him, in one way or another. What he expects is hurt, being cheated on, manipulation, or humiliation.
3. **Emotional Deprivation:** She believes that others won't meet her primary needs adequately, or perhaps at all. This includes her physical needs and her need for empathy, affection, protection, companionship, and emotional care. The most common kinds of feared deprivation are of nurturance, empathy, and protection.
4. **Defectiveness-Shame:** He feels incomplete and bad. As others get to know him better, his defects will be discovered. Then they will want nothing to do with him. No one will find him worthy of love. He's overconcerned with the judgment of others. A sense of shame is always present.
5. **Social Isolation (alienation):** She has the feeling that she's isolated from the rest of the world, is different from others, and doesn't fit in anywhere.

Second domain: Impaired autonomy and performance

This individual believes that he's incapable of functioning and performing independently. He may come from a clinging family, from which he couldn't break free. He was overprotected, he lacked support, or he was repeatedly discouraged.

6. **Dependence-Incompetence:** She's not capable of taking on normal responsibilities and cannot function independently. She feels dependent on others in a variety of situations. She may lack confidence to make decisions on simple problems or to attempt anything new. The feeling is one of complete helplessness.
7. **Vulnerability (to harm or illness):** He's convinced that at any moment something terrible might happen and there's no protection. Both medical and psychological catastrophes are feared. He takes extraordinary precautions.
8. **Enmeshment (undeveloped self):** She's overinvolved with one or more of her caregivers. Because of this fused relationship, she's unable to develop her own identity. At times, she has the idea that she cannot exist without the other person. She may feel empty and without goals.

9. **Failure (to achieve):** He's convinced that he's not capable of performing at the same level as his peers in his career, education, sport, or whatever he values. He feels stupid, foolish, ignorant, and talentless. He doesn't even attempt to succeed because of an abiding conviction that it will lead to nothing.

Third domain: Impaired limits

This individual has inadequate boundaries, a lack of a sense of responsibility, and poor tolerance of frustration. She's not good at setting realistic long-range goals and has difficulty working with others. Perhaps she came from a family that offered little direction or gave her the feeling of being superior to the rest of the world.

10. **Entitlement-Grandiosity:** He thinks that he's superior to others and has special rights. There's no need for him to follow the normal social rules or meet the normal expectations of society. He can get away with what he wants without taking others into consideration. The main theme here is power and control over situations and individuals. Rarely is there any empathy.

11. **Insufficient Self-control (or self-discipline):** She cannot tolerate any frustration in achieving her goals and gives up quickly. She has little capacity to suppress feelings or impulses. It's possible that she's attempting to avoid being uncomfortable in any way.

Fourth domain: Other-directedness

This individual always takes the needs of others into consideration and represses his needs. He does so in order to receive love and approval. His family background is often one of conditional love. The needs and status of the parents took priority over what was important to the child.

12. **Subjugation:** She gives herself over to the will of others to avoid negative consequences. This can include denying most of her emotional needs. She thinks that her desires, opinions, and feelings won't be important to others. This often leads to pent-up rage, which is then expressed inadequately through passive-aggressive or psychosomatic symptoms.

13. **Self-sacrifice:** He voluntarily and regularly sacrifices his needs for others whom he views as weaker. If he does act to meet his personal needs, he's likely to feel guilty. Being oversensitive to the pain of others is part of the presentation. In the long term, he may feel some resentment towards those for whom he has cared and sacrificed.

14. **Approval Seeking (recognition seeking):** She searches for approval, appreciation, acknowledgment, or admiration. This is at the cost of her personal needs. Sometimes this results in an excessive desire for status, beauty, and social approval.

Fifth domain: Over-vigilance and inhibition

At the cost of self-expression and self-care, the individual suppresses his spontaneous feelings and needs and follows his own strict set of rules and values. It's likely that his family stressed achievement, perfection, and the repression of emotions. Caregivers were critical, pessimistic, and moralistic, while at the same time expecting an unreasonably high standard of achievement.

15. **Negativity-Pessimism:** She always sees the negative side of things while ignoring the positive. Eventually, everything will go wrong even if it's currently going well. She may be constantly worried and hyper-alert. She often complains and doesn't dare to make decisions.

16. **Emotional Inhibition:** He holds tight control over his emotions and impulses, as he thinks that expressing them will damage others and lead to feelings of shame, abandonment, or loss of self-worth. This leads him to avoid spontaneous expressions of emotions such as anger, sadness, and joy. It also involves avoiding conflict. Often, he'll present as very detached and overly rational.

17. **Unrelenting Standards (hypercriticalness):** She believes that she'll never be good enough and must try harder. She'll try to satisfy unusually high personal standards to avoid criticism. She's critical of herself as well as those around her. This results in perfectionism, rigid rules, and sometimes a preoccupation with time and efficiency. She does this at the cost of enjoying herself, relaxing, and maintaining social contacts.

18. **Punitiveness:** He feels that individuals must be severely punished for their mistakes. He's aggressive, intolerant, and impatient. There's no forgiveness for mistakes. Individual circumstances or feelings are not taken into account.

Social Undesirability, a 19th schema, has been suggested, but only the 18 listed are currently assessed by the *Young Schema Questionnaire, version 3* (YSQ-3), which is used to assess the most relevant schemas for treatment.

Maladaptive schemas hinder people from recognizing, experiencing, and fulfilling their own needs.

To do: Fill out the YSQ-3 (see www.schematherapy.com). It's a very useful short form for identifying characteristic thought patterns associated with the various schemas, but tends to neglect factors such as emotions, physiology, behavior, and motivation. Note the three or four items that you score most highly on.

You will have to buy the YSQ-3 short form, as it is copyrighted. However, you can also add a 1 to 6 score to the schemas listed above for a rough overview or fill out the 11 listings in Young's book, *Reinventing Your Life.*

Think about schemas as areas of emotional learning. They're the deeply entrenched assumptions we have about ourselves and life in general. Understanding schemas will help you understand what is happening in your life. Domains 1 to 3 contain *unconditional* or *core* schemas. They represent the direct impact on the child and the child's emotional reactions. Domains 4 and 5 contain conditional or compensatory schema coping responses that are reactions to schemas in the first two domains. For example, you can sacrifice yourself (#13), preventing Emotional Deprivation (#3), or develop Unrelenting Standards (#17), saving you from Failure (#9). Or you might develop a Negativity-Pessimism schema (#15), preventing Vulnerability (#7).

Reflect: Use the list of schemas to identify those that might be operating for Nancy, Monte, Barbie, and Brett, who all have personal problems:

Nancy was abused in childhood. She has profound difficulties with trust. She has met someone and is strongly attracted to him, but she's very jealous. She thinks he'll leave her for a "more attractive option."

Monte is very self-important. He was recruited by a merchant bank straight out of college and it has gone to his head. He looks down on his less successful friends.

Barbie is too anxious to leave home, even though she's in her late thirties. She says, "I have to look after my mother. She needs me. Oh, I know she's in good health, but I'm a good daughter and need to be around the place."

Brett is excessively hard on his teenage sons. They complain about his put-downs and how he embarrasses them in front of their friends. Brett's oldest son has recently started talking to a counselor at school, who thinks that this treatment is "abusive."

Reflect: Another way of thinking about schemas is to consider them as ghosts that will haunt you and your relationships.

We see the following schemas in the examples:

Nancy has Mistrust-Abuse and Defectiveness-Shame schemas. She's not able to trust in her new relationship because of previous experiences.

Monte has an Entitlement-Grandiosity schema. He has to be important and be constantly recognized for his achievements. He looks at his job as proof of his superiority as a person.

Barbie has Enmeshment and Self-sacrifice schemas operating in her relationship with her mother.

Brett has Punitiveness and possibly Unrelenting Standards schemas.

It's easy to see how such patterns will undermine your stability and life satisfaction. They form traits of your personality. Their potential influence on your relationships is obvious.

Reflect: Think about the list of schemas and try to identify any that seem familiar to you. Ask your partner or members of your family. With your partner, play a game of "spot the schema" with a few TV shows or movies (this helps to familiarize you with the schemas).

Responses to Schemas

Young also looked at patterns of response to schema vulnerability, including surrender, avoidance, and compensation.

Susan came from a dysfunctional family. Her mother was an alcoholic who neglected all the children when intoxicated, which was most of the time. She never knew her father, and an older brother was a drug addict. She was date-raped when she was 17. Understandably, she has a Mistrust-Abuse schema that she responds to in different ways. At times, she withdraws from men, suspecting even the most innocent of malicious intent. Recently, she began dating a man she met at a prison fellowship meeting, who was recently paroled from prison for violent offences. She also smokes cannabis.

Susan illustrates all three of the potential reactions to Mistrust-Abuse schema activation: *avoidance* when she resorts to substances; *compensation* when she becomes oversuspicious and mistrusting; *surrender* when she considers having an intimate relationship with a very risky man and possibly being abused again. So the core of the schema is being abused, and mistrust is already a kind of compensation preventing her from being abused.

The reactions to schemas are also called *coping styles*. In summary, coping styles include surrender, avoidance, and compensation.

Surrender   A person gives in to the schema. This includes:

Behavior: He repeats behavioral patterns from childhood by looking for people and situations that are similar to those that led to the formation of the schema.

Thoughts: She processes information selectively, seeing only what confirms the schema and not what counters it.

Feelings: She directly experiences the emotional pain of the schema.

Avoidance   He avoids activities that trigger the schema and emotional reactions. The result is that the schema is not engaged. He has no access to the schema to change or revise it.

Behavior: She actively and passively avoids all kinds of situations that might trigger the schema.

Thoughts: He can deny traumatic events or memories. He can use psychological defenses, such as emotional detachment.

Feelings: She can smooth over feelings or escape into numbness.

Compensation   A person goes in the opposite direction to the schema. This results in underestimating the strength or influence of the schema. Aggressively independent behavior is often a give-away of this coping style.

Behavior: He acts in a way that is opposite to the schema.

Thoughts: Her thoughts are opposite to the content of the schema. She denies the schema.

Feelings: He feels uncomfortable with feelings associated with the schema. The feelings may return if the compensation fails.

Consider the following example:

> *Vince* had an Emotional Deprivation schema. There was never enough love for him, so he started compensating with dating. But he tended to lose interest in women after the first date because he did not find what he was really looking for. Finally, he ended up surrendering to his schema by mixing up sex with love. He felt guilty about such promiscuity: "I don't feel I have a choice. I feel empty all the time." At times, Vince would also watch internet porn as a way of avoidance in a self-soothing way, although mostly he was surrendering to the quick fix of Emotional Deprivation.

Minny had a very strong Self-sacrifice schema, which was rewarded in her employment as a nurse. However, she would find herself resentful about the excessive demands of supervisors, as a form of compensation. At times, she would surrender to Self-sacrifice, but at other times she avoided her negative feelings through excessive exercise at the gym. Hers was a mixed response.

Reflect: Think about the following and try to identify operating schemas and styles of schema coping:

Claire would often text her husband at work, "just to keep in touch." She was highly anxious if he was called away to work commitments, and would try to distract herself with online gambling and impulse shopping. She also felt she was inadequate and undeserving of anyone's love.

Hint: For Claire there's a possible Abandonment schema, but look at the various ways she tries to cope. Can you identify other schemas perhaps indicated by her being hard on herself? List how she tries to cope.

Coping styles are not always stable but change over time depending on the situation. Try to look at coping styles from a longitudinal perspective and see the pattern in relation to possible schemas.

Reflect: Can you think of figures from pop culture who might exhibit schemas? Look through a popular magazine or newspaper and discuss this with a friend.

Challenge of schema attunement

Think for a moment about any schemas in the list that might feel very familiar to you. Can you identify your own schemas? This will relate to intense emotional reactions or "hot beliefs" about yourself. What schemas are probably operating in your partner? Is there a chance that you can check the schema listing together with your partner, finding out what schemas you both have?

Reflect: Think about a recent time when you felt strongly. Intense feelings indicate that a schema has been triggered, especially when your reaction is stronger compared to others in the same situation. What did you feel? Think? How did you behave? Did this indicate attitudes you have about yourself?

To do: Do a schema identification exercise: Move to a quiet place, calm down, close your eyes, and start a journey through the events of the past days. Let the images pass by in front of your closed eyes. Where did strong feelings pop up? In which of these situations have you eventually been triggered? What was the trigger? Which schema has been activated?

Go into the activated feelings and let yourself float back into your childhood days. Do any scenes pop up where you had these feelings before? This could be the origin of your schema.

> *Charles* reflected on a recent work assessment. He was flooded with feelings of guilt and thought, "I didn't try hard enough in my job." He felt helpless to improve in any way. He withdrew into himself and didn't share this "defeat" with anyone he knew at church. He identified schemas of Failure and Social Isolation.

Now try to recognize any triggers.

> Charles saw that being evaluated was the trigger. He said, "I've never done well with exams. I worry about how I've performed. Perhaps it's more how I'm seen to have done. I'm very self-conscious."

Then the coping style is relevant.

> Charles saw that he would surrender to feelings of failure and would withdraw from friends who could emotionally support him. He also had some avoidance, playing computer games late into the night. He didn't think that he compensated. But then he realized that sometimes he had almost grandiose thoughts about his faith, and wondered if this was a compensating mechanism against his deflated self-esteem.

This illustrates a process of schema attunement. Charles was able to identify when his schemas have been activated ("I feel overwhelmed, almost on autopilot with my feelings"). He saw the trigger and identified a weakness from childhood about being self-conscious during evaluations. And finally he recognized how he would react to a schema activation with a coping style.

To do: List five schemas you can recognize as the ones you most commonly activate. You might ask your partner or family members or best friend to help you with this. Notice any triggers. Does anything make a difference in how overwhelming it may feel? Are there times when you're more robust? Times when you feel very fragile? Carefully describe to yourself any steps you go through from the trigger to schema activation to coping style to resolution.

Note: This skill of self-awareness is very important. What we'll identify is unique to each of us. Take time—weeks, even a month or two—to become very aware of your schemas. But do not feel ashamed. We all have schemas as legacies from our past. It's better to become aware and consciously deal with them than to always fall into the same life-traps again.

Gottman wrote about "gridlocked problems" (unresolvable problems) that might be understood in terms of clashing schemas. But they're not unresolvable. Once you manage to identify the relevant schemas within you and your partner, you can establish a working alliance, mutually detecting schema activations. Blame it on the schema—not on the partner.

Theoretical note: Young's 18 schemas are very comprehensive, especially when coupled with the three response patterns, but keeping all this in mind can be a challenge. The simple mathematics of potentially one schema leading to a response is 18 × 3 = 54. And we can easily activate multiple schemas at the same time! Later, we introduce the concept of *modes*, or states of schema activation, which will add to your understanding and give you an easier way to deal with schema activation.

Emotional learning

You can think about schemas in terms of what has been learned unconsciously in childhood. The schemas identify areas of emotional learning. For example, the learning associated with, say, Mistrust-Abuse can be distinguished from Defectiveness-Shame. Mistrust-Abuse is about others; Defectiveness-Shame relates to the self. This is explored further in a later chapter.

Think about this example:

> *Mandy* felt like a failure in everything she did. She dropped out of part-time university studies. She had a menial job, which she did for a number of years, and believed it was all she was capable of doing. She began to keep a journal and found an underlying emotional learning: "My mother said I would never amount to anything. She believed it was risky to expect anything out of life since it always led to disappointment. She said she loved me, and maybe she wanted to protect me, but this was her 'truth,' not mine."

This is an emotional belief within the domain of Failure. Once Mandy saw the origins of her Failure schema and the meaning, she was able to question whether it was relevant to her. She was encouraged to re-enroll in college by some friends she had made through a local social club.

Challenge: If you can identify areas of schema vulnerability and attune to the triggers and your coping styles, can you go further and ask yourself what core beliefs you have associated with those areas?

Emotional learning is a very important concept that is developed through this book. Often, we learn something in childhood but are hardly aware that it's a "truth" we live by. We may be barely conscious of it, but that doesn't stop us living as if it were a divine commandment. Understanding schemas can give us a language for this early learning.

Review: Young's list of maladaptive schemas provides potentially the most comprehensive framework for understanding psychological problems. If you're seeking to understand yourself and interactions in a relationship, complexity can become less of a barrier, since you know yourself and have time to think about complex dynamics.

Reflect: You now have the basic schema model. This would be a good time to more fully identify your schema vulnerability and your characteristic coping styles and think about which schemas are likely to be core (unconditional) and which compensatory (conditional). Which core schemas are hidden behind a compensatory or coping schema? Use your journal and try mapping out the schemas and their interaction. Simply do your best. Share your work with your partner or a close friend once you feel that it's 90% complete (as a reality check, but feedback from a partner risks being distorted). This is one of the most important self-awareness exercises you'll do. Remember that it's open-ended: You can refine and add to (or correct) your basic schema model as you work through this book.

Further reflection: As you identify your schemas, can you make this more vivid by associating a color with each schema? What feelings do you have with the schema? Locate those feelings in your body. This will help you to "ground" the schema in your sense of self.

More reflection: Think about your experience of relationship complementarity in terms of schemas. What evokes what? Try to track sequences of schema activation in your relationship. Try getting a sense of looking behind the coping schema on the front stage and accessing the backstage schemas. There are also potential compensating schemas; for example, a person with Abandonment may have a compensating Self-sacrifice schema that is then played out in the couple relationship with patterns of de-selfing. Of course, it's a relatively complex task to track all possible schema activations in a relationship, especially when multiple schemas may activate at the same time, but take your time. Try to collaborate with your partner. Four eyes see more than two, and we usually have blind spots when we're looking at ourselves.

Exploring your schemas together can become a mutual expedition to an unknown territory and connect you more deeply, but try this only when you're in a peaceful mood, not during an argument. Do not use your knowledge about your partner's schemas and coping styles as a weapon. That would be an abuse of schema therapy! Your partner and friends might contribute to a much clearer picture. Make use of their contributions. They're not accusing you as a person—they're talking about your schemas.

Schema patterns

Once you identify which schemas most easily activate, try to understand the dynamic interaction of schemas with family members or close friends, including "schema chemistry," "schema clashes," and "being locked in schemas." These are terms used in schema therapy to describe interactions driven by our schemas. This will be most obvious in intimate relationships.

> *Kell* had a history of child sexual abuse by a neighbor. She was quick to activate schemas of Mistrust-Abuse and Defectiveness-Shame. There was a part of her that believed that she deserved to be treated badly. There was instant attraction when she met Billy. He was very dogmatic and judgmental. He had Punitiveness and Unrelenting Standards schemas. Kell was attracted to his strength and offered a pattern of Subjugation. What caused problems was the emergence of his punitive and controlling relationship style, which soon grated on her. They became locked in her sense of Defectiveness-Shame and his inability to respond because of Emotional Inhibition.

This example illustrates how schema therapy can be used to explore why and how people interact. Schema therapy provides a way to understand complex couple dynamics.

It's helpful to understand that current feelings may be driven by schemas rather than by the environment. Being aware of schema vulnerability will get you closer to the source of your problems, inside yourself instead of in the behavior of others. Take responsibility for your schemas and coping styles instead of blaming others. They won't understand your schema activations and will withdraw from or fight with your "strange" reactions. You'll find yourself in your old life-traps. But this is not gridlock—there's a way out!

For now, it is enough to simply note that the schemas originate in childhood through adverse experiences, and that an individual's consciousness associated with an activated schema is determined by developmental factors.

Visualize your personal potential

You have already taken an important step to a different future by reading this book. You may have begun working with a schema therapist. Well done! Both will provide an effective way to make changes for the better.

Exercise: Close your eyes and calm down a little bit. Then visualize yourself in a stressful situation. It may be something that happens often. Next step: Can you now picture yourself coping well, acting the way you want and in line with your most deeply held convictions and values? What do you see happening in this visualization that doesn't happen now? What is different? Write this out in your journal. What are the values you most want to live out in a consistent way?

This is the direction we want to take: Schema therapy has the goal of moving us away from maladaptive schemas to living in the healthy side of the self by using our internal resources.

Visualize your potential as a couple

As a couple, you hope you're moving toward a better future. Almost every relationship has some potential. Where would you like to be in 6 to 12 months? We encourage you, as a couple, to do the following exercise (from Wendy Behary, ISST couples workgroup):

Couple exercise: Do this exercise with your partner. Move to a place where you won't be disturbed for at least 15 minutes. Both of you should close your eyes and visualize yourselves as a couple having a satisfying encounter. This may be as simple as enjoying an activity together. You may be affectionate but not necessarily sexual with each other. What do you see happening? Why are you happy or content? Share what you have visualized with your partner. What is in common; what is different? What could be the first step going in this direction?

Variation: If you're in trouble with your partner right now, you can draw back to the time of the beginning of your relationship. What did attract you in those days? Try to get a vivid picture of your partner and remember what you did exactly. How does that resonate within you now? Is there something that you could do again today? What would be the first steps to take? If your partner is in reach, go and tell them. If you like, you could do this exercise together during one of your "connect talk" meetings (we discuss connect talk in Chapter 14).

Reflect: What do you see happening in this visualization that doesn't happen now in your relationship? This may identify currently unmet needs. You can now set important goals for your relationship. You may, for example, see yourself talking easily, with a sense of safety and no trace of a power struggle.

To do: Return to your list of most easily activated maladaptive schemas. Consider working out a work plan to potentially transform maladaptive schemas into healthy coping.

> *Walter* identified Abandonment as a core problem in finding a satisfying romantic relationship. He found that any women he met at work soon felt overwhelmed by his emotional needs, so he had to accept that learning to

soothe himself was the first step to take. He couldn't hand over responsibility for his child needs to a potential romantic partner. It was his responsibility to "adopt" the emotional part of himself and care for it as if it were his son. Preparing himself for this challenge of being a good parent for himself, he found that he was able to use some mindfulness resources he had learned in a meditation group to soothe himself when he became anxious about a girlfriend. He learned to talk to himself as a good parent would do. This helped, but he acknowledged that "I still felt very anxious, but I had identified the problem. I had to 'fake it before I make it.' Strange as it may sound, it did help."

Mary was hyperdemanding of herself. She had a list of expectations of herself that could fill pages in her notebook, and often did! She rated how much she expected of her own performance ("100%, actually"). She saw that it was all overwhelming and began to try to better tolerate less than perfection. She started with her work practices and made a contract with herself to give it a try. She disciplined herself to proofread her written work only once (instead of three or four times) and then see what would happen. She wrote down the expectations of her Unrelenting Standards schema: You'll make a lot of mistakes and will be fired! Then she rated as a percentage how likely that would be: 90%! While she occasionally missed a typo, she also observed that she was getting more done, especially when under time pressure. The result of this experiment was that she performed even better than before. And she wasn't fired! In this way, she weakened her Unrelenting Standards schema.

For an example of a working plan to deal with maladaptive schemas in a relationship, see Figure 1.1 (fill out the bottom section for yourself).

Reflect: Clearly identify the goal of working toward healthy coping. What steps would be needed to either make progress or complete the transformation of a maladaptive schema into a healthy one? Be aware that schemas do not fade merely because of insight. It will take behavior trials to discover that they're false guides. The experiment reveals the truth. The first step is to overcome emotional avoidance and decide to challenge your schemas and automatic coping responses by behavior experiments. And don't forget the percentage rating! How this is possible is addressed in the chapters that follow.

To do: Keep a separate "positive journal" to record healthy and happy experiences. In this record, collect observations that are contrary to your maladaptive schemas.

Reflect: What have you noticed in being introduced to the concepts of schema therapy? Do you have some tools to think about your intimate relationship in a different way? Any "A-ha's" of recognition or insight?

Core schema—Walter:	Abandonment
Ways I compensate for that schema:	Opening up very quickly to potential partners to see if they will stick with me (testing them?)
Healthy ways of managing or soothing that schema:	Adopt my vulnerable side and look after him.
What do I need to do when triggered?	Use mindfulness to sooth the fear
What do I need to hear my Healthy Adult side say?	"I'll stay, I'm not going anywhere"

Core schema—Mary:	Unrelenting Standards
Ways I compensate for that schema:	Writing lists of expectations, telling myself "it's perfect or it's terrible", proof reading multiple times
Healthy ways of managing or soothing that schema:	Try doing things "less than perfect" to have more time and energy for me
What do I need to do when triggered?	Limit my proofreading as an "experiment"
What do I need to hear my Healthy Adult side say?	"Perfect is not all it's cracked up to be. How about 'good enough'?" and "I am more than my last typo."

My core schema:	
Ways I compensate for that schema:	
Healthy ways of managing or soothing that schema:	
What do I need to do when triggered?	
What do I need to hear my Healthy Adult side say?	

Figure 1.1   Working plan to transform maladaptive schemas. Source: Worksheet by Ruth Holt

Summary

If you're seeing a schema therapist, you may already be very familiar with the language of schemas. Perhaps they're helping you to become aware of your schema vulnerability. Alternatively, your therapist may be talking more about modes, which are the focus in the rest of this book. Schemas show emotional depth and reveal your history; modes are easier to track in the here and now when you're unstable. Both are important, and each completes the picture in different ways.

You'll also be encouraged to see your relationship from a number of different perspectives. This will give you a more encompassing view of what is happening.

The next chapter explores assessment tools such as the genogram, contributions from important current theories such as attachment theory and systems theory, and interventions from evidence-based therapies such as emotion-focused therapy and schema therapy. Each provides a different vantage point, but the real application is potentially changing dysfunctional relationships to become more stable and satisfying. This challenge is addressed in the following chapters.

To Read Further

- A recent book on schema therapy and modes: Arntz and Jacob (2013)
- Evidence for schema therapy's effectiveness with borderline personality disorder: Bamelis, Bloo, Bernstein, and Arntz (2012), Farrell and Shaw (2012)
- The effectiveness of schema therapy with histrionic, narcissistic, and avoidant personality disorder: Bamelis, Evers, Spinhoven, and Arntz (2014)
- The beginning of cognitive behavioral therapy: Beck (1963)
- The nature of schemas: Edwards (2014)
- The advantages of schema therapy: Edwards and Arntz (2012)
- Schemas becoming "worn and rigid" and patterns of schemas: van Genderen, Rijkeboer, and Arntz (2012, p. 29)
- The 15 adaptive schemas and the Social Undesirability schema: Lockwood and Perris (2012)
- Evaluating the YSQ-3: Sheffield and Waller (2012)
- Positive schemas: Wright, Basco, and Thase (2006)
- Frequency of personality disorder in the population: Yang, Coid, and Tyrer (2010)
- The beginning of modes in schema therapy: Young, Klosko, and Weishaar (2003).

Note

1 We are alternating genders to give a sense of comprehensiveness. Men and women share a common schema vulnerability.

References

Arntz, A., & Jacob, G. (2013). *Schema therapy in practice: An introductory guide to the schema mode approach.* Oxford, UK: Wiley-Blackwell.

Bamelis, L., Bloo, J., Bernstein, D., & Arntz, A. (2012). Effectiveness studies. In M. van Vreeswijk, J. Broersen, & M. Nadort (Eds.), *The Wiley-Blackwell handbook of schema therapy: Theory, research and practice* (pp. 495–510). Oxford, UK: Wiley-Blackwell.

Bamelis, L., Evers, S., Spinhoven, P., & Arntz, A. (2014). Results of a multicenter randomized controlled trial of the clinical effectiveness of schema therapy for personality disorders. *American Journal of Psychiatry in Advance*, ajp. psychiatryoneline.org, 1–18.

Beck, A. (1963). Thinking and depression. *Archives of General Psychiatry, 9*, 324–333.

Edwards, D. (2014). Schemas in clinical practice: What they are and how we can change them. *Bulletin of Psychologists in Independent Practice, 34*(1), 10–13.

Edwards, D., & Arntz, A. (2012). Schema therapy in historical perspective. In M. van Vreeswijk, J. Broersen, & M. Nadort (Eds.), *The Wiley-Blackwell handbook of schema therapy: Theory, research and practice* (pp. 3–26). Oxford, UK: Wiley-Blackwell.

Farrell, J., & Shaw, I. (2012). *Group schema therapy for borderline personality disorder: A step-by-step treatment manual with patient workbook.* Oxford, UK: Wiley-Blackwell.

Lockwood, G., & Perris, P. (2012). A new look at core emotional needs. In M. van Vreeswijk, J. Broersen, & M. Nadort (Eds.), *The Wiley-Blackwell handbook of schema therapy: Theory, research and practice* (pp. 41–66). Oxford, UK: Wiley-Blackwell.

Sheffield, A., & Waller, G. (2012). Clinical use of schema inventories. In M. van Vreeswijk, J. Broersen, & M. Nadort (Eds.), *The Wiley-Blackwell handbook of schema therapy: Theory, research and practice* (pp. 111–124). Oxford, UK: Wiley-Blackwell.

van Genderen, H., Rijkeboer, M., & Arntz, A. (2012). Theoretical model: Schemas, coping styles and modes. In M. van Vreeswijk, J. Broersen, & M. Nadort (Eds.), *The Wiley-Blackwell handbook of schema therapy: Theory, research and practice* (pp. 27–40). Oxford, UK: Wiley-Blackwell.

Wright, J., Basco, M., & Thase, M. (2006). *Learning cognitive-behavior therapy: An illustrated guide*, Washington, DC: American Psychiatric Publishing.

Yang, M., Coid, J., & Tyrer, P. (2010). Personality pathology recorded by severity: National survey. *British Journal of Psychiatry, 197*, 193–199.

Young, J. E., & Klosko, J. S. (1993). *Reinventing your life.* New York, NY: Plume.

Young, J. E., Klosko, J. S., & Weishaar, M. E. (2003). *Schema therapy: A practitioner's guide.* New York, NY: Guilford Press.

2

Past Tense, Present Tense
Understanding Family Patterns

Family. We join at birth. This has been likened to arriving two hours late for a party. Most of what is important has already happened and we see its effects on the people around us secondhand. And often we do not know what is *really* happening.

How do we come to terms with this? If you're to understand the dynamics of your own family, you'll need some tools. One is the genogram, which is a way of mapping the family over the generations. Another is doing an autobiography of relationships. This chapter examines both before introducing the attachment model.

The Genogram

The genogram gives a picture of your family over three generations. The symbols create a kind of family tree. The genogram was developed in family therapy, but is now used more widely. It's helpful in maintaining an overall perspective, including on the influence of individuals on each other, and in identifying repetitive dynamics in your family system.

In the genogram in Figure 2.1, we see that both Bert and Nancy grew up in alcoholic homes. Bert had a previous marriage to Jane, which ended in divorce; Jane later died of breast cancer. Nancy lives much closer to her immediate family and tends to get involved in their dramas. In 1986, the year after the stillbirth of her daughter Ann, she had multiple stresses following the death of her mother: Her father increased his drinking, and her younger brother was admitted to hospital with a

Breaking Negative Relationship Patterns: A Schema Therapy Self-help and Support Book,
First Edition. Bruce A. Stevens and Eckhard Roediger.
© 2017 John Wiley & Sons, Ltd. Published 2017 by John Wiley & Sons, Ltd.

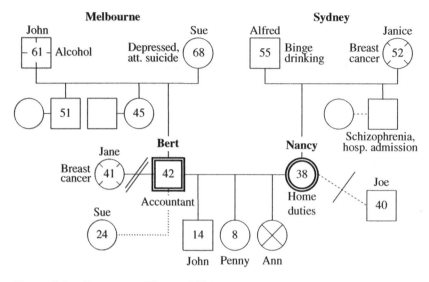

Figure 2.1   Genogram of Bert and Nancy

diagnosis of schizophrenia. This might explain her need for additional support, which she sought in her brief affair with Joe. Bert and Nancy have gone to relationship counseling because Bert is "having feelings" for Sue, a temporary administrative assistant in his accountancy firm. Nancy complains that Bert works long hours, neglecting his family and household tasks.

The symbols in the diagram (such as squares for males, circles for females, dotted lines for a relationship, solid lines for marriages, one cutting line for a separation, two for a divorce, crossed out for death, and so on) can be adapted to what interests you about your family history.

Draw your own genogram and include the following:

1. Name, age, highest level of education, occupation, and any significant problems.
2. Relationship status (single, married, in a common-law marriage, separated, divorced).
3. Transitions (dates of birth, death, marriage, divorce, separation—anniversaries tend to raise anxiety or cause sadness), any other significant stressors or transitions (accident, illness, change of job, moved house), especially if any occurred just before an event such as work-related stress, separation, or injury.

4. The geographical location of parents and other family members; patterns of migration.
5. Ethnic and religious affiliation.

Now add the same details for your partner. Don't worry if you have to redraw it to fit everyone on one page. Everyone makes a mess of their first attempt at a genogram.

Family problems

Identify any problems, including alcohol abuse, drug or other addictions, genetic defects, suicide, violence, accidents, job instability, betrayal, gambling, sexual abuse, criminal behavior, mental illness, or psychosomatic disorders. It's easy to use a shorthand symbol such as "@" for alcoholism, but make up your own for any theme that you think might be significant.

If all this provides the bones, then emotional patterns are the flesh. Think about anyone who might be enmeshed or overinvolved, or who is not talking to whom (emotional cutoffs), and any triangles (two people close at the expense of a more distant third person). Who are the success stories in the family? What are the criteria (business, academic, sport, or financial success)? Are there clear gender roles? How important are sibling positions? Who are the black sheep or the scapegoats? Who are the failures (and by what criteria)? What are the family's rules, taboos, hot issues, secrets, and scripts? Add any other emotional patterns that interest you.

The wider context can also be considered. What historical forces have shaped each generation? What wars, economic conditions, birthrate changes, cultural forces, and new technologies were influential? Have notions about gender changed or remained the same? If there was a migration, what differences in culture were introduced? One cultural value that influences self-care is selflessness versus self-consideration. Did this change in the family? How has the meaning of work changed through the generations? Use the genogram to think about your family history.

Practical application

Doing a genogram has considerable advantages:

1. *Representation:* The genogram can visually represent of a lot of information. It allows you to see the generations and to notice, perhaps for the first time, distinctive family patterns.

2. *Context:* It provides a context for any problem, including a difficult relationship. Think about any relationship difficulties in the light of what was modeled by your parents. Your family history may give an indication of stresses on a generation and the possible impact of traumas, such as war or forced migration.

3. *Themes:* You can identify dysfunctional themes that run through the family, such as antisocial behavior, violence, neglect, physical or sexual abuse, and addictions. Do you notice this repeating in subsequent generations? Were your needs met as a child? What strengths can you identify in individuals or family groups? What is the contribution to the family of people who joined through marriage or relationship? Do you notice anything surprising?

4. *Problems:* Think about who has a problem, such as being anxious or easily stressed. Is this an intergenerational problem handed down in the family?

5. *Tracking:* You can track emotional patterns. What emotions were expressed; what were repressed? Who were close? Who were distant? Did anyone "escape" the family, never to return? When you're in a low mood, or unreasonably angry, can you see the origins of such emotions in your childhood?

6. *Analysis:* Choose a different color to overlay your genogram with some indications of the quality of relationships. You can use a zig-zag line /\/\/\ to indicate a conflicted relationship, three parallel lines to indicate an enmeshed relationship and -| |- to show an emotional cutoff. Again, be creative and think up your own symbols to indicate different kinds of relationship in the genogram.

7. *Prediction:* You can predict how difficult it will be to recover from problems. If there are strong intergenerational themes of dysfunction, you can assume that any improvement will be more labored. This may also be an indication of personality disorder or serious mental health issues.

8. *Thinking:* Think about what your parents modeled to the children of your generation. Consider patterns of nurturing. You might also want to think about attachment styles (see below). What schemas were most obvious in people and in each generation?

9. *Spirituality:* Identify those with a religious faith. Who would you consider a good role model? Are there any whom you consider hypocritical? Can you see patterns in the spiritual commitments in your family? Or does unbelief, perhaps atheism, run through the generations?

Reflect: Draw your own genogram and reflect on family themes. Interview the elders in your family. They're often the keepers of the family's oral history, sometimes knowing the family secrets, and this can help you to understand themes and patterns that have shaped the family over the generations. It's a good idea to interview the oldest members of your family soon, because people can become senile or die suddenly.

Schema transmission through the generations

Schemas indicate that a child's needs weren't met. Can you see patterns of neglect, lack of protection, abuse, violence, and possibly antisocial behavior? This will indicate a chronic lack of regard for the welfare of children.

Identify, if you can, the most important schemas in each generation. Begin with your parents and grandparents on both sides. Can you see which two or three schemas dominated for each person? Can you see their coping styles: surrender, compensation, or avoidance? This not only provides modeling but also indicates which schemas were most commonly activated. From the genogram above:

> *Bert's* father John was a bank manager. His most obvious schemas (and coping styles) were Unrelenting Standards (surrender) and Punitiveness (surrender). His mother Sue was an alcoholic and had Emotional Deprivation and Defectiveness-Shame (avoidance through alcohol). Nancy's father Alfred's schemas included Social Isolation (surrender) and Entitlement-Grandiosity (surrender). His binge drinking was an occasional avoidance. Her mother Janice had Enmeshment (surrender) with her son, who was schizophrenic.

Your tracking of schemas will give you a dynamic understanding of the psychological forces that have shaped your family and relationships.

To do: Mark your genogram with colored logos to indicate who exhibited which schemas. Can you draw lines to indicate influence on others? Compare the generations. What schemas tend to repeat in each generation? Is there a pattern of, say, Unrelenting Standards among oldest children? And so on ...

Reflect: Schema vulnerability provides clues to emotional learning as a child. What messages were present in your family? What did you hear about yourself? What did you accept as "gospel"? Did your siblings accept the same messages or believe something different? Think about what "scripts" have shaped your life and relationships. Try a sentence completion exercise: "I learned this about myself in my family ...," then add your own words. Repeat until something you add "clicks" or feels very significant.

Autobiography of Relationships

Relationships are not meant to be easy. This cliché is of course true (as well as remaining a cliché), but people mostly live their relationships for better or worse, gaining the experience but missing the meaning. We suggest the following exercise. Write your autobiography of relationships. This can begin with your early experiences of your parents (the foundational relationships), but include experiences of your first love or early attraction, group dating, pairing off, first kiss, first committed relationship, and marriage experiences. Write it with a focus on your emotional highs and lows and try to get a sense of repeating patterns.

What influenced you to become who you are? Include successes and failures. How did you adapt to early responsibilities? Continue until the present.

Hargrave recommended the use of questionnaires. While this can be a simple information-gathering exercise, answering a list of questions can also help you think about yourself. He suggested questions about parental discipline, how and when there was teaching about sexuality, and descriptions of relationships in the family of origin. He also included the following questions:

- As a result of growing up in your family, what did you learn about how lovable or important you are?
- In your family, what was the most important thing to do or be?
- In your family, how did you know you were loved?
- What was the most important thing about being a family?
- What did you learn about being a man or woman?
- Who taught you about God? Or to doubt? Were there any models of spiritual maturity?

But this is what he thought was important:

- What questions most interest you?
- What expectations do you have for relationships?

Think about these questions in relation to your autobiography.

Neil thought about how he got messages about being loved. He said, "I went to boarding school and my parents wrote letters every week. I really looked forward to getting the mail and learning what was happening at home. The letters were regular, no matter what was happening on the farm. This was an important message to me about expressing yourself and being constant."

Reflection: As you thought about your personal history "from the inside" by writing the autobiography, what did you learn about yourself emotionally? Try any of the following sentence completions:

- As a child, I learned that I must …
- I always accepted that I have to … in relationships.
- If I do something different, then the results will be …
- What I never question about myself is …

Think about this in terms of schema vulnerability and what you might like to change.

Reflect: Think about your history of relationships. Can you form a sentence about what you learned from each relationship? This can be challenging if you have had a long marriage or a series of longer relationships, but the challenge is to boil it down to a single sentence.

Infant Attachment Styles

Attachment theory now plays an important role in most approaches to relationship therapy. This theory recognizes that the brain of an infant develops in important ways in the first year or 18 months. Immature at birth, the brain is wax in the hands of the infant's caregivers. When the child's fundamental need for attachment is met, the child develops a secure attachment style for life. If it isn't met, the attachment remains insecure.

To get a sense about your attachment style and your sense of safety and trust towards other people, some fundamental questions about your family system might be helpful:

1. Was your family stable?
2. Whom did you feel closest to in your family?
3. Who met your needs?
4. How about other family members, including grandparents, aunts, and uncles?
5. How would you describe your earliest experiences as a child with your parents?
6. Did you feel basically safe?

7. Was somebody there when you needed them?
8. Were the people around you reliable, or sometimes present and sometimes not?
9. Did the mood of your caregivers change dramatically?
10. Was their behavior toward you predictable?
11. Were they honest, or did they tell you lies sometimes?

Here's the example of Nellie:

> *Nellie* described her father as distant, absent, busy, judgmental, and self-centered. She then recalled an incident in which he was distant: "When he got home he would read the paper. I got the message he didn't want to be bothered." In relation to his absence: "I was selected to give a speech at school. It was an honor, but he didn't rearrange his schedule to be there." She recalled her father being busy "all the time, with too many things to do to worry about me or my sister." She remembered her report cards, "which were an ordeal. I was always nervous if I didn't have all A's." And about him being self-centered: "It's hard to say it, but I think he only cared about himself. I remember he went on a holiday overseas by himself. We didn't get any family time at the beach that year, but he got the trip."

She repeated this with her mother. Then she considered which parent she felt closest to and why.

> Nellie continued: "I was closest to my mother. She was there emotionally. I could talk about school and she would listen. I never found my dad to be patient enough to listen, even to the end of a sentence. I would have to be in real trouble for him to even notice me. Mom had emotional words, but not Dad."

Nellie was asked what she did when she was upset as a child:

> She recalled falling off her bike and injuring her arm: "We thought it might be broken. My mother left her friends and took me to the hospital." She added, "I think I was confident that she could meet my needs."

The questions could now become more searching. What was the first time she remembers being separated from her parents? How did she respond? Did she remember how her parents responded? Were there any other separations that came to mind?

> Nellie said, "I remember I went on my first school camping trip. I was scared I might wet the bed. But my mother gave me my favorite stuffed

animal and it went OK. I was nervous, but I coped. Mom said she was proud of me when I got back."

Reflect: Given this information, what schemas would have been expected? Any surprises? Ask yourself the same questions. Any surprises there?

Attachment patterns are based on research on infants. It was found that young children relate emotionally to adults in a variety of ways. You can think about this in terms of how young children bond to caretakers. The range identified by theorists includes the following:

- *Style A is avoidant.* This person is comfortable being alone. She uses her resources to meet personal needs. The basic assumption could be: "Better rely on your own strengths than needing somebody!"
- *Style B is healthy.* There's enough relational stability for him to use others or to rely on himself in a flexible way.
- *Style C is ambivalent.* She needs to attach to others, basically having no confidence in herself to find the resources for self-regulation. The core belief could be: "You have to take care that people like you, but you can never fully trust them!"
- *Style D is mixed (disorganized).* He has a confused style of attachment with little internal consistency. This is often present in survivors of childhood trauma and severe neglect. His mood and behavior often change in an unpredictable way.

The attachment styles are considered at length in a later chapter. This listing is just meant to give you an overview for now.

Reflect: Do you have any children? Or young relations? What style of attachment have you observed in the next generation of your family?

Note: Attachment theory has been very influential because it adds a layer of understanding of current behavior patterns derived from early childhood experiences. Thus, the schema concept is very similar to attachment ideas. Persisting schemas are highly influential on our current behavior. It's also possible to think about spirituality in terms of this theory, too. If you believe in God, consider what your style of attachment to God might be.

A Note About Theory

Why theory? The answer is simple. A good theory will explain what is currently confusing. It will provide a pattern and ultimately a sense of meaning that ties together seemingly unrelated "facts." Theory also tells you what to notice about yourself.

So far, we have mentioned a few theories. Emotion-focused therapy has a focus on primary emotions (we tend to value what we feel strongly about). Attachment theory notes longstanding patterns of human attachment. The genogram, which is a tool of systems theory, attempts to understand family dynamics more or less as a whole. However, the main focus of this book is schema therapy, which identifies underlying schemas that influence emotions, thoughts, and resulting coping behaviors in all relationships.

We think it's helpful to think about some of the theories we have introduced and we explore them more fully in the pages that follow. What resonates with you? Maybe this will assist you in *noticing*, then *identifying* what is important in your relationship, and then finally *making some changes*. In this way, you're creating your own theory about you—authoring your own story—and imagining a different ending.

Summary

We have introduced some important tools to help you to understand some of the ways your family has shaped you as an adult. This includes the genogram, which gives a picture of the generations. You can reflect through a biography, questionnaires, and some questions taken from the adult attachment interview. It helps to understand the four attachment styles: avoidant, healthy, ambivalent, and mixed. All of this is essential information that you can use to better understand your patterns, healthy and unhealthy, in relationships.

To Read Further

- Research on attachment: Cohen (1996)
- The adult attachment interview, from which some questions in this chapter were taken: George, Kaplan, and Main (1984–1996)
- Clinical application of the adult attachment interview: Solomon and Tatkin (2011)
- Attachment and God: Granqvist, Mikulincer, and Shaver (2010)
- Questionnaires: Hargrave (2000)
- The origins of negative emotions in childhood: Jacob, van Genderen, and Seebauer (2015)
- Monica McGoldrick and Randy Gerson's book *Genograms in Family Assessment* (1985) is very useful. While it's now slightly dated, it shows what can be understood from a genogram.

References

Cohen, V. (1996). *Human attachment.* New York, NY: McGraw Hill.

George, C., Kaplan, N., & Main, M. (1984–1996). *The attachment interview for adults.* Unpublished manuscript. Berkeley, CA.

Granqvist, P., Mikulincer, M., & Shaver, P. R. (2010). Religion as attachment: Normative processes and individual differences. *Personality and Social Sciences Review, 14.* doi:10.1177/1088868309348618.

Hargrave, T. D. (2000). *The essential humility of marriage.* Phoenix, AZ: Zeig, Tucker & Theisen.

Jacob, G., van Genderen, H., & Seebauer, L. (2015). *Breaking negative thought patterns: A schema therapy self-help and support book.* Malden, MA: Wiley-Blackwell.

McGoldrick, M., & Gerson, R. (1985). *Genograms in family assessment.* New York, NY: W. W. Norton.

Solomon, M., & Tatkin, S. (2011). *Love and war in intimate relationships: Connection, disconnection and mutual regulation.* New York, NY: W. W. Norton.

3

Attraction, Romance, and Schema Chemistry

If your romantic relationship history was made into a movie, what would it be? Melodrama, comedy, tragedy? Perhaps all three? You might feel you have been given lines to recite by a bad director. It's all very confusing. In this chapter, we look at possible sources of confusion in relationships.

There seem to be at least two layers. The first is attraction. What does Kylie see in Justin? This question is often asked but, as everyone who has a friend knows, it's hard to answer. Attraction is no easier for therapists to understand.

The second layer is illusion. At the risk of sounding cynical, this includes the almost universally believed myth of romantic love. Bear with us—we won't leave you in the wilderness but offer an explanation in terms of "schema chemistry."

Attraction: Where Opposites Meet

What do people find sexually attractive about others? As a game, with your partner or a friend, rate the following celebrities on attractiveness, using a scale from 1 to 10:

- George Clooney
- Julia Roberts
- Barack Obama
- Woody Allen

Breaking Negative Relationship Patterns: A Schema Therapy Self-help and Support Book, First Edition. Bruce A. Stevens and Eckhard Roediger.
© 2017 John Wiley & Sons, Ltd. Published 2017 by John Wiley & Sons, Ltd.

- Kylie Minogue
- Madonna
- Professor Stephen Hawking
- Pope Francis (and anyone else you can think of).

What makes a person attractive to you? Is it good looks? Power and status? Money? Talent? Personality attributes, such as a sense of humor? Intelligence? Virtues, such as honesty or spirituality? Most of us are reasonably clear about our likes and dislikes, but there are other forces at work that influence the choice of a lover or marital partner. Attraction operates in less obvious ways.

Reflect: What figure from literature or film would represent an ideal for you? Mr. Darcy from *Pride and Prejudice*? Portia from *The Merchant of Venice*? If you like classic movies, you might think of Audrey Hepburn as Holly Golightly in *Breakfast at Tiffany's*. But who are you drawn to in recent movies? Now think about why.

> *Nancy* watched all the James Bond movies. She could discuss for hours which actor made the best Bond. She thought that her attraction had something to do with male strength, but maybe she was also attracted by a hint of malice.

Is there a dark edge to people you find attractive?

Unconscious Aspects

The notion of attraction takes us to the edge of our psychological awareness. It's where the light of understanding meets the twilight of what is just out of sight. This is like Carl Jung's (1938) notion of a shadow side to the personality. Harville Hendrix (1988) considered attraction to be an unconscious dynamic in a relationship.

> Take, for example, *Mark*, who as a young child wasn't allowed to be angry. He forced these forbidden feelings behind a screen of repression and denial. He grew up with hardly any awareness of an angry impulse. When it came to choosing a partner, he arrived at a fork in the road. He found himself very much at ease with Amanda, a colleague who also repressed anger, "She's 'my kind of person,' I feel comfortable with her." On the other hand, he was attracted to Marje, who was easily enraged.

No prize for guessing which would be the more interesting relationship!

Reflect: What emotions were taboo when you were growing up? Were you allowed to express anger? Sadness? Exuberant joy? Were you inhibited by guilt and shame? Make a list of the emotions you have difficulty expressing. Have you chosen a partner who exhibits those emotions? Or are you both "compatible" in avoiding such emotions?

The first layer, attraction, leads to more questions than answers. There are forces that have great influence but from a seemingly hidden realm. Maybe we'll learn more from the next layer, illusion.

Romantic Love Through the Ages

Romantic love raises the stakes. What is puzzling about attraction becomes mystifying in romantic love. Love tends to intensify the dynamics, with reasoning even more irrational and perhaps ultimately destructive.

> *Nancy* thought it had been "so romantic" even from the start—just like in the TV show *Perfect Match*. Brett had walked up to her on the street with a bunch of flowers and told her he loved her at first sight! Initially, she thought he was crazy, but then thought "What could be more romantic?" Although her parents opposed the marriage, they went ahead and had a church wedding four months later. The honeymoon was a dream, but then things began to go wrong.

Romantic love has been likened to the seraphim in the book of Isaiah (6:2): "Each had six wings, with two he covered his face, and with two he covered his feet, and with two he flew." "So you don't know where you're going, and you can't see clearly who you are with, but, oh my heavens, you do fly!" (*The Age*, May 3, 1989).

We'll try to put romantic love in context. This may help us to understand that it's an idea that is relatively recent in Western civilization.

Sexual attraction has been celebrated through the ages. The Song of Solomon in the Old Testament is an ancient example: "O fairest among women" (1:8) and "Ah, you are beautiful, my love; ah, you are beautiful; your eyes are doves. Ah, you are beautiful, my beloved, truly lovely" (1:15–16). Before the Middle Ages, the dominant form of love was "heroic love" with the central theme of the pursuit and capture of the woman. Perhaps as early as the 12th century, an ideology of love began to develop, with an enormous impact on Western culture.

Romantic love came from courtly love in the Middle Ages. It was a time when only the aristocracy had time for leisure, the arts, musical appreciation, companionship, and refined manners. An idealized notion evolved in which love was equated with the ecstatic adoration of the perfect woman. Troubadours were inspired to sing romantic ballads and to tell long stories, such as that of Tristan and Isolde. The ideal was a spiritual love that couldn't mix with the clay of married life.

The combination of romantic love and marriage is much more recent. The stronger link historically was love and adultery. Maybe this was inevitable when most marriages were arranged by parents for reasons of name, family, property, social status, and commercial and diplomatic agreements. Love may have been the result, but rarely the cause, of such marriages.

In the 16th century, there was a rediscovery of the ancient Greek concept of democracy and individual rights. This led to profound political changes in which individuals felt that they could decide their own destiny, which included the right to marry someone of their own choice—thus radically changing marriage from a sociopolitical institution into a psychological and spiritual one.

Romantic love has been noted for its inherent blindness. As Shakespeare wrote, "Reason and love keep little company together now-a-days; the more the pity, that some honest neighbours will not make them friends" (*A Midsummer Night's Dream*, 3.1). In jazz standards, it was a kind of spell—that "old black magic."

Being in love is a natural high. It's a powerful cocktail with a dash of ecstasy. The initial pretense involves both lovers trying to appear more mature and less needy. Negative aspects of the partner are either ignored or denied.

> *Mary* was convinced that she had at last found the man of her dreams. She invited Mark to her apartment for a meal that she had worked all day to prepare; there were candles on the table and soft music. Everything had to be perfect. She asked her sister to babysit Nathan, her 4-year-old son. After all, she reasoned, "Why have anyone around to spoil the evening?"

Some people get addicted to the "rush" of this drug, resulting in serial relationships with little commitment.

Our Western culture is the first to make such love the basis for marriage. There's almost a disparaging attitude to using reason to think about this most important of life decisions.

How romantic are your attitudes?

List A   1. I believe that there is just one perfect person for me.

2. Being in love is primarily a feeling.

3. If my partner really loves me, he or she will know what I need without me having to ask.

4. If a woman has an affair, that means that she was never really in love with her husband.

5. When a relationship loses its sparkle, it's over.

6. Fate brings lovers together.

7. There is no point in working on a relationship when you are no longer in love.

List B   1. I do not believe that there is only one special person for me.

2. Love is not just a feeling; it's an act of the will.

3. Marriage is too important not to think about family background, religion, and job prospects.

4. It's important that you keep working on a relationship and not give up easily.

5. I am not surprised that some arranged marriages work well.

6. It's too easy to "fall out of love" these days.

7. Commitment has little to do with how you feel.

How many of these statements do you agree with? Compare the number of items from each list. If you agree with more items in the first list, then you are more romantic in your attitudes. Now ask your partner to fill it out. Compare your answers. Which are the same; which are different? What does this suggest about how each of you comes to your relationship?

A Hidden Agenda

Romantic love masks unrealistic expectations. The agenda is the healing of childhood wounds: "The lovers believe they are going to be healed—not by hard work or painful self-realization—but by the simple act of merging with someone" (Hendrix, 1988).

Unrealistic expectations of romance can be illustrated using one of the highest grossing romantic movies of all time, *Pretty Woman* (1990). It was a remake of the Pygmalion theme, but beautifully crafted in true Hollywood style. It is the story of the transformation of a sex worker, played by Julia Roberts. George Bernard Shaw had Professor Henry Higgins work full-time with a flower girl for a few months, but in the fantasy of Hollywood "adding class" can be done in less than a week! Even more interesting is the equally miraculous change in the character played by Richard Gere, from a heartless corporate pirate into a compassionate financier. In a subtle way, Gere was also healed of his fear of heights, symbolized by being able to go out on the balcony. He was later able to commit himself to a relationship. All this happens through the magic of romantic love. *Pretty Woman* is a typical feel-good movie because it confirms deeply held beliefs about love in our culture.

There's an aura of magic about romantic love. This is seen in the unconscious assumption that a lover can read minds.

> *Sue* had a difficult day caring for toddlers at home. She thought to herself, "Wouldn't it be nice if John rang to say that he was thinking about me." John was preoccupied with problems in keeping an advertising client, and when he arrived home Sue was visibly upset. He asked, "What's wrong?" She accused him, "Why don't you ever think about me?"

This may sound silly, but unspoken expectations are a central dynamic in many relationships—and an endless source of conflict. Think about how often you have heard, "If he loved me, he would know what I really want." Such attitudes provide an endless source of work for marriage therapists!

In the example above, Sue has an unconscious belief that John has the capacity to meet her every need. He "has it all." There must be a malevolent reason for his withholding the thoughtful reminders of his love that she so desperately needs. This adds to her frustration, resentment, and bitterness.

Sadly, this logic can lead to tantrums, financial and sexual blackmail, bullying, even violence. Such negative behavior comes from desperation and using an infantile tactic, "If only I can cause my partner enough pain, he'll return to his loving ways." Gradually, it may dawn on Sue that her husband has neither the skills nor the motivation to meet her deepest needs. Of course, an even deeper realization is possible: He has attributes of a wounding parent and is a most unlikely candidate to be able to meet such needs.

Reflect: What do you expect from your partner but rarely ask for? Does your partner complain about what you neglect to do? Try to ask for what you really want. It doesn't cheapen the gift, but makes it possible. Ask them to be specific and not to brush you off with a generalization such as "I just want you to be more considerate." This is the only way to get out of the pin-the-tail-on-the-donkey mentality of guessing the what, when, and how of what is desired.

Again and Again …

There's something profoundly repetitive about relationships:

> *Anna* agonized, "How could I have been so blind? My father was an alcoholic and violent, and now I find that my husband hits me as well." Her friend Bruce asked her, "Did you have any indication when you first went out with Tony?" She thought for a moment, "Well, yes. The night before we got married he threw me on the ground in the parking lot. I just thought that things would change because I loved him."

There have been various explanations. Freud, for example, observed patterns of behavior as repetitive and somewhat compulsive. He described the tendency of adults to repeat the traumatic events of childhood with the unconscious hope of later "changing the script." The initial trauma may have been caused by neglect, violence, abandonment, or abuse, or in some cases by a combination of many such factors. Thus, a young girl hurt by repeated disappointments and shameful incidents involving an alcoholic father may choose a high-risk spouse to replay the old dramas. She's easily hooked, usually with thoughts like "This is someone who really needs me." It's easy to repeat, and hard to change.

Unresolved needs from childhood are replayed in current relationships. When the dynamics of attraction and love are out of our awareness, it's inevitable that we'll keep repeating destructive patterns with little or no understanding.

Reflect: Can you recall a time when you were madly in love? How did you feel? What were your thoughts about your beloved? How would you rate the accuracy of your reading of their character, their suitability for a committed relationship, and your shared values? Use a 1 to 10 scale, with 10 being very accurate. Discuss this with your partner.

Schema Chemistry

Now we return to schema therapy and its contribution to understanding these dynamics. Both attraction and romantic love can be understood in terms of "schema chemistry." What adds to the chemistry is passion, immediate attraction, the idealization of the partner, and possibly the unavailability of the desired partner. This chemistry is also generated by the activation of core schemas. Indeed, couples often choose each other on the basis of their schemas, often by re-experiencing familiar childhood emotions or recalling situations that were distressing. Unlike Freud, we don't need to speculate about an unconscious will at work. We just feel attracted to a kind of person and assume what we (nonconsciously) know. It's just a matter of priming the pump. This is similar to how commercials work on us: We buy what we know or we tend to choose what we're familiar with. This is why Jeffrey Young called such schema-based behaviors "life-traps."

> *Victor* knew that he was attracted to macho men. He would go to gay bars and sometimes find himself in dangerous situations: "I seem to pick guys who can't accept their orientation. I have been assaulted, once ending up in intensive care in the hospital."

Victor had a Defectiveness-Shame schema, which was confirmed in abusive relationships. There was also a Subjugation schema. This would be a good fit for someone with a lot of aggression, with an underlying Entitlement-Grandiosity schema.

Schema therapy explores the concept of interlocking schemas. Clearly, there are schema pairs that might be *dysfunctional* but *compatible*. This is how schema chemistry works: It just fits!

> *Mike* was raised in an abusive home. His father abused alcohol and was violent to all the children. His mother was passive and unable to protect them. Mike found Angie, who was intense, lively, and warm. She also had dark moods in which she could lash out in uncontrolled fury at the slightest provocation. She was emotionally abusive, and rarely if ever apologized.

Mike has a Mistrust-Abuse schema, almost expecting abusive behavior, and with Angie's Punitiveness schema this is virtually guaranteed. Both schemas have origins in childhood but tend to fit in familiar adult patterns. We can understand Mike and Angie's schema chemistry as their compatibility, what feels familiar to both, and perhaps their attraction as a nonconscious knowing that their relationship will involve interlocking schemas.

There are potentially many interlocking schemas. The following examples give an indication of possible combinations:

> *Danny* had a history of unreliable parenting through various foster families. He was acutely sensitive to abandonment and tended to be very controlling as compensation. This usually pushed partners away, until he met Cindy, who thrived on his dependence on her. They were inseparable. Danny had an Abandonment schema and Cindy Enmeshment. The result, for different reasons, was that they were always together.
>
> *Ben* was a successful lawyer. He wanted the best of everything and felt it was his due. It was his optimism that attracted Suzi, who said, "I always expect everything to go wrong." She was raised caring for younger siblings. Ben had an Entitlement schema making him think, "I will get that going," which fit in with her general Negativity-Pessimism, Subjugation, and Self-sacrifice schemas.
>
> *Amanda* didn't get her needs met as a child. She was a forgotten child in every family and social context. As an adult, she was a bottomless pit of need but generally acted as if she expected nothing. She felt at ease with Ned, who had "something of a gambling problem," but she was shattered when she found out he was having affairs. Amanda had an Emotional Deprivation schema, which at times she surrendered to and at times compensated for. Ned had an Insufficient Self-control schema.
>
> *Kylie* developed an eating disorder in her early adolescence. She remained obsessed about her body image even though she was slim, to the envy of her friends. Her negative view of her body was reinforced by the hypercritical attitude of Larry, who constantly pointed to imaginary faults and was relentless in his pressure for her to resume dieting. He could also be harsh when easily angered. Kylie had a Defectiveness-Shame schema that dominated her self-image and tied in with Larry's Unrelenting Standards and Punitiveness schemas.
>
> *Chaz* was "hopelessly neurotic." He was on long-term disability after developing a multi-point pain disorder for vague work-related reasons. He almost needed a full-time caregiver, which he found in Bridget, who was unceasingly attentive to his physical needs. Chaz had a Vulnerability schema, which fitted in well with Bridget's Self-sacrifice schema.

These examples illustrate how schemas can match and interlock.

Reflect: Think about your last few relationships. By now, you have some awareness of your schema vulnerability. Look at the list and try to identify any that your partners exhibited. Can you see any interlocking pairs or clusters of schemas? Think about it in terms of a time line: Was there a period of complementary schemas, which deteriorated over time? Any signs that this destructive cycle had commenced, become problematic, and led to a final deterioration in your relationship? Can you see a similar pattern in past relationships? Do you recognize some traits you're familiar with from one of your parents?

Young's idea of schema chemistry can help to explain attraction in a couple's relationship. It also provides some understanding of psychological compatibility in longer-term relationships. Of course, we would add that schema compatibility may not result in a healthy relationship. There can be underlying pathology while the relationship is nevertheless stable and satisfying for the couple—especially if there's a good fit of underlying needs. But usually so-called complementary relationships include some rigidity: As soon as one partner tries to change their patterns, the situation becomes unstable. This might be an intervention point to review the relationship and eventually ground it less on chemistry than a conscious mutual encounter between what we call Healthy Adults. This might open up a new space of development for both partners, including more flexibility and role changes leading to a richer life.

Reflect: Think about your current relationship. Do you often find yourself in a specific role? What schemas can you see operating? Can you see how they fit together? Can you identify schema chemistry, schema locking, and possible schema clashes? Can you understand your attraction in terms of matching schemas? Do you see the "gain" of that matching for each of you? Despite that, do you sometimes dream of a change?

Here's a longer example of a relationship with schema analysis:

Terrence was a stiff "Victorian gentleman" who always dressed in a three-piece suit, even to mow the lawn. He prided himself in having a stiff upper lip, since he was English and had a stoic philosophy of life. He met Wanda at a diplomatic function and for a number of years they had a warm friendship. She exuded warmth, verging on being gushy, and it was easy to see how they complemented each other in their different emotional styles. In schema terms, this was Terrence's Emotional Inhibition schema matched with Wanda's Dependence-Incompetence schema. This provided them with comfortable schema chemistry. There were other matching schemas: Terrence's Negativity-Pessimism and Unrelenting Standards matched Wanda's Subjugation, Self-sacrifice, and Approval Seeking.

But when they considered the possibility of marriage there was a significant schema clash. Terrence felt a lot of anxiety, which tended to put his Unrelenting Standards into hyperdrive and which interacted with Wanda's Approval Seeking. They presented for couples counseling because Terrence was constantly picking at her with his criticisms on points that Wanda felt she had no control over. She was in tears, saying, "I want to please Terrence, but the goalposts keep changing. I just don't know what he wants anymore." This illustrates a progression from a reasonable fit, at lower levels of anxiety, to a schema clash.

The Possibility of Change

At this point, you might feel some helplessness in the face of dominating schemas from your childhood. It's true that unrecognized schemas may determine the quality of adult relationships, but that is not a given. All this can change. The formula is simple: If schemas influence later interactions, then changing schemas can change your vulnerability in adult relationships. And that is very good news!

This can even change attraction and the dark side of romantic love.

Debbie realized that she had long-standing Failure and Subjugation schemas that added to her chronically low self-esteem. She tended to be attracted to men with Unrelenting Standards and painfully Punitive schemas. She talked about this with a psychiatrist she was seeing, who helped her with childhood memories of an impossible-to-please mother and an absent father. What made the most difference was assertiveness training. Therapeutic gains were eventually generalized in her life, first affecting her role as office manager in a small business. She was no longer as accommodating to every whim of management and even her staff.

When she met Roger, she was initially attracted but then reflected, "He was an old schema fit. I was attracted to his self-confidence but then noticed how controlling he was. I was quickly irritated by his manner. Any interest I had quickly disappeared. I think that this means that something is changing for me." Her psychiatrist agreed.

There's also a way of changing established patterns that sabotage relationships.

Brett was overly intense in relationships. His last male partner justified leaving by saying that Brett was "too needy" and that he felt like an "empty well." Brett entered therapy with a clinical psychologist who specialized in schema therapy. They identified Abandonment and Emotional Deprivation as problematic schemas. Brett recalled a very troubled relationship with his mother, who had a number of addictions. He listed about 10 key memories and over the next six months had weekly therapy, learning mindfulness and having limited reparenting, which began to make significant differences.

Brett then met Matt. He told his therapist, "I think I'm handling this relationship much better. I still feel needy and it distresses me when he's away on business trips, but I have learned to better soothe myself. I don't escalate with phone calls and texting; I can stop myself, observe my reactions, and begin to take responsibility for what I need. I know Matt does what he can, and I know he genuinely cares for me, but there's always something that I have to manage for myself. But what's most important is that I'm not driving him away by my irrational demands. I feel that there's a stability in our relationship that I haven't noticed before."

Schema awareness is an important part of what can be a foundation for a different way of looking at relationships. Understanding such dynamics can change long-established dysfunctional patterns. This is the central theme of the rest of this book, although we have to also dig deeper into the soil of emotional learning.

Summary

Unconscious factors affect our most intimate relationships. What we may consider a rational choice is more complex when we're under the influence of romance. Calm surface water masks swirling currents beneath. But understanding attraction and romantic love in schema terms leads to potential clarity—and a way forward.

To Read Further

- History of romance and marriage: Coontz (2005)
- Compulsion to repeat childhood events as an adult or in relationships: Freud (1920)
- Unconscious aspects of relationships: Hendrix (1988)
- Jung's shadow side to personality: Jung (1938).

References

Coontz, S. (2005). *Marriage: a history.* New York, NY: Penguin Books.

Freud, S. (1920). *Beyond the pleasure principle. In the Standard edition of the complete psychological works of Sigmund Freud, 18,* 7–64.

Hendrix, H. (1988). *Getting the love you want.* Melbourne, Australia: Schwartz & Wilkinson.

Jung, C. (1938). *Psychology and religion.* In *Collected works,* Vol. 11.

Young, J. E., & Klosko, J. S. (1993). *Reinventing your life.* New York, NY: Plume.

4

Back to the Future

Janus, the Roman god, was always pictured looking both backwards and forwards. We need to do the same. First backwards to understand our personal history, what we bring into a relationship, appreciating strengths and vulnerabilities, understanding key life-changing events that have formed us, and determining our range of responses. Then forward to a future with new options. And hope for change.

Schema therapy helps us to identify our patterns of emotional reactivity. These are our schemas. Understanding this can provide a map to meeting our emotional needs in healthy ways.

Schemas and Childhood Needs

Jeffrey Young, the founder of schema therapy, identified five primary tasks of childhood: connection and acceptance; autonomy and performance; realistic limits; inner-directedness and self-expression; and spontaneity and pleasure. These areas include what a child needs from others, what they need to learn to do, and how to make a contribution. With optimal care, a child will develop in a healthy way in all five domains.

Schemas are created when childhood needs aren't met. Again, the 18 schemas:

Abandonment (instability), Mistrust-Abuse, Emotional Deprivation, Defectiveness-Shame, Social Isolation (alienation), Dependence-Incompetence, Vulnerability (to harm or illness), Enmeshment (undeveloped self), Failure (to achieve), Entitlement-Grandiosity, Insufficient

Breaking Negative Relationship Patterns: A Schema Therapy Self-help and Support Book, First Edition. Bruce A. Stevens and Eckhard Roediger.
© 2017 John Wiley & Sons, Ltd. Published 2017 by John Wiley & Sons, Ltd.

Self-control (or self-discipline), Subjugation, Self-sacrifice, Approval Seeking (recognition seeking), Negativity-Pessimism, Emotional Inhibition, Unrelenting Standards (hypercriticalness), and Punitiveness.

To do: Rate your childhood experience on a scale of 1 to 10 (1 would be associated with abuse and/or neglect, 5 would be an average meeting of needs compared to your friends growing up, and 10 would indicate a sensitive, child-focused environment in which your needs were fully met). Give a rating for each of the five domains: disconnection and rejection; impaired autonomy and performance; impaired limits; other-directedness; and over-vigilance and inhibition. Ask your partner to do the same and then compare your results.

Failure to have childhood needs met can be linked to dysfunctional schemas:

1. Basic safety and stability (schemas: Abandonment, Mistrust-Abuse, Vulnerability [to harm or illness])
2. Close connection to another (Emotional Deprivation of nurturing, empathy, protection; Social Isolation)
3. Self-determination and self-expression (Enmeshment, Subjugation, Dependence-Incompetence, Failure [to achieve])
4. Self-actualization (Unrelenting Standards, Enmeshment, Approval Seeking, and maybe Negativity-Pessimism, Self-sacrifice)
5. Acceptance and self-esteem (Defectiveness-Shame, Punitiveness)
6. Realistic limits and concern for others (Entitlement-Grandiosity, Insufficient Self-control)

These areas provide criteria for emotionally healthy development. Of course, no one gets everything they need as a child (or adult!). But we're shaped by early experiences and that is our emotional bedrock. First, let us consider what happens when the needs of a child are neglected in a catastrophic way.

Emotional Themes from Childhood Chaos

There's really no escaping a troubled childhood. Sadly, early emotional damage can last a lifetime. There's no doubt that many people continue to suffer as adults when their parents failed to meet even their basic needs as children. This can leave a legacy of emotional fragility and badly attempted solutions involving addictive substances.

We begin with a wide lens, looking at general emotional themes.

Amanda and Victor had a troubled relationship. Initially there was "chemistry": "We were madly in love." As a child, Amanda had been sexually abused by a neighbor, and she had a child with an older boyfriend when she was 14. Her family insisted that the child be put up for adoption. She later married Victor, but they began to have sexual difficulties when planning to start a family.

Amanda said, "I am worried about having a child. I lost my first child, which broke my heart, and I can't help but think it could happen again. Or Victor could suddenly leave me."

Victor brought his own problems to the relationship as well. His father was violent, and Victor tried to protect his younger siblings. He was impatient with Amanda not feeling secure enough to have children.

Both Amanda and Victor brought baggage into their relationship. It's usual to expect a lot in a new relationship. But if the past is confused with the present, it will be nearly impossible to find a healthy way forward.

Amanda needed therapy to deal with the grief of losing her child as a teenager. Only then could she emotionally separate what happened *then* and what they were trying to do *now*. She had trauma therapy to deal with intrusive thoughts and images. Gradually, this enabled her to create a "safe place" for a different sexual experience.

Victor was able to talk with a close friend, now a mental health nurse, and through his journal he revisited his childhood experiences and found he could better leave them behind. He could now see the support Amanda needed in her journey of recovery from trauma. This mutual understanding drew them closer together.

Reflect: What do you expect from your friends? Family? Lover? One way to think about this is to ask what frustrates you or makes you most angry in relationships. Think also about your partner.

Underlying Agendas

The legacy from childhood can be disabling. But individuals may or may not be aware of this.

Sandy was neglected. His mother became pregnant after a drunken one-night stand. She was mostly single, except for periodic turbulent and often violent relationships. She was an alcoholic and mostly withdrawn "into the bottle," and he was left to fend for himself. He did develop a coping veneer from his early years, but as he became an adult cracks began to appear. He was reckless, with a penchant for driving souped-up cars. He said, "I just need a lot of excitement in my life."

Kelly was severely bullied at school because she was "different." She left home and was drug dependent by the age of 15, financing her habit by working in the sex industry. She later went into a residential drug program led by Teen Challenge, a Christian organization, and became clean. She said, "That program really saved my life. It helped me take responsibility for my life and not blame others."

In these examples, Sandy wasn't aware of the influence of his past; Kelly has begun to understand and come to terms with her history.

Reflect: Can you identify what you may have missed as a child and whether this relates to any difficulties you have had since adolescence? Might this be replaying in romantic relationships? Ask some friends who know you well.

You can think about this as emotional learning from childhood. What themes have you identified as powerful for you?

Children in a Disaster Zone

Some children were completely failed. Not even their basic needs were met. They received only conditional love and no consistent nurturing. Additionally, there may have been a failure to protect them against sexual abuse; they may have seen domestic violence, and lacked discipline or guidance. There could have been a reversal of roles, in which the child was expected to support or even parent his adult caregivers. This results in what has been called the "parentified" child. Some parents will even blame their child when *their* needs haven't been met. Such experiences add up to a loss of safety, security, and self-esteem.

Children from chaotic homes become adults with emotional deficits and a sense of violation. Consider the case of Sandy:

Sandy raced cars on the weekends. He had a couple of near misses and then a serious accident that he was lucky to survive. In a rare moment of self-reflection, he said, "Nothing really satisfies, but it's a distraction."

Hargrave observed that a child with a disturbed childhood will grow up with either rage or a sense of entitlement, or possibly both. This makes psychological sense. They may be stuck emotionally in childhood and acting out unconscious needs. A damaged adult, when in a relationship, will take almost any action to gain the nurturing and care needed. This can lead to destructive behavior, including manipulation, threats, and abuse. It has been called "destructive entitlement."

How do you deal with this history? Think about what is "onstage" and what is "backstage." The actors in the relationship dramas, now adults, play out destructive behaviors through manipulative acts, threats, abuse, and being sexually promiscuous. The bad behavior is obvious. But this is only the coping behavior on the front stage. Backstage, behind this layer of self-centered behavior there are still the unconditional schemas and old wounds.

Today's maladaptive coping behavior is often based on learning from childhood: People usually do what works best to meet even a few of their needs. As a child, lashing out or being dominant, controlling, or threatening was more successful than showing vulnerability or weakness ("If the going gets tough, the tough get going").

This can be the real clue to why a person *feels justified* in showing antisocial behavior. Why? The adult is emotionally still a child trapped in family dynamics. Naturally, the result will be a profound instability in life and relationships. This is a matter of facing hidden agendas. What worked in childhood is not likely to be optimal for the adult living in different circumstances. This is one of the reasons we end up matching our childhood coping styles instead of finding a more adaptive way to live.

We'll say a few words about both rage and entitlement. Rage may be externalized with verbal abuse, threats, violence, or any combination of them. It may also be internalized by being locked in dark depression or self-destructive acts such as cutting, binge eating, or attempting suicide. Clearly, this is very stressful to family members and anyone else who is close, so it must be addressed.

Perhaps equally destructive is a sense of entitlement. This is expressed in the maxim "What's mine is mine and what's yours is mine as well!" Entitlement is usually self-focused or narcissistic. There may also be a dynamic of shame in the background, with assumptions such as "I was unworthy of love" and "If I don't fight for my rights, no one will care about me." In the latter case, the entitlement is a compensation for the underlying Defectiveness-Shame schema. It makes a huge difference if you're able not to judge the book by the cover and add the hidden scene of Defectiveness-Shame to the entitled persona. It's a kind of high road to dealing with undersocialized narcissists, telling them that you dislike their onstage presentation but that you like their backstage vulnerable side.

Reflect: Can you identify any strong themes here? If you recognize a failed childhood, what have you learned about yourself? Can you see evidence of either rage or entitlement? Can you sense the vulnerable core within the hard shell?

On the other end of the personality spectrum, we find people who learned to please others to survive, such as those we identified above as parentified children. They had to submit to other people's needs and demands to gain a minimum of approval or attachment. They were born servants! They often find themselves ending up in such roles, asking themselves, "Why is it always me?" This indicates that they haven't faced up to their personal script ("You have to be nice to others to survive!"). This is conditional love: You're not loved for who you are but for what you do. If you recognize yourself in this description, you might consider whether you have been oversocialized.

Warning: Some people believe that they always have to be nice to others. But we can come from terrible backgrounds and under cover be as entitled or enraged as anyone else. The needs for assertiveness and attachment are innate to all people, and how they play out depends on early childhood experiences. Looked at this way, we're all birds of a similar feather. Dealing with difficult people is much easier if you're able to address their hidden side.

Dealing with the Past

It's an important first step if you recognize yourself in this description of childhood deprivation and resulting schemas leading to feelings of rage, entitlement, or both.

To do: Take the time to write your story of violation or neglect and carefully describe what you see as its impact on your adult relationships. Perhaps add this account to your autobiography. This will take insight and honesty (with yourself—the hardest kind!). Can you share this story with your partner or your best friend? Perhaps they will have a similar story. This could be a good starting point for looking at each other differently.

A child will have a tantrum if their needs are not met. So, too, will adults who have a needy child within:

> *Jessica* was described as "Mount Vesuvius" by her friends. She would quickly explode for seemingly no cause, and she was finding that friends quickly lost patience with her. She said, "I'm just being me. I allow my friends to be themselves. Love it or leave it!"

Bart remarked, "I enjoy building up my body. The girls are interested in me. I just return their interest—nothing wrong with that!"

Jessica and Bart, in different ways, are responding to a sense of unmet need with entitlement: "I must be happy." They seem to have minimal awareness of the cost to others. The cue for getting a clearer understanding of the price of this behavior is thinking about its long-term effects. In the end, such behavior will push away people who do not want to fight or to submit. This reduces the number of possible friends and partners significantly. Eventually, you might be in control but more or less alone. Jessica and Bart are stressing their assertiveness leg too much and denying their need for attachment.

You need to work out a strategy to deal with all this. Only then can the past be left in the past. If you aren't in therapy, think again carefully about taking this step. Realistically, it's hard to work through such issues on your own.

We want to acknowledge that *it was natural to expect more as a child.* Indeed, it was your human right. And biology supports this "deal": The baby's neediness activates the caregiver's attachment or caregiving system so that they finally have no choice other than to soothe the baby, at least as long as they're more or less healthy. And the baby's smile rewards them, reinforcing a functional attachment cycle. This is how things are meant to be.

When this natural expectation failed, for whatever reason, in your family, it's far more difficult to make up for the lost love. There are limits to what you can expect from friends or a marriage. You don't look as cute as a baby does, and your expression of anger doesn't activate people's attachment systems but their assertiveness systems, forcing them to escape from you to protect themselves!

Blaming others for what you didn't get as a child is a trap that you can avoid. It's essential to understand the childhood origins of adult problems and keep those issues where they belong. A lot of conflict masquerades as adult issues, when a resolution can only be achieved by addressing what began in childhood. Thus, it's essential to separate schema-driven impacts from environmental influences on your current way of feeling. If you're aware that the way your partner feels and acts is schema driven, it will be much easier not to take their criticisms or accusations personally. A helpful way to separate one from the other is to try to shift to an observer's perspective to get an idea of how a healthy or wise person would react in the given situation (deviations are usually schema driven). On the other hand, it takes a lot of the burden off your partner if you don't expect them to deal with your schema-driven feelings and don't get angry when they're unwilling to fulfill your childlike needs. It just won't work in the long run if you expect others to do so.

> *Cindy* has a severe Abandonment schema that she compensates for with controlling and bossing her partner, *Bert*. No matter what Bert does, she'll never really trust him. It would be helpful to remove the burden from Bert of constantly reassuring her. On the other hand, Bert has a Mistrust-Abuse schema resulting from his coercive mother. Whenever Cindy says anything critical about him, he feels that he's being bossed around and tends to react by withdrawing from her to avoid the activation of his schema. This is exactly what triggers Cindy's Abandonment schema.

It's not hard to tell that there's only a small space left for Cindy and Bert to meet in without falling into their old life-traps. Nevertheless, they felt attracted by each other because they each found what they already knew from their parents. This is schema chemistry.

When we appreciate the backstage dynamics, the play begins to make sense. Once this is understood, it can lead you to greater emotional stability. Finally you're in charge of working on that yourself. Once you depend less on others, your relationships will work better. Love is a child of freedom—not of dependency.

Reflect: Who are the backstage characters in the theater of your life? What are they saying to you? Do you have a sense of what kind of play you're in? Is it a comedy, a melodrama, or a tragedy?

Start with Schemas

Now a suggestion about a possible way forward using the idea of emotional learning. Think about the two or three most troubling schemas you have.

> *Michael* thought about Emotional Inhibition, Failure, and Social Isolation.

These areas describe schema vulnerability. They can also be understood as domains in which emotional learning has occurred. You can think of emotional learning as "what I know about myself."

> Michael sought to be more specific about what he had learned in each domain. He said in relation to Emotional Inhibition, "I'm not safe to feel emotions." With Failure, the message was, "I can try all I want but nothing will ever change." And with Social Isolation, "My safety is in avoiding people."

In this example, there has been a shift from the neighborhood of schema identification to the "street" of a statement about the self. In a later chapter, we go further, using a process of discovery proposed by Bruce Ecker. That can take us to an even more accurate "house" level statement of emotional learning.

Summary

In schema therapy, the past is not past. There are a range of powerful techniques to change the grip of past emotional deficits, traumatic experiences, and behavior patterns. You might plan to change extreme swings from being overcontrolling to being chaotic. It's easy to see that some behavior made sense in dysfunctional families but becomes problematic in adult relationships.

While schema therapy is a very effective way to deal with the past, it's not the only effective therapy. There's nothing prescriptive here. Indeed, any therapy that manages to put the past in its place is useful to deal with issues that can overwhelm you in your current situation. Family-of-origin work will help you to recognize how prior hurts continue to play out in your life, to understand your or your partner's automatic responses and, we hope, to interrupt dysfunctional processes. You can be a detective and discover what was missing in your past, but even more important is an enduring commitment to make changes to improve your present and future. Also be aware of how important these same dynamics might be for your partner. Think about how growth is a challenge both to you as an individual and to you in a relationship. It's a matter of *both/and*.

To Read Further

- The cognitive exercise is from Andrew Bernstein (2010). See www. resilienceacademy.com
- Destructive entitlement: Boszormenyi-Nagy and Krasner (1986)
- Rage and entitlement: Hargrave (2000)
- The five tasks of childhood: Young (1999).

References

Bernstein, A. (2010). *The myth of stress: Where stress really comes from and how to live a happier, healthier life.* London, UK: Piaktus.

Boszormenyi-Nagy, I., & Krasner, B. (1986). *Between give and take.* New York, NY: Brunner/Mazel.

Hargrave, T. D. (2000). *The essential humility of marriage.* Phoenix, AZ: Zeig, Tucker & Theisen.

Young, J. (1999). *Cognitive therapy for personality disorders: A schema-focused approach.* Sarasota, FL: Professional Resources Press.

Young, J. E., Klosko, J. S., & Weishaar, M. E. (2003). *Schema therapy: A practitioner's guide.* New York, NY: Guilford Press.

5

Modes
In the Present Tense

Language makes us human, and schema therapy has created a language for psychological things. It's important that we devote time to understanding our psyche: what works and what so easily goes wrong. This will help us to better understand not only ourselves but our romantic relationships.

We already have some background understanding of being human, based on our experiences. Now we'll look more closely at how we function in relationships in the here and now. The first goal is to become *mode aware*, both as an individual and, importantly, as a couple. In later chapters, the shift will be to *mode management* and *mode change* through the Healthy Adult mode and the practical application of these techniques to relationship growth.

From Schemas to Modes

There has been a shift in language and models in schema therapy circles. Initially, it was all about *schemas*, naturally, but then *modes* came to center stage. This happened for some very good reasons.

We know that we're changeable beings. Our inner state is generally in flux over the course of time. This is described by modes. Modes comprise activated schemas and coping responses in one unit. Modes are what you *see*. This can include behaviors as well as cognitions, emotions, and

Breaking Negative Relationship Patterns: A Schema Therapy Self-help and Support Book, First Edition. Bruce A. Stevens and Eckhard Roediger.
© 2017 John Wiley & Sons, Ltd. Published 2017 by John Wiley & Sons, Ltd.

bodily sensations. Noticing a mode is like looking at the surface of a pond. Deep in the water are the underlying schemas.

This might be easier to explain with an example:

> *Nell* worried about her health. She felt that she could easily get cancer, so she had frequent medical examinations. She would often get a second opinion when she felt that her doctor had not been careful enough. All this indicated a Vulnerability schema, which could appear on the surface as a Suspicious Overcontroller mode and at times as a Vulnerable Child mode when she felt defenseless.

The idea of a mode includes our current state of feelings, thoughts, and how we act. It's helpful to understand that we do not actually see or feel a schema, but only the mode, which is the activation of the schema in the here and now. In the traditional language of psychology, a schema is a trait, while a mode is a state. So a schema is a vulnerability; a mode is an actuality. While you *have* a schema; you *are in* a mode.

It's much easier to work with what you see. This is why most schema therapists look for modes in clinical sessions. But you won't understand the modes unless you see the schemas that drive them. There's always a causal link between schemas and modes.

Schemas point to the emotional depth of the mode and to its developmental origins. This is a core difference from other therapy models, which describe parts of the self. Modes are in the present but signal the past. We can only fully understand a current mode while seeing it as a reactivation of old wounds in the here and now. When the schemas behind the modes are missed, modes seem to float without any foundation (and become arbitrary). A mode appears in the present, but its drivers come from the past.

Reflect: It's easier for you to change what you *see yourself doing* or *feeling* or *thinking*. This will help you become aware of your modes. Think about your partner. When you see that they're distressed, what you see is a mode. Although this is the activation of a schema expressed through a coping style, the result is the mode you see.

To do: Make mode awareness a goal for your growth (some tools are introduced below). It may take weeks or even a month or two. You'll come to quickly recognize mode shifts in yourself and your partner. And of course in everybody else: colleagues at work, drivers on the highway, shoppers in the supermarket, and people everywhere. You cannot *not* be in a mode.

Types of Modes

There are four major kinds of modes (see Figure 5.1):

- child modes
- internal parent modes
- coping modes
- Healthy Adult mode.

In the mode model, we have the introduction of positive states of mind. Maladaptive schemas are negative, but with Healthy Adult and Happy Child there's an important positive extension to the model. Healthy Adult and Happy Child provide the building blocks of healthy functioning and well-being.

First, we introduce the *range* of modes.

Child modes in this book—based on a description by Young—are understood in terms of basic emotions we experience deep inside of us. We can see this in facial expressions in all cultures: sadness, fear, anger, disgust, surprise, and happiness. Happiness is the goal. When we feel

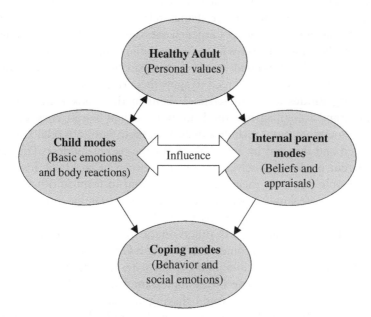

Figure 5.1   The basic mode model

sadness or fear (in the sense of panic), we're at the Vulnerable Child end of the emotional spectrum. These emotions are a sign that our attachment need has been threatened and activated. In a state of panic, we tend to cling to anyone. Think of a child in a playground who cannot find her mother. You see pure panic in her eyes. When we feel disgust or anger, this is an indication that our self-assertiveness, our need to protect our autonomy, is challenged, so emotionally we shift between Vulnerable and Angry Child modes. The other child modes capture emotions in the range between. When our needs are met in a balanced way, we're in Happy Child mode. Just for clarification: Disgust on an emotional level appears more as disliking something or feeling annoyed and trying to get away from it. Fear of something (for example, entering a plane or an elevator) is more "disgust" than "fear" in the sense of panic. We try to get away from something that we do not like or that threatens us. We try to protect ourselves. This is more an expression of the assertiveness or self-protection need than the attachment need because attachment means trying to connect with somebody (or something). The Defiant Child mode is close to Angry Child and is defending autonomy.

Internal parent modes are the traces of what was said by authority figures, mostly our parents, during our childhood. But such an internal commentary can also come from older siblings, relatives, peers, teachers, or sports coaches. Sometimes we grasp unspoken messages from the family atmosphere. We hear them as voices in our heads commenting in a critical way on every step we take. This builds up the biggest part of our automatic appraisal and belief system. We usually tend to apply these rules to others, too!

Coping modes as we understand them in this book include visible behavior and accompanying social emotions such as hatred, envy, guilt, or shame. Social emotions include a nucleus of basic emotions (child modes) modified and directed by appraisals (from the parent modes). The child and parent modes themselves can remain unseen or backstage inside us. Most people don't act their basic emotions out in front of other people (except for close family or when under stress). For example, do you always let people know what you actually think about them? The coping modes describe the way we act towards others on the front stage. This is the point where schema therapy becomes interpersonal. Our current coping modes are often replays of our childhood coping styles. In childhood, this may have been our best way to deal with unpleasant situations, but as adults we have additional resources to avoid behaving in maladaptive ways.

Healthy Adult mode represents a mindful and self-reflective level of functioning based on our personal values. This state of mind is able to bring rational and functional behavior into the present. In this mode, we're able to recognize and fulfill the needs of the child modes of ourselves or others in a well-balanced way, just as we normally stand on both our legs, not one. We can also reappraise and block the parent mode voices. So instead of sinking down into our old automatic coping modes we can rise to a new level of functional behavior.

In a nutshell: The child modes in their essence represent basic emotions and are closely related to body sensations. In a child mode, we still feel as we felt as a child. These circuits are still present in the so-called limbic (or animal-like) part of our brain. The dysfunctional parent modes are the voices of significant others, including for core beliefs and recurring negative automatic thoughts, and are often experienced as toxic messages. The maladaptive coping modes are coping reactions to early childhood experiences accompanied by social emotions such as disgust, shame, guilt, or feeling superior. This includes behavioral reactions. The front-stage behavior is fed by both basic emotions (from child modes) and cognitions or beliefs (from parent modes).

Note: You can also think of the child modes as an emotional part of you that is yet to grow up or to be integrated by your Healthy Adult mode.

Don't be surprised if the description of the model we present in this book differs a bit from those you find in other books about schema therapy. Our perspective is closer to psychodynamic thinking, neurobiology, and consistency theory. Not all of our colleagues share this conceptualization, with the two levels (backstage and front stage) and the interaction between the modes. Some see all modes on one stage only and just describe them. However, the essential ideas of the model remain the same.

In our interpersonal schema therapy model, there's always an interpersonal meaning when we're in a coping mode, defining the relationship to the other person: either "I'm on top" (overcompensation striving for control), "I surrender" (to gain attachment), or "I withdraw from a relationship" passively (Detached Protector, as freezing behavior to avoid harm) or actively (Detached Self-soother, as a flight reaction to emotionally protect or soothe oneself). The unconscious selection of coping modes depends on the current internal activation of the child and parent modes.

Narelle had an anxious child mode (Vulnerable Child) with a harsh Punitive Parent, so she reacted with Detached Protector. She complained that she "rarely felt anything." Her partner thought something was wrong with her.

Brad had chronic problems in his romantic relationship. He had an Angry Child when feeling rejected, which came out when he resorted to alcohol in Detached Self-soother.

The coping mode is not basically maladaptive, but pathways can become too rigid, alternatives can be lacking, and modes can be highly unstable or flipping from moment to moment. We'll see below how in a Healthy Adult mode we use the essence of the coping modes in a more adaptive and flexible way.

Theoretical note: Freud (1923) in his structural theory distinguished *ego*, *superego*, and *id*. There are some similarities with schema therapy's understanding of modes: Roughly, superego is close to the parent modes of Demanding and Punitive Parent, ego is like Healthy Adult (although Healthy Adult in schema therapy is more integrative and not just aware of external reality), and id has components of the child modes, though more instinctual. The defense mechanisms parallel to a certain extent avoidant coping modes. What is missing in Freud is the surrendering and compensatory coping modes, although Self-aggrandizer has parallels to his idea of narcissism and some of the coping modes might be considered defense mechanisms. However, Freud's concept of conscious and unconscious processes and their dynamics differs a lot from the schema therapy model.

Once you become familiar with the mode model, you'll have a comprehensive map to understand yourself and your relationships with others. You'll see your behavior and that of others in a new light, especially when you're able to anticipate the hidden child modes behind an acted-out behavior. You'll better understand personal and interpersonal deficits by not judging the book by its cover. This will help you to find a path to more healthy and adaptive functioning. Healthy means being well balanced, remaining flexible, and having a realistic perspective. You'll be able to see all options and use them in a socially adaptive way when you need to.

Modes are important as concepts, but their real value emerges when you recognize them easily and adopt change strategies. Modes are user-friendly. An understanding of them gives language to the visible expressions of our inner states even when we're most unstable. And modes have been found to be a reliable guide to what we might need in a family or an intimate relationship (such as validation or limit setting).

In contrast, there's an inherent difficulty in using schemas. As we have mentioned, there are potentially 54 combinations of a single schema activation and coping styles (and countless combinations among them). With unstable individuals, it's the norm to have a vulnerability to many schemas with unstable patterns of schema activation. The emotional pathway to a single mode, such as Vulnerable Child, can involve a number of schemas such as Abandonment, Mistrust-Abuse, Defectiveness-Shame, and so on. The schemas are each expressed through a coping style and the result is a single mode. The advantage of thinking in terms of modes is that the end point, a single mode, limits complexity and potential confusion.

Remember: Modes are what you see—in yourself and others. Keep asking yourself, "What mode am I in right now?" Try to identify the general categories of child, parent and coping modes, and Healthy Adult.

Introducing the Individual Modes

The following is a list of the 14 most important schema modes.

Child modes

Vulnerability

1. **Vulnerable Child:** Vulnerable Child feels like a lonely child. Because his most important emotional needs have generally not been met, he'll usually feel empty, alone, socially unacceptable, undeserving of love, unloved, and unlovable. His feelings of emotional pain, fear of being abandoned, and shame are linked to childhood experiences.

Anger

2. **Angry Child:** Angry Child feels intensely angry, infuriated, frustrated, or impatient because her core emotional (or physical) needs or her need for autonomy are not being met. She'll vent her suppressed anger in inappropriate ways. She may make demands that seem entitled or spoiled and that alienate others, or act like a child throwing a temper tantrum. Be aware that an Angry Child mode can cover an underlying Vulnerable Child mode. Especially when you're highly energized, falling into anger feels better than getting in touch with your underlying sadness. So, once more: Dig deeper!
3. **Enraged Child:** Enraged Child experiences intense feelings of anger that results in him hurting or damaging people or objects. This displayed anger is out of control, and has the goal of destroying the aggressor, sometimes literally, mostly when his assertiveness need or his autonomy is threatened. This can be seen as the Enraged Child screaming or acting out impulsively.

Lack of discipline

4. **Impulsive Child:** Impulsive Child acts on her desires or impulses from moment to moment in a selfish or uncontrolled manner to get her own way, without regard to possible consequences for herself or others. She often has difficulty delaying her gratification, cannot tolerate limits, and may appear spoiled. Note that doing things that are healthy for you is often initially boring.

5. **Undisciplined Child:** Undisciplined Child cannot force himself to finish routine or boring tasks, gets frustrated quickly, and gives up.

Happiness

6. **Happy Child:** Happy Child feels at peace because her core emotional needs are being met in a well-balanced way. She feels loved, contented, connected, satisfied, fulfilled, protected, praised, worthwhile, nurtured, guided, understood, validated, self-confident, competent, appropriately autonomous or self-reliant, safe, resilient, strong, in control, adaptable, optimistic, and spontaneous.

Maladaptive coping modes

Surrender

7. **Compliant Surrender:** He acts in a passive, subservient, submissive, reassurance-seeking, or self-deprecating way towards others out of fear of conflict or rejection. He gives in to the perceived expectations of others, especially those seen as more powerful, and passively allows himself to be mistreated, or doesn't take steps to get healthy needs met. He selects people or engages in other behavior that directly maintains his self-defeating schema-driven pattern. He may feel a lot of resentment.

Avoidance

8. **Detached Protector:** She withdraws psychologically from the pain of schema activations by emotionally detaching. She shuts off all emotions, disconnects from others, rejects their help, and functions in an almost robotic manner. She feels "nothing" and appears emotionally distant, and avoids getting close to people. Signs and symptoms include depersonalization, emptiness, boredom, substance abuse, bingeing, self-mutilation, psychosomatic complaints, and "blankness." She shuts off from her inner needs, emotions, and thoughts, and usually feels aempty.

9. **Detached Self-soother:** He shuts off his emotions by engaging in activities or taking substances that will somehow soothe, stimulate, or distract him from feeling. His activities are generally pleasurable or exciting but he does them in an addictive or compulsive way. They can include workaholism, excessive exercise, gambling, dangerous sports, promiscuous sex, internet addiction, or drug abuse. Others will compulsively engage in solitary interests that are more self-soothing than self-stimulating, such as playing computer games, overeating, watching television, or fantasizing.

Overcompensation

10. **Self-aggrandizer:** She feels superior, special, and powerful, and behaves in an entitled, competitive, grandiose, abusive, or status-seeking way in order to have whatever she wants. She sees the world in terms of "top dog" and "underdog." What is most obvious may be a drive for dominance or control, so overcontrolling is a related overcompensatory mode. She's concerned about appearances rather than feelings, is almost completely self-absorbed, and shows little empathy for the needs or feelings of others. She demonstrates superiority and expects to be treated as special, and doesn't believe she should have to follow the rules that apply to everyone else. She craves admiration and frequently brags or behaves in a self-aggrandizing manner to inflate her sense of self. This compensates for her inner feelings of inferiority, inadequacy, or doubt.

11. **Bully and Attack:** He uses threats, intimidation, aggression, and coercion to get what he wants, including retaliation, and directly harms other people in a controlled and strategic way emotionally, physically, sexually, verbally, or through antisocial or criminal acts. He wants to assert a dominant position, but has the edge of threat. The motivation may be to compensate for or prevent abuse or humiliation. There may be an element of sadism.

Maladaptive parent modes

12. **Punitive Parent:** This is the internalized voice of the parent, criticizing and punishing the person. She'll become angry with herself and feel that she deserves punishment for having or showing normal needs that her parents didn't allow her to express. The tone of this mode is harsh, critical, and unforgiving. Signs and symptoms include self-loathing, self-criticism, self-denial, self-mutilation, suicidal fantasies,

and other self-destructive behavior. In our interpretation of the mode model, like the underlying schemas these expectations can be directed to others, too.

13. **Demanding Parent:** The Demanding Parent continually pushes and pressures the child (or other people) to meet excessively high standards. He feels that the "right" way to be is to be perfect or achieve at a very high level, to keep everything in order, to strive for high status, to be humble, to put other's needs before one's own or to be efficient or avoid wasting time. He feels that it's wrong to express feelings or to act in a spontaneous way.

Healthy Adult mode

14. **Healthy Adult:** The Healthy Adult nurtures, validates, and affirms the Vulnerable Child mode and sets limits for the Angry and Impulsive Child modes. She combats and eventually replaces the maladaptive coping modes with functional coping behavior. She performs appropriate adult functions, such as working, parenting, taking responsibility, and committing. She pursues pleasurable adult activities, such as "good" sex; intellectual, esthetic, and cultural interests; health maintenance; and athletic activities. There's a good balance of her own and others' needs.

To do: First of all, reflect on the list of modes. What modes have you seen in others? In your partner? Do any seem familiar when you think about yourself? Can family members recognize that you might operate in some of the modes described here? How well does this model describe you in family or intimate relationships? For example, are child modes or coping modes more common? Play the "mode detecting game" wherever you are, with yourself and the people around you, just for fun and to sharpen your diagnostic eye. This will make you and your partner more mode aware.

Individual exercise: For any modes that you have identified, can you think of what that mode would say? Use your imagination. Try to find three or four sentences for each.

Reflect: Can you see the Healthy Adult mode in someone you admire? You might consider some amazing examples, like Nelson Mandela or Desmond Tutu from South Africa.

Couple exercise: Draw a pie chart of yourself in terms of modes. The size of each piece of the pie shows how much of your adult life you spend in that state. Include only the most common modes you find in yourself. Do the same for your partner. If they do the same, you can compare the results and discuss them. Or, even better, do it together right away!

To do: Download, answer, and score the Schema Mode Inventory version 1.1 (SMI 1.1). Does this inventory agree with your self-assessment? Where are the differences? To access the SMI 1.1, go to www.schematherapy. com. You may have to pay for the right to download it.

Additional Modes

The canon of modes has not been settled. Additional modes are continually being suggested and debated in schema therapy circles. See Figure 5.2 for a diagram of modes (including some suggested ones). We tend to consider the following in our clinical work:

1. **Defiant Child** is a mode every parent will recognize. The angry message is "I'm not going to do what you say!"
2. **Angry Protector** is a global irritation for everyone. The message is "Keep away." *Henny* had an important executive position in which she always felt stressed. Her staff knew when to avoid her.
3. **Suspicious Overcontroller** mode is a "me against the world" state of mind. Everything is dangerous and the only way to cope is to try to manage every detail, but any sense of safety is illusory.
4. **Perfectionist Overcontroller** mode is based on the belief that nobody will do it as well as you, and that you have to control others to make sure they do it right.
5. **Over-analyzer** mode is typical of some people in computing or academia. *Ben* is a very intelligent person but highly ruminative, and never gets to a solution.
6. **Fantasy** mode lets a person get lost in a make-believe world of endless daydreams. *Brenda* read romance novels and tagged the pages for certain kinds of romantic interactions. She was endlessly imagining Mr. Right and when he would turn up. She said, "God already has him picked out for me."
7. **Avoidant Protector** is about avoiding everything. It's a state of mind in withdrawal. There's no engagement with people or even life.
8. **Accusing Protector** blames others for not treating him fairly and giving him what he deserves. He abstains from taking the responsibility for his own life and stays passive.

9. Forensic modes such as **Conning-manipulative** and **Predator** modes
    are more typical in prisoners and antisocial groups such as motorcycle
    gangs. David Bernstein has developed this understanding.

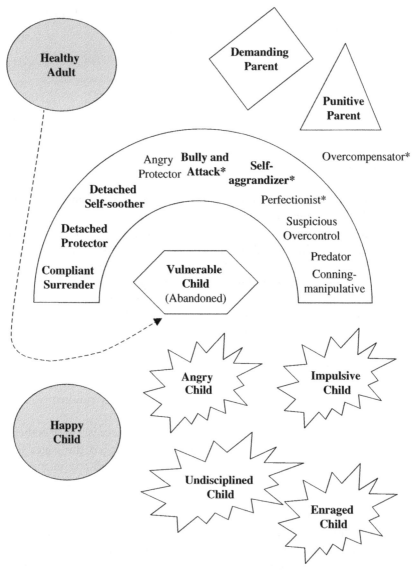

Figure 5.2 The generally accepted modes. Note: Modes in bold are in SMI 1.1

Figure 5.2 pictures these modes in a spectrum of coping modes. The modes in bold are in SMI 1.1, which is widely available. There are some other proposed modes, which are explained in later chapters.

To do: Find a photograph of yourself at a young age. Choose something to represent your Vulnerable Child. Do you have a photo of your partner as a child? *Marie* found a photo of herself at age 8 looking lonely. She had it framed and put it on her bedroom table to remind her to better care for her vulnerable self.

Integrating Schemas and Modes

Initially, schemas and modes are like two different languages. However, it's possible to integrate the two. Think about the following:

Schemas < > Schema coping styles < > Modes

This represents a constantly moving awareness, shifting from schemas to modes or from modes backwards to schemas, but through the filter of schema coping styles (surrender, compensation, or avoidance). This is illustrated in the following example, which links the three areas:

> *Vince* has schema vulnerability with Abandonment, Emotional Deprivation, and Mistrust-Abuse. He'll characteristically compensate Abandonment by becoming clingy and overcontrolling in relationships, using avoidance to manage Emotional Deprivation with alcohol abuse, and surrendering with Mistrust-Abuse by too quickly trusting strangers. This provides pathways to Vulnerable Child through Abandonment, Detached Self-soother using alcohol, and overcompensating by controlling others but also going into Compliant Surrender in relationships, about which he should be more cautious.

Understanding the schema and coping style background gives psychological depth to the mode model. Also, when you consider rescripting (introduced below), use your awareness of schema vulnerability to make sure you meet the needs of the Vulnerable Child. For example, with Abandonment there's a need for physical presence and emotional nurturing, with Mistrust-Abuse the need for reassurance and protection, and with Emotional Deprivation the child's emotional needs are prioritized. This will be what will be guiding your therapist in schema therapy.

Summary

The mode model was introduced in this chapter. Modes are activated schemas and coping styles—basically what we see. There are four kinds: child modes, parent modes, coping modes, and Healthy Adult mode. The list of modes is not yet fixed and is open for additions. The challenge is to become aware of your modes and those of people close to you. It's possibly easier to recognize modes in others, but don't stop there. Seeing your own modes through mode awareness is one of the most important skills you'll need to master. Also challenge yourself to not forget your schemas but remember the two-way path from schemas to coping styles to modes. This will provide a deeper understanding of your mental states and help in changing out of dysfunctional relational patterns. Mode awareness is a very important first step to improving your relationships.

To Read Further

- The structural theory of Freud: Freud (1923)
- The Schema Mode Inventory version 1.1: see ISST website (www. SchemaTherapySociety.org)
- Patterns of couple mode interactions: Atkinson (2012)
- Defiant Child mode: Jacob, van Genderen, and Seebauer (2015).

References

Atkinson, T. (2012). Schema therapy for couples: Healing partners in a relationship. In M. van Vreeswijk, J. Broersen, & M. Nadort (Eds.), *The Wiley-Blackwell handbook of schema therapy: Theory, research and practice* (pp. 323–335). Oxford, UK: Wiley-Blackwell.

Bernstein, D., Arntz, A., & de Vos, M. (2007). Schema focused therapy in forensic settings: Theoretical model and recommendations for best clinical practice. *International Journal of Forensic Mental Health, 6*(2), 169–183.

Freud, S. (1923). *The ego and the id*. In the *Standard edition of the complete psychological works of Sigmund Freud, 19*, 3–66.

Jacob, G., van Genderen, H., & Seebauer, L. (2015). *Breaking negative thought patterns: A schema therapy self-help and support book*. Malden, MA: Wiley-Blackwell.

Young, J. E., Klosko, J. S., & Weishaar, M. E. (2003). *Schema therapy: A practitioner's guide*. New York, NY: Guilford Press.

6

Mode Awareness

We have been described as a "tool-using animal" (Thomas Carlyle). While some animals use simple tools like a stick to dig for ants, we use more complex tools to extend our effectiveness. So, too, in schema therapy, as we explore in this chapter.

Introduction to Mode Dynamics

The mode map based on the extended mode model was developed to show the interaction of modes (Figure 6.1).

This conceptualization allows you to visualize yourself. Are you sinking down into a coping mode on the bottom level? Are you in a child mode, almost emotionally drowned or haunted by parental mode thoughts or beliefs? Or are you well balanced in your Healthy Adult mode, rising to the top of the figure, aware of your inner emotions and having a good distance from your intrusive beliefs? Think about how you function over time. If you remain more in Healthy Adult, you can track when you're being driven by emotions and activated beliefs leading to the coping modes. The integrative and realistic perspective of Healthy Adult is essential to better functioning. Knowing these dynamics is an aspect of being more mode aware.

> *Kerry* noted a feeling of overwhelming fear and identified her Vulnerable Child. She told her husband, Brad, "I'm really scared to go out of the house without you."

Breaking Negative Relationship Patterns: A Schema Therapy Self-help and Support Book, First Edition. Bruce A. Stevens and Eckhard Roediger.
© 2017 John Wiley & Sons, Ltd. Published 2017 by John Wiley & Sons, Ltd.

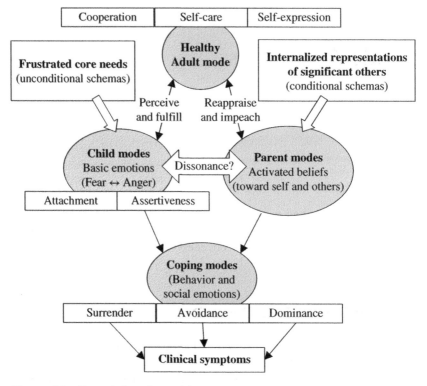

Figure 6.1   Extended mode model

Bill needed to feel connected to himself. He did adventure sports. Only when he parachuted did he feel completely alive. He reconnected with a sensual Happy Child to stop spending more time in Detached Protector mode.

You may be troubled by your parent modes. Such messages come as the voice of an inner critic (inside your head). These are internalized messages from the past. Often, such messages will contradict your child-related needs.

Sam had a strong Punitive Parent mode, which was merciless in condemning him. He said, "This voice attacks me. I'm worthless, worth nothing."

Sam listened to the parental voice and neglected his child-related needs for self-care. He thought about his success in the military and thought this was evidence of his "superior intelligence" (Self-aggrandizer mode).

He also thought about how he had an internalized voice of his abusive father. The only respite was his time at school, when he enjoyed being in the cadets. This continued with a career in the army, where he was quickly promoted. But he also stuck with his coping style when it no longer served the same need. These modes caused difficulties with his wife, who threatened to leave him.

Brenda was in her early thirties. She was already a successful solicitor but she was bullying, which gave her a bulldog reputation and intimidated others. This caused problems in her family life. Her partner asked, "Why do you have to get so angry just to get your way?"

We can use the extended mode model to see that Brenda had a Bully and Attack (dominant) coping mode. This was justified by her Demanding Parent mode with rigid rules about what is "right." What was hidden, and protected, was her Vulnerable Child. If she was to grow into a more flexible adult, her Vulnerable Child mode would have to be recognized and those needs better met.

Usually, people don't see a problem with their coping behavior. This style of interacting is understood as part of personality and experienced as "just being me." This is one reason why people typically believe that they're normal and everyone else in their life has to change. Brenda, in the case above, was happy with her way of interacting with people. She was convinced that she was justified in how she related. Developing a mode map (see Figure 6.1) based on the extended mode model is an important tool for understanding mode dynamics. It reveals excesses and deficits in our behavior and allows some comparison with others. Like a street map, it shows us where we're standing and which road to take to become more balanced. Note the risks as well. You may find that changing your behavior can lead to conflict. But there are benefits in making a realistic appraisal, and even accountability.

In everyday life we usually find ourselves in some kind of coping mode—more or less adaptive and functional. Coping modes can be linked to social emotions such as shame and guilt on the internalizing pole, or hatred and envy on the externalizing pole.

Sometimes it's more difficult to be aware of our child modes "backstage." Getting in touch with our emotions is the way in. The child modes are linked to our basic emotions. We enter a child mode when our core emotional needs are not met.

Note: The child modes have a way of seeing the world that is like the view of a child. Gitta Jacob also added that one's reactions to situations are childlike when in a child mode. The implication for couples is that when we're in a child mode our thinking tends to be very black and white or absolute.

Exercise: Think about an emotionally intense situation. Then take a multiple-choice test and ask yourself which of the four emotions fits best: anger, disgust (feeling annoyed), sadness, or fear (in the sense of panic)?

To be aware: Since basic emotions are an expression of a biological activation, they're closely linked with body sensations. This is why it's helpful to identify how your body feels. Is there some pressure on your chest or a butterfly feeling in your stomach? This might be fear. Do you feel a weight on your heart? This could express grief. Heavy weights on your shoulders are usually caused by overwhelming Demanding Parent modes. Is something pushing from inside, below your belly? This is probably anger. If your throat feels sour, this can be a sign of Detached Protector avoiding anger. This landscape of emotions is reliable because we have learned how the body expresses itself, but sometimes we need training to get in touch with these basic emotions again. Men seem to have the greatest difficulty in this area.

To do: When you notice you're in a child mode, ask yourself what you need. Can you meet that need in a healthy way? Can you think of ways to invite someone close to you to meet such needs? Involve your partner. All this has a lot to do with being healthy in relationships. We desperately hope that our child needs will be met in our closest relationships. If we're stuck in a coping mode or externalizing Punitive Parent in our intimate relationship, that will have repercussions. At the very least, our partner will be unhappy. The only way forward is to become more aware of our mode states. See how the modes work—or don't work—in your relationship and then try to find healthy solutions.

From Unhealthy to Healthy Modes

In schema therapy, the goal is to strengthen the Healthy Adult mode. Staying in Healthy Adult enables us to cope in a flexible and integrated way. Some emotional distance through Detached Protector is useful, but to remain there is to shut out the world. As with medication, what is the right dosage? The negative automatic thoughts of the parent modes have to be reappraised and the needs of the child modes have to be acknowledged and fulfilled when possible. This is the way to psychological growth.

Imagine a child whose needs are always perfectly met. While such a child won't be well prepared to survive, she would not feel sad, anxious, or angry. So basic emotions are signals to our caregivers (and later to ourselves) that our needs are not fully met. When the child's needs are satisfied, Vulnerable Child becomes an open, fearless, and sensitive child again, willing to socialize with others. The Angry Child, when his needs are met, calms down and becomes an empowered child ready for exploration with realistic assertiveness. It's the job of the Healthy Adult to reappraise the old beliefs and care for the child in a balanced way and then develop functional and flexible coping behavior for a successful performance in life. This is what you see in the top level of Figure 6.1.

Reflect: Think about yourself in various settings: home, leisure, work, social, church, and so on. What modes are you commonly in? For example, where are you most likely to be in Demanding Parent mode? Or in a child mode? How much of your time are you in a coping mode? Reflecting on your modes is an essential part of mode awareness. Think about your partner as well. Can you see how your modes might interact?

Drawing Your Own Mode Map

To do: In order to think about your mode dynamics, we'll begin with the mode map diagram. Make up your own individualized diagram first. Figure 6.2 is an empty mode map that you might find useful.

This mode map is based on the extended mode model and may appear complex at first sight, but don't be put off. It's easier when you start to fill in the squares. Also, it's the whole model summarized in one clear diagram. So keep looking until you see beyond the parts and get familiar with the whole interacting model.

Start with the blank mode map. Perhaps photocopy it so you have a few copies to work on. Begin to insert the information in the boxes. Typically, some will remain blank, which reveals the gaps in your understanding. The bottom row shows your coping behavior, the middle "hidden emotions" and thoughts, and the top the goal to remain as long as possible in Healthy Adult mode. You can also add schemas into the boxes (see Figure 6.3).

Advice to fill out the diagram: Typically, you might begin this exercise in a coping mode, which might not take you very far. But then make your way up and look at the boxes in the middle level. You come to the underlying basic emotions and beliefs. To use a metaphor, what we do in analyzing coping modes is like a painter who knows color. All the colors we see are mixed out of the primary colors red, blue, and yellow (shaded by black and lightened by white). Blue could stand for the Vulnerable Child, red for the Angry Child, and yellow for the beliefs. All visible behavior is composed out of these components.

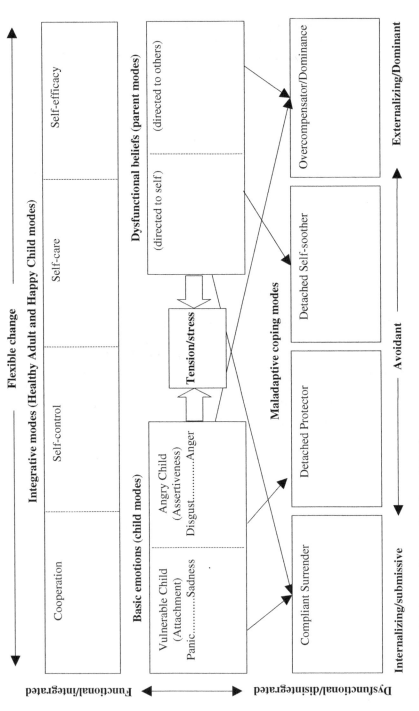

Figure 6.2 Mode map. Source: Roediger (2012)

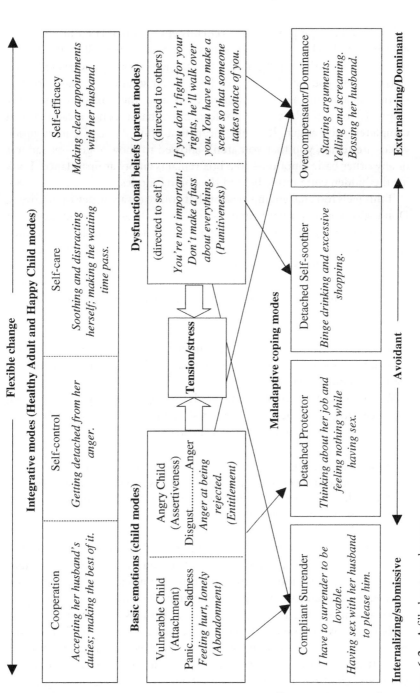

Figure 6.3 A filled-out mode map

Usually, if a coping mode box remains empty, the related boxes in the intermediate level will be more or less empty, too. Just follow the arrows backwards from the coping modes to the motivational "backstage" level. This is where you can find the key for a better solution. It may currently be out of sight in the empty boxes. Of course, the boxes are not really empty. If, for example, you do not feel angry, that does not mean that you completely lack anger. It could mean that your Punitive Parent mode voices are telling you that you aren't allowed to show anger—or sadness or any other basic emotion—so a box remains empty at first glance. Look for the hidden child mode behind the coping modes.

If this feels too challenging, accept that you're on a journey of discovery. Don't give yourself a hard time, as you are making important steps just by noticing what isn't in your awareness. Just take a break, or continue reading but keep returning to the diagram. Perhaps come back when you feel distressed; that's likely to be when you're in a child mode and can identify a Vulnerable Child mode cycle. All it takes is that you don't push your basic emotions aside even if your self-critical parent modes dislike them. Shift into a self-accepting, healthy observer mode and you will begin to see the basic emotions.

To do: After you have a shot at the mode map, if you're seeing a schema therapist ask them to assist you. Also look carefully at Cindy's mode map for ideas about how to fill out yours.

When you can see your coping modes, accept that they're present but may need to be softened and integrated in a more functional and flexible way. But if a coping mode works, don't worry.

> *Nikki* went through a crisis after her best friend committed suicide. She blamed herself for not seeing that her friend was in difficulty. She survived in Detached Protector mode until she was strong enough to feel the intense emotions of the grieving process.

In schema therapy, we try to "ride the tide" and to use what we have in a more adaptive manner. Use your style of coping in the best way possible. The Healthy Adult mode is your trainer. In that mode, you'll get a realistic perspective and find a way to perform better. The direction of your coping mode might not be basically wrong, but sometimes less is more!

To do: Look at yourself through the eyes of a good friend (or a wise person). They see you with the potential to be all you can become. Another idea: It may help to look at your child modes as if you are looking at your own children. Try loving yourself and kick your devaluating parent modes out!

Now: Fill out the mode map from the perspective of your Healthy Adult. Then take a moment to get into a state of spiritual awareness, getting in touch with the best, most positive part of you, and look again at your map. Do you want to make any changes?

Tracking Mode Changes

The mode map can be used to explore your relationship dynamics. For example, it's possible to link the coping mode you may be in to the internal activation of a child or parent mode: An Anxious Child with an inward-directed parent mode will lead to surrender. An Angry Child and an outward-directed parent mode will result in an overcompensation coping mode, such as Bully and Attack. If an Angry Child's tendency to fight is blocked by a Punitive Parent, that might result in an avoidant coping mode such as Detached Protector or Detached Self-soother. Sometimes both ends of the spectrum of basic emotions are activated simultaneously.

> *May* was unhappy in her life. She fought against an awareness of distressing emotions. Instead, she retreated into the numbness of Detached Protector, but then she realized, "I don't really feel anything. I exist in a kind of emotional fog." This protected her against having to face questions, such as whether she wanted to remain in her relationship with Ralf.

> *Toby* could see that he always tried to please his wife. He would do whatever she insisted on. But eventually after frustration built up his Enraged Child mode erupted: "This is too much! I've done so much for her and she's not grateful at all. So I'll stop being so nice! She'll get what she deserves!" Such overcompensatory explosions would surprise him (and her!). Then he would feel shame afterwards. His Punitive Parent would say, "Shame on you for letting yourself go that way. You'll lose your marriage!" Then Toby would surrender again, but feel worthless. And the cycle continued with even greater intensity.

Of course, some people (for example, narcissists or antisocial people) are more on the right-hand end of the coping mode spectrum and rarely surrender. Others never break out and remain highly contained and submissive. Interestingly, these expressive/unexpressive types of personality match well as a couple, as long as both agree to the unwritten contract—that one is the top dog and the other is the underdog remaining in Compliant Surrender.

Further advice on filling out the mode map: If you look at the box for the integrative modes (Healthy Adult and Happy Child) above the child and parent modes you'll recognize that there are types of coping, like the four boxes in the bottom line. These are your possible relationship styles of fight, flight, freeze, and surrender. But the Healthy Adult is able to soften the edges and use these basic tools in skilled, flexible, and socially adaptive ways.

Reflect: If a police officer stops your car, it's perhaps wise to adopt a moderate form of surrender. In an argument with your partner, "avoiding" by going for a 10-minute walk might ease the tension. If you have to wait for a train, some distraction skills are helpful. When a colleague ends up bossing you around, there's probably a need for limit setting. And if you lack assertiveness skills, you'll never get a higher salary.

In Healthy Adult mode, we use these options in a flexible way. We watch for the reactions of others. We can shift gears if necessary. There's a balance of attachment and assertiveness. We remain centered and adaptive. We're part of a social network and have our place. We're integrated and accepted. This gives us a feeling of safety and allows the Happy Child to be expressed.

Exercise: Do either of the following to assist you in visualizing your modes:

- Draw a representation of your common modes. You might use a large piece of paper and represent visually the interaction of your modes.
- Look through a stack of popular magazines. Find and cut out pictures that represent your common modes. Label them and with your partner make a poster to represent your relationship. Be creative; anything to represent your mutual identity is fine.

To do: Think about a recent incident in which you reacted strongly. Can you identify which modes were activated? What was the action sequence? Dialectical behavior therapy encourages "chain analysis" back from an incident. Try it and see what you discover.

Reflect: Can you think about a sequence of mode activation that led to Healthy Adult? Think about this pathway and whether you can more easily shift gears into a balanced perspective.

Triggers

An important aspect of mode awareness is to be able to identify triggers that result in our being in a mode.

Gary grew up listening to the Beatles. He found that some of their ballads, such as "Yesterday," quickly brought tears to his eyes. It reminded him of being frightened for his mother and living with the uncertainty of a violent father. He felt sadness: "I think of lost years of childhood, sad for my mother who deserved better, but anxious for myself." He was able to recognize that he was in Vulnerable Child mode.

A trigger can be anything that evokes a mode. A leads to B.

Jorja attended a university Bible study. The leader was very conservative, in a harsh, judging way. The message was more about judgment than God's love, but Jorja was lonely and valued her new group of friends. However, she found that the studies gave voice to her Punitive Parent and gradually she became more depressed. She talked to a Christian medical doctor who gently advised her to think about changing to a different Bible study group.

Once you identify triggers, it's easier to see why you shift into certain modes. This is an important aspect of mode awareness.

Reflect: Can you identify a common trigger for you? What is the mode you tend to shift from, and to what? It's like changing gears in a car. Can you make a choice, or is the shift automatic?

The Healthy Adult is Self-aware

Building awareness of your modes is essential in schema therapy. This mode awareness is similar to self-awareness. Our colleague Robert Brockman has noted that Healthy Adult mode can only act to overcome the influence of unhelpful modes if it's able to *notice them* when they're activated. We often find ourselves on autopilot. All too often, we're taken down a mode-driven pathway without any knowledge of the influence of that mode. We find ourselves in that mode too late, and it feels like we have almost no chance to change it. Becoming aware of your own modes at least gives you the chance to shift gears; without mode awareness you'll find it very difficult.

Sandy found herself crying for seemingly no reason. She thought, "I'm really sad and I'm feeling alone. Unprotected, as if no one cares for me." She had been reading about schema therapy and realized, "I feel very young, maybe five or six years old. I'm in a child mode." She looked at the mode list and saw that she was in Vulnerable Child.

Schema Therapy Flash Card

The schema therapy flash card developed by Jeffrey Young (Figure 6.4) is a very useful resource.

To do: Make a number of copies of the schema therapy flash card. Use them as you become aware that you're upset or angry. Figure 6.5 shows a flash card filled out for Cindy.

Right now I feel _____ (*emotion*)

because _____

_____ (*triggering situation*).

However, I know that this is probably my _____

_____ (*schema/backstage modes*),

which I learned through_____

_____ (*childhood experience*).

These schemas and modes lead me to _____

_____ (*coping mode*).

Reality testing (healthy mode):

Even though I believe _____

_____ (*parent mode message*),

the reality is that _____

_____ (*Healthy Adult message*)

The evidence in my life supporting the healthy view includes:

* _____

* _____

* _____.

Therefore, even though I feel like _____

_____ (*maladaptive coping mode*),

I could instead_____

_____

_____ (*functional coping mode*).

Figure 6.4 Schema therapy flash card. Source: Adapted from Young, Klosko, & Weishaar (2003)

Right now I feel ___*extremely angry*_____ (*emotion*)

because ___*Bert isn't showing up for dinner, even though he promised to be on time*_____

_____ (*triggering situation*).

However, I know that this is probably my ___*Abandonment schema, triggering my Angry*____

*Child mode*_____ (*schema/backstage modes*),

which I learned through___*being left alone by my mother all the time*_____

_____ (*childhood experience*).

These schemas and modes lead me to ___*exaggerate the situation and start yelling at Bert and*__

*fighting with him*_____ (*coping mode*).

Reality testing (healthy mode):

Even though I believe ___*that Bert being late proves that he doesn't love me and that*_____

*fighting with him is the only way to get his attention*_____ (*parent mode message*),

the reality is that ___*there might be other reasons for him being late, and I had better ask*____

*him before I immediately start lashing out at him when he comes in*___ (*Healthy Adult message*)

The evidence in my life supporting the healthy view includes:

* *He's told me before that he has a stressful situation at work for a few weeks*_____

* *We spent a beautiful weekend together recently, and he was very kind to me*_____

* _____.

Therefore, even though I feel like ___*I have to explode*_____

_____ (*maladaptive coping mode*),

I could instead___*take a few deep breaths and give him the benefit of the doubt. I could ask him*__

_*why he's late, instead of screwing myself up with negative thoughts. It would be better to go*___

*for a jog and leave him a message*_____ (*functional coping mode*).

Figure 6.5 Schema therapy flash filled out for Cindy

To do: Identify an emotionally charged exchange you have had with your partner. Can you both use the schema therapy flash card? Can you experience yourself shifting into Healthy Adult—perhaps together, as a couple? Try it just once before you finish with this chapter. It can be a very useful resource for your couple relationship.

Exercise: First you need to have drawn up your own mode map and familiarized yourself with it. If it's safe to do so, perhaps leave it somewhere fairly prominent, like in the front of your diary or in your study pinned to your computer. Once you're fairly clear *theoretically* on the modes in your mode map, you can use the schema therapy flash card to help you to become aware of what they're like while you're *experiencing* them in your daily life.

To do: Make a commitment to monitor what's happening whenever you're in a triggering situation. What mode are you in?

- Start by identifying the triggering situation.
- Then notice your thoughts or interpretation of that situation at the time.
- Now label and then rate the intensity of your emotional response.
- Finally, considering your thoughts and feelings in this situation, what did you feel like doing in response to those thoughts and feelings?

Now that you've identified the trigger, thoughts, feelings, and behavioral urges associated with the mode, take a guess at the mode or modes you might be in, or have been in. The mode map shows you all relevant modes, but feel free to label your own modes with personal names (like "the fighter," "the servant," "the sad Cindy," or "the dictator"). Essentially, you're training yourself here to step out of whatever mode you are in by asking yourself, "What mode am I in right now?" This can give you access to the Healthy Adult, at least temporarily, and in that moment let you gain some awareness of what's happening for you.

Now that you've gained some insight into the modes that might be in play, the final part of the flash card helps you to further strengthen and consolidate yourself in Healthy Adult mode. Ask yourself, "Now that I know these feelings are a result of the (insert mode) mode, what would my Healthy Adult think, say and do in this situation?"

Tip: If you've been keeping a journal (or therapeutic diary) while reading this book, you can integrate aspects of the flash card into the diary. For example, as you express your thoughts, feelings, and urges in your diary, try to add in parentheses when you notice a mode shift in the narrative. If you can't do so *as* you initially express yourself, try to go back later and give it another try by adding the mode in parentheses; for example, "I can't believe Jan could do this to me. I hate her for it. She makes my blood boil" (Angry Child).

Summary

This chapter has introduced the important step of mode awareness. This is the first practical step in schema therapy. Be patient. Allow yourself time to become tuned in to your modes. It will certainly take weeks, usually a month or two, so give yourself the time to be able to observe the modes and triggers and to slow down the flipping between modes. This chapter has also introduced the important tool of mode mapping and the schema therapy flash card. We have discussed ways to identify different kinds of emotions and emphasized the importance of Healthy Adult mode, which is a central theme of the rest of this book. In the next chapter, we shift to mode management and examine the potential of Healthy Adult for eventually changing dysfunctional modes.

To Read Further

- Modes often play out in particular patterns: Bernstein, Arntz, and de Vos (2007)
- Child and other modes: Jacob, van Genderen, and Seebauer (2015)
- Bodily maps of emotions: Nummenmaaa, Glereana, Harib, and Hietanend (2014).

References

Bernstein, D., Arntz, A., & de Vos, M. (2007). Schema focused therapy in forensic settings: Theoretical model and recommendations for best clinical practice. *International Journal of Forensic Mental Health, 6*(2), 169–183.

Jacob, G., van Genderen, H., & Seebauer, L. (2015). *Breaking negative thought patterns: A schema therapy self-help and support book.* Malden, MA: Wiley-Blackwell.

Nummenmaaa, L., Glereana, E., Harib, R., & Hietanend, J. K. (2014). Bodily maps of emotions. *PANS, 111*(2), 646–651.

7

Managing the Modes

"The map is not the territory," as Gregory Bateson once observed. But we need maps or we'll soon get lost. Schema therapy can provide both a psychological understanding of life-traps and powerful techniques for change, but first we must manage dysfunction. If you get stuck at any point, we recommend that you see a therapist trained in schema therapy to help you find a way forward.

Don't speed-read the next few chapters, because we'll now pay close attention to how to manage the modes in your couple relationship using mindfulness strategies. Give yourself plenty of time to try out the suggested exercises. Select what grabs your interest. The idea is to become emotionally engaged in the principles to effect lasting change. You may be tempted to believe that understanding or insight will be enough, but the process of change is not just cognitive. Lasting change means that you experience something new and this leads to different behaviors. Schema therapists work "hot" in sessions, so that too must be part of what you do. These exercises will work equally well with both schemas and modes.

Compassion

Compassion is the ultimate goal for a couple. It can be elusive but when it's present, even in small doses, it can make a huge difference. Compassion adds qualities such as understanding and goodwill—both of which not only influence how a couple can change but encourage them to grow toward each other. This is why we spend so much time encouraging you

Breaking Negative Relationship Patterns: A Schema Therapy Self-help and Support Book,
First Edition. Bruce A. Stevens and Eckhard Roediger.
© 2017 John Wiley & Sons, Ltd. Published 2017 by John Wiley & Sons, Ltd.

to discover your personal background and underpinnings before coming to the interaction with your partner. It's not possible to start building a house on the second floor. The foundations and first floor have to be built first.

It's easy to think that you're an expert on your partner. You *see* a lot of them, but it's harder to *see* yourself. This is why we ask you to hold a mirror up to see yourself more clearly. Once this happens, you'll have a better understanding of your intimate relationship and of course begin with what you can change—yourself!

Identify Trigger Points in Your Relationship

There's always emotional garbage in a couple relationship. What are your sensitivities? Young recommends in his training DVD that couples identify prototypical conflicts (conflicts that keep repeating). They're likely to be based on interlocking schemas and coping styles. This also highlights what is important in your relationship.

Couple exercise A: List the "hot" issues for both of you. Then individually rearrange your list in order of importance. Finally, compare your list with your partner's. What is similar and what is different?

When you think about your relationship, try to identify trigger points. This is a good indication that a schema may have been activated. If you can maintain some objectivity, do a chain analysis of what led to a recent incident (identify and trace the steps that led up to the clash). Are there other influences? Why are you both hot on the issue? Can you reflect on how you were treated as a child, perhaps in related experiences, and how that might have led to unhealthy schemas?

Couple exercise B: Return to your list of hot topics. Think about the trigger points for any sudden escalation of conflict. Think about using a 10-point scale of intensity of conflict (about 8 is losing control). How would you rate each topic? Can you maintain a two-point buffer zone before losing control? How about not going past 6? It's very useful to find mutual strategies to calm conflict at the various levels, especially by catching it early.

Danny had a bad temper. He said things that he later regretted. Occasionally, he would throw things in a fit of rage. He had never hit Zandra—but she was frightened. Danny worked out his scale, recognizing that he would regret his actions if he got to 8 or beyond. He decided to have a buffer zone: "I must not go past 6. If I notice that I've exceeded my cutoff, say by reaching 6.5, then I immediately leave the house and go for a 20-minute walk. At about 4, I drink a glass of water to slow myself down; at 5, I stop talking about the hot issue and practice the skill of progressive muscle relaxation that I learned at a stress workshop."

You might also try a mindfulness response to schema activation. Simply observe that you're feeling abandoned or that mistrust has overwhelmed you. This may provide a buffer. Mindfulness techniques are more fully discussed later.

Stop Clashing First!

Couple exercise: You might think about developing a "stop sign" to interrupt the cycle of conflict. Whoever is the first to notice that a clash is getting too heated shows the sign (for example, by raising their hands to form a T, like the sign to interrupt a basketball game). By prior agreement, you are both *committed* to stop instantly without saying something more. You can retire to separate rooms or one of you can go for a walk. This eliminates any further triggering cues, giving your brain a chance to readjust itself. Even deep sighs or finger tapping can be triggers!

A conflict is usually based on mutual activation of your assertiveness needs. While strengthening your assertiveness leg, getting control seems more important than remaining connected. Once your partner is literally out of sight, your sense of control is regained and that need sinks down in your internal hierarchy of needs.

But now you're alone! Your attachment need becomes activated and your longing for the other increases. However, now you probably have a better balance and are ready for reconciliation. Generally, it's best for the person breaking off conflict to nominate a time to return for further discussion, preferably soon to avoid frustrating the partner. So don't forget to make an appointment to meet again (for example, in an hour, for dinner, or for a longer talk on the weekend); otherwise, the separation might activate an Abandonment schema!

Exercise: Think in terms of a traffic light. Red means you're not ready to reconcile. Yellow means you're close to reconciliation but still need a little more time to calm down. Green gives your partner a "go" signal. When your partner tries to approach you but you're still not ready, tell them which color your traffic light is. Or pin a traffic light at your door and mark the color you are in in order to avoid frustrating reconciliation attempts. Once your partner's attempt fails, they will probably fall back into anger and detachment. This means an unnecessary extra loop in reconnection. Avoiding this saves time and energy.

Looking at modes as a third party allows you to see things differently. *The enemy is the coping modes, not your partner!* The dyadic relation between the two of you can become a triad. You can reconnect with your partner against bad schemas from the past as expressed in maladaptive coping modes. This is a way to escape the gridlock problem, the way a river flows around a rock.

Exercise: You might try a meditation exercise. Sit in a quiet place and simply follow your thoughts. This includes normal thoughts, such as you might have standing in line waiting to pay a bill. But this time turn your head left when you think about past thoughts, keep it straight ahead when thinking present thoughts, and turn to the right with future thoughts. Do this for 10 minutes. Do you notice anything? This will help you to identify the center of gravity for your thoughts and strengthen your internal observer.

You might also try a mindfulness response to schema activation. Simply observe that you're feeling abandoned or that mistrust has overwhelmed you, but abstain from an immediate reaction. What you observe are just temporary thoughts and feelings—ghosts from the past. Do not feed them with your attention but let them go. Observe what mode you're in. Shift into some manual work (like dishwashing or tidying). Give yourself and your brain some time to readjust. This may provide a buffer.

Urge surfing exercise: This is a mindfulness exercise. You may find that you have an intense urge to do a behavior that needs to change. This encourages you to pay attention to the urge while "surfing" on top of it, rather than being drawn into the behavior. You can also simply observe the urge and watch how it increases with time and diminishes after peaking. If you like this idea but have difficulties in practicing it, you might enroll in a mindfulness-based stress reduction (MBSR) program. It's a commitment for about eight weeks and is widely available.

Acceptance

Sometimes it's best to use acceptance strategies with modes rather than striving for substantial change. This will help with mode management, especially if there are conditions that you aren't free to change.

Frankie had difficulty with her Demanding Parent mode. Her internalized voice said, "You must be a perfect mother. Always be responsive to your daughter." But she felt exhausted by her child's needs and expectations. She found it better to take an acceptance stance, mindfully observe and not judge (either the voices or herself): "The demanding messages are there, but I accept them as if I were watching cars go past me on the road. I visualize myself in a roadside coffee shop, enjoying a cup of coffee and watching the traffic. Then it doesn't seem to matter and I don't have to obey the dictates of my parental mode." This is a technique from acceptance and commitment therapy called "thought diffusion," which separates thoughts from emotions.

Remember: Frankie's behavior could be misunderstood as a Detached Protector. The difference between acceptance or a healthy protector is that a Detached Protector is detached and unaware of the underlying feelings, while in a state of acceptance we know what our feelings are but try to keep our head above the water and not allow our emotions to take over.

More on Mindfulness

We don't easily control our thoughts. If I told you to *not* think of a pink elephant in a tutu, it would be the first thing you would find yourself thinking about. This is normal. Brains simply produce thoughts. Usually, we cannot stop them, but we can stop listening to them and giving them our time and attention. What counts is what you actually *do*.

Exercise: As a simple mindfulness exercise for emotional stabilization and to strengthen your observer state, write a detailed description of the room you're in. Don't judge what you see, such as by writing "That's messy." Simply describe exactly what you see—for example, by counting the bricks in a wall. What you do must attract more of your attention than the activated schema. If you can do something mundane like this, there's no space left for angry feelings or despair. Just suck the mental energy out of the dysfunctional thoughts and direct your attention to something emotionally neutral. Guiding your attention onto neutral content cools down the activation in your emotional brain. Try this exercise when you're next upset. Rate your distress level using the Subjective Units of Distress Scale of 1 to 10 (discussed in Chapter 11) before and after. Is there a difference?

To do: Try to do a regular activity each day *mindfully*. Have a mindful shower. You can feel the tactile sensation of lathering up your body and the warm water washing over you. Or do your dishes while concentrating on each plate. When your attention drifts away, gently guide it back to the plate you're currently working on. Look at it, feel it in your hand, watch your hand moving in circles. Let all other upcoming thoughts pass by. Be present. After an initial irritation, this actually feels relaxing. You escape from your mental treadmill for a moment. This feels like a little vacation. Aim to do a mindful activity a few times a day, even for just a few minutes. Mindfulness can be a powerful counter to schema activation.

Mindfulness is a very useful skill to learn. It can be challenging to practice when alone, but is much harder in an emotionally tense situation with your partner. You need to practice the skill to the point that it becomes natural and even second nature. It can then become a safety release, even in a couple relationship.

In a nutshell: The outcome is often poor if we act out spontaneously. We *feel* the urge to do something when we're emotionally driven, but then our automatic pilot holds the steering wheel. Let your Healthy Adult become the boss! If you feel the urge to do something, train yourself to *not* react. Take a few deep breaths first. Try watching yourself from a bird's perspective, or through a camera lens. Picture your best friend at your side. What would they recommend doing? Think about tomorrow: How will you think about the situation then? Refocus your attention to describe the room you're in. Eventually, stand up, taking some steps. You aren't trapped, like you were in childhood. Nowadays there's room to move. Moving your body helps to change your mood state. Once you cool down and your Healthy Adult holds the steering wheel, you can try to get connected again. The result will be much better!

Summary

In this brief chapter we have raised the importance of managing your modes from your Healthy Adult side. This can be done by using mindfulness and acceptance strategies. The next three chapters further explore the theme of mode management with special reference to the parent, coping, and child modes.

To Read Further

- Mindfulness-based stress reduction programs: www.mindfulness.org.au
- Mindfulness and schema therapy: van Vreeswijk, Broersen, and Schurink (2014)
- Schema therapy for couples training DVD: Young (2012)
- Mindfulness and acceptance in schema therapy: Roediger (2012).

References

Roediger, E. (2012). Why are mindfulness and acceptance central elements for therapeutic change in ST too? An integrative perspective. In M. van Vreeswijk, J. Broersen, & M. Nadort (Eds.), *The Wiley-Blackwell handbook of schema therapy: Theory, research and practice* (pp. 239–247). Oxford, UK: Wiley-Blackwell.

van Vreeswijk, M., Broersen, J., & Schurink, G. (2014). *Mindfulness and schema therapy: A practical guide.* Oxford, UK: Wiley-Blackwell.

Young, J. (2012). *Schema therapy with couples* [DVD]. (APA Series IV, Relationships, hosted with Jon Carlson). www.apa.org/pubs/videos/4310895.aspx.

8

Past Tense
Managing the Parent Modes

The inner critic. Sound familiar? Almost all of us, at times, suffer from this intrusive commentary or voice of condemnation. Schema therapy will help you deal with this voice of the damaging parent modes. It can be inner directed, leading to psychological distress, including depression. It can also be outer directed, leading to unrealistic demands or even punitive treatment of your partner or other people. Remember what you sometimes think about your children when they drive you mad, or about other car drivers! In this chapter, we carefully examine the parent modes and find ways to lessen their influence.

While we talk about parent modes, they may or may not correspond to the experience you had with your parents. There are many different authority figures, such as schoolteachers, who can contribute to parent modes. And sometimes children grasp unspoken messages.

> *Sammy* had a depressive mother who used to lie in bed when he came home from school. She would stare at the ceiling without speaking a word to him or even turning her head. So he internalized messages like: "You can't expect anything from me. So you'd better rely on yourself and not bother me!"

Demanding Parent

The Demanding Parent mode is that part of you that's never satisfied. This voice will remind you that there's a "right" or "only" way to do things. Achievement must be at the highest level. The goal may be high status or it can be more humble: Always put the needs of others first.

Breaking Negative Relationship Patterns: A Schema Therapy Self-help and Support Book,
First Edition. Bruce A. Stevens and Eckhard Roediger.
© 2017 John Wiley & Sons, Ltd. Published 2017 by John Wiley & Sons, Ltd.

This is the realm of the ideal. But no matter how good you are at meeting demands, it's *never enough*. This mode refers to the nature of your internalized standards or strict personal rules.

This is hard to dispute, because Demanding Parent can keep our standards high.

> *Brit* was doing well as a first-year medical student. She found it hard to relax and do quilting: "I have to keep pushing myself. There's always something to learn or revise. But I've always enjoyed being creative and my crafts keep me sane. My brother talked to me about self-care and this seems important or I'll never 'go the distance.'"

Don't look at the content of the thought (it might appear right, at least at first glance). Look at the consequences: Demanding Parent is never satisfied. It will drive us mercilessly until we're exhausted. This is what counts! So it's up to our Healthy Adult to negotiate with its demands and find a path that will realistically meet our expectations as well as allow us to care for ourselves.

> Brit thought about what was most healthy for her. She talked to an elder in her local church, who reminded her that "Even God rested on the seventh day." She was able to organize herself to take the period between Christmas and New Year's Day off. She said that it was against her instincts but she felt refreshed and passed her oral exam in anatomy.

This can also be expressed as unrealistic expectations of a relationship.

> *Stan* expected Tracey to retain her youthful figure. She said, reasonably, "But it's now over 20 years since we both said 'I do.'" Stan continued, "But how do we keep that 'in love' feeling if you're not as physically attractive to me?"

Demanding Parent can be easily aligned with spiritual values. In this way, the demands seem to come as "divine guidance."

> *Claire* is a practicing Buddhist. It had always been her intent to keep up her spiritual disciplines. However, when she was promoted to a position of greater responsibility, with frequent travel, that became increasingly difficult. She sought the advice of her mentor, who sensibly told her, "It's good to do what you can, when you can. You shouldn't feel a failure when your meditation time is not possible."

Reflect: Write a list of the standards you expect of yourself. In your journal, give a rating on how satisfied you are with meeting each one listed. Maybe give a score from 1 to 10. Do your goals and standards allow you to rest? This is an important way to distinguish unhealthy Demanding Parent from healthy ambition. Constructive self-criticism can be a good thing; destructive self-criticism can only tear you down. The effect counts.

The emotion test: Demanding Parent has a built-in standard, usually too high to be attained, but nevertheless there. You'll feel *guilty* in response to its messages, so that feeling is a clear indicator of its presence. So think about when you feel guilty. What are the messages in your head? Can you see a wise person or a religious figure, such as Jesus, saying it to you? If not, then it's probably not a divine standard but a human one put arbitrarily on you.

To do: Take an observer's stance and realize how your inner voice constantly comments on what you're doing. Do not be surprised if the voice talks almost all the time! List the demands the voice makes of you. Can you put them in order of priority? Did you include self-care? If not, why not? Try playing with the voice: Can you say the demands in a pirate voice (which is recommended in acceptance and commitment therapy)? Or a chipmunk voice? How does that feel? It will usually at least make you smile, and humor is the beginning of subverting the authoritative demands of the Demanding Parent.

To do: In order to get some distance from the voice, put it on an empty chair and stand up in front of it, looking down on the voice. From a Healthy Adult stance, what comments about it do you make? If unsure, ask your best friend. Or imagine your child sitting on a chair in front of the voice and the voice pushing your child. What do you feel and how do you respond to the voice now? Perspective change increases mental flexibility. Write the Healthy Adult answers down in your records.

Consider: Demanding Parent feels many of the following:

- The right way to be is to be perfect or to achieve at the highest level. Everything has to be in order.
- Strive for high status, to be humble, to put others' needs first, and to be efficient and avoid wasting time.
- Another person is wrong to express feelings or act spontaneously.

Punitive Parent

The Punitive Parent mode can be easily mistaken for Demanding Parent, but its tone of voice is different. It's more aggressive ("You're worthless. Pathetic. Everything you do shows what a loser you are!"). It attacks any remnant of self-esteem. It wins when you're reduced to nothing.

You might think about it as an inner critic, but it's darker, more like an inner assassin. People with eating disorders, those who have been sexually abused, and severely depressive people suffer from extreme Punitive Parent modes. Some call it an inner dictator that throws them into a concentration camp, with no escape. A dungeon of despair!

First consider the direction of the Punitive Parent's voice. Is the voice directed against you or others? When you're the target, this voice can drive you to self-injury or suicidal despair. Unlike with Demanding Parent, there's no negotiation. You must vigorously resist this voice and "impeach" its influence in your mental space.

The voice of Punitive Parent can also be directed at others (for example, in antisocial modes) and can easily poison romantic relationships. Watch any signs that you or someone else thinks that someone deserves punishment or blame!

Self-assessment: What do you think about others when you're very angry? Do you make personal attacks in your fantasies? Do you find yourself saying to others what your Punitive Parent says to you? Reflect on a recent "hot" argument in your romantic relationship. Was the tone more demanding—say, for change—or punishing by attacking the other's self-worth? A demand can lead to negotiation, but a punitive attack cannot.

To do: Think about how you were treated as a child. Did you have parents who expected a lot of you and were never satisfied? Maybe you brought home a report card from school with five As and one B. Were you immediately interrogated about the lapse? Or did you suffer punitive messages from your parents, essentially communicating how worthless you were? Or have you been punished with stonewalling, which is a very severe punishment for a child? If you haven't done this in your autobiography take a moment to write out a typical dialogue between you and the parent who was most often angry. Imagine he or she is angry, like when you were a child. What do you hear that person saying to you?

Emotional test: While feelings of guilt indicate the presence of Demanding Parent, the emotion that shows Punitive Parent is *shame*. Shame is a very uncomfortable feeling that makes you want to hide and escape the gaze of others. Guilt is specific ("You've done this wrong"); shame is an experience of the whole self as defective or inferior.

Note: If you experienced neglect or abuse as a child, it's likely that your Punitive Parent has a louder voice than your Demanding Parent. Does Punitive Parent speak more often? Does Punitive Parent have a more authoritative tone and do you find the accusations more believable?

Michael was homeless at 15. He was a delinquent who stole cars and had a long list of juvenile convictions. He had an addiction to cannabis and was admitted to a residential treatment facility. There he was introduced to schema therapy. He was able to distinguish the voice of Punitive Parent: "It's so harsh. I don't think Punitive Parent would be satisfied unless I committed suicide."

Reflect: Compare the Punitive Parent and Demanding Parent voices. How much time do you spend in each? Maybe draw a pie chart with Punitive Parent, Demanding Parent, and Healthy Adult.

Consider: Punitive Parent feels that you and/or others deserve punishment. In this state, a person will often blame or abuse others. This voice may also drive self-destructive urges—be warned!

About Accessing and Externalizing Parent Modes

Parent modes are usually easy to detect (simply tune in to the commentary in your head), but sometimes their presence is subtle. For example, the expectations of Demanding Parent can hide in Healthy Adult.

Cindy thought it was healthy ambition. She said, "I really expected to get 'Outstanding' in every category of my work performance review. I wouldn't be satisfied with even 'Fully Effective.'" But she realized that there was a rigidity more typical of Demanding Parent than Healthy Adult.

It's harder, of course, when the message is partly true. In this case, performing well at work is highly desirable. Remember: Look at the effect. If it makes you feel worse, it can't be a Healthy Adult voice.

Reflect: Make a list of statements about what you must achieve or standards you must reach. Compare the list with what others expect from themselves. If the voice says, "This is OK for *them* but not for *you*," it's a Demanding Parent mode. Can you identify the unreasonableness of Demanding Parent in what you have accepted as healthy? Can you hear positive messages? If not, it may be that Punitive Parent is blocking that feedback.

Note: Some of us completely identify with these voices. We regard them as genuine parts of ourselves. You might be amazed at this, but the background is rather simple: It is almost impossible for a child to object to their parents. Our parents are too important! It's difficult to stand up to them, so identifying ourselves with their values is a good way of getting out of the combat zone. The cost is you having to deny your assertiveness needs and surrender, but sometimes surrendering is better than getting battered by an abusive parent.

Avoid being too emotionally involved with the voices, stay cognitive and to some degree detached.

Chair-dialogues to Manage the Parent Modes

Schema therapists often use chair-dialogues. This enables the person in therapy to literally shift their position and speak from two sides of an issue.

> *Brad* was thinking about leaving his marriage. His therapist encouraged him to speak from the "I'm leaving" chair, and later he gave equal time to the "I'm staying" position in a different chair. This enabled him to explore how he felt about the issue from both sides. It clarified the issue in a balanced way.

To do: Use chair-dialogues as a journal exercise. Simply write from the coping mode and then change into Demanding Parent or Punitive Parent. Then write dialogue between the modes as outlined above.

> *Cordi* began in Detached Protector: "I feel nothing. It's comforting, but I also feel like a zombie. I want to be more alive. But I hear critical voices."
>
> Critical voice in the head: "I'm worthless and don't deserve to take up space."

Now put this voice on an extra chair and change the wording into second person. Let the parent voice chair talk to an empty chair in front of it: "You're worthless and don't deserve to take up space."

If you feel strong enough, you can sit down on this Vulnerable Child chair and let the words resonate within you. How do you feel? Probably very suppressed, overwhelmed, and sad. This is where your depressive feelings come from. And what do you need now? Probably somebody who's there to take care of you and whom you belong to.

Now stand up and change into Healthy Adult mode. What do you feel looking down on the three chairs below? Can you feel anger towards the punitive or demanding voice? Do you feel compassion for the Vulnerable Child chair? If so, you're actually in a Healthy Adult mode and you can talk back to the parent mode chair. If not, you're probably identified with the parent mode voice.

In a next step, you can picture your best friend standing beside you. Put yourself in their shoes and try to feel how they would feel about this voice. Or put a photo of your own son or daughter or another real child whom you love on the child chair. What do you feel if the voices beat this child up? If you shift into Punitive Parent, you had better stop the exercise and reconsider going into therapy. If you feel a constructive anger toward the parent voice and compassion for the child mode, you may say to the child mode: "I can look after your needs. I'll block the voice of Punitive Parent and assure you that you're lovable. I want to care for you and I'm always around."

Once you get better at distancing from the parent voice and shifting into Healthy Adult, you can use a journal with two columns: one for the parent voice and one for the Healthy Adult response. You might try this journal exercise and see if it's a better fit for you than chair-work. It can be very effective, but some people find the technique of sitting in different chairs more activating (once they get over feeling self-conscious).

Warning: Be very careful when getting into a chair to represent Punitive Parent. Instead, use an empty chair to represent that mode and speak back to it. Try being loud and aggressive in rebutting its voice. Stand firmly, put your hands on your hips, and get a well-grounded feeling first. When you are dealing with traumatic experiences or self-injuring behavior, abstain from sitting in the Punitive Parent chair.

But: Don't beat yourself up when you identify the Punitive Parent inside of you. Once you have discovered it, there's help in sight. Just distance yourself from it, and visualize putting it on a bus and seeing it driven out of the city. The Punitive Parent is not you! It's just a toxic part planted in your psyche when you were young. Maybe other people around you behaved like that. But Punitive Parent is not friendly. Throw it out of the door every time it shows up. You're free to choose!

While the ways to manage Demanding Parent and Punitive Parent modes are similar, be more vigorous in pushing away Punitive Parent. There's some space for negotiating with Demanding Parent. One way to leave Demanding Parent mode is choosing your own values and making your own rules and rituals to replace Demanding Parent's voice by shifting into Healthy Adult. This is a resource activation technique: We adopt a wise person's voice reminding us of this act of self-care. Maybe you promised yourself to do some exercises every day. So do that now. The ritual helps you take on healthy patterns. You can make a rule out of it, which can help you get into action in the face of the Undisciplined Child mode.

Talking Back to Your Parent Modes

To do: Journal the voices of the various modes and return to Healthy Adult to respond. Think about whether you find it helpful to change where you sit to fully enter into the mode, or to stand up and take some steps across the room to support mental perspective changes. Is there someone you can ask to sit beside you to form an alliance against the mode? Then write in your journal from the Healthy Adult mode.

> *Margaret* was plagued by her Punitive Parent mode. She decided to write from that perspective in her journal. Punitive Parent: "Margaret, you're a useless wimp. You never stand up for yourself, and you just let your mother, family, and friends walk all over you. No wonder no one respects you! You're a useless piece of #$@#! Do everyone a favor and die!"
>
> While Margaret was familiar with this voice, she was shocked at the intensity of its self-hate. She wrote from Healthy Adult: "Wow, I really don't have a friend in Punitive Parent. It's just that this scathing voice is so familiar. But I didn't know how disturbed it was and how it couldn't be satisfied until I was dead. I now realize that there's no compromise with this voice. It's like having a psychopath inside of me. I have to find a mute button for this voice!"

Use your Healthy Adult to engage in what has been called "cognitive restructuring" (to be honest, we both like the term "reappraisal" better). The parent modes tend to have black-and-white thinking. Picture someone you love: Can you think about them in a more moderate, complex, nuanced, and reality-based way?

To do: You might want to respond with a compassion letter addressed to your Vulnerable Child. Ask yourself what it needs to hear, such as "You're loved and accepted just as you are." Eventually, picture yourself looking at your own child. How does that feel? Then write to Vulnerable Child. You might start with, "You're completely loveable ..." Use that sentence to prime the pump and then write more, keeping the needs of Vulnerable Child in focus.

Also: Return to your mode list and give voice to the modes in your journal. Then, when each mode has had its say, switch back to Healthy Adult to respond to what was said. Can you use thought diffusion ("It's just a thought") to make the voices just like background noise?

Mindfulness and Parental Voices

Note that the more punitive a parent mode is, the more it must be dealt with in some way. Try to weed out such comments from your relationship. This is essential, or the goodwill in your relationship will diminish.

How to deal with the voices? There are two general approaches. Try both and see what works best for you. You can try to dispute them. Some colleagues recommend fighting the parent modes. Simply argue against them, like an advocate in a courtroom. But this doesn't always work, because you might find that such fighting is too engaging and may empower the mode. In that case, try to use any of the mindfulness techniques to be more grounded and less emotionally bound to the negative thoughts.

Use urge surfing to deal with unpleasant thoughts and feelings: Watch the thought or feeling coming, acknowledge it, make a reality check (a reappraisal) and, if it represents a ghost from the past, just let it go. You'll find with these steps that you can neutralize the domination of the modes. Ultimately, try to disempower the voices by just letting them go. Turn your attention away. Don't worry if what is said is right or wrong. Try to see its influence and the unwanted consequences. Note that Punitive Parent will often interpret even neutral comments from a self-punishing perspective. And don't be surprised if you find that Punitive Parent voices talk and comment almost all the time. This is common.

To do: Let the messages of Punitive Parent be like chatter in the background. Or see yourself having coffee at a roadside café. The thoughts are just cars passing by.

Another metaphor: Imagine a cow with flies on her back. How does the cow react? Right, she gently waves her tail. The flies go away for a moment, but will come back soon. What is the cow doing? Exactly: She waves her tail again! Is the cow depressed? No, she has accepted that flies are part of her life, but she has found a way to deal with them (one could think of cows as reincarnated Buddhists).

Also: Write out a list of typical messages you get from Demanding Parent or Punitive Parent. Maybe 5 or 10. Write them in capital letters or in a strange script. Then look at them with detached interest. Can you visualize them on a movie screen? See yourself in a plane looking out the window at clouds beneath you. Write the messages on the clouds. Try saying the messages in a pirate voice. Usually, when you stop laughing, the messages do not seem so powerful.

It's the role of the Healthy Adult to raise your head above the water. The goal is to use whatever you can to weaken intrusive thoughts, calm down or soothe child modes, and lead your attention and action in the desired direction.

Exercise: Use mindfulness on modes. Listen for messages and then identify the mode. Sit with the mode to see how it feels. How does it feel to distance yourself from negative messages in the mode?

About Couple Relationships

It's easy for a couple relationship to become dominated by parental messages. These include the "ought" messages:

> *Marie* was certain that "a good husband will do ..." She was dogmatic and certain about "the right thing to do." Barry didn't actively challenge this but quietly withdrew in the face of her disapproval. This led progressively to a chill, which soon dominated the early years of their marriage.

Judgmental and punitive attitudes come from parent modes, and such communication will soon be toxic in a relationship. This needs to be identified. It's one thing to have an internal focus, but such inner voices can cripple you and bruise the people you love. External expressions of those attitudes will burden your relationship and possibly make it mutually intolerable. Again: Although it might feel right in the moment standing fully on your assertiveness leg, if it's destructive, it's not healthy, because it undermines your attachment need.

To do: Become more vigilant about the input of the parent modes turned toward your partner. Understand how they can easily intrude in your intimate relationship.

Relationship researcher John Gottman identified "Four Horsemen of the Apocalypse" that can accurately predict relationship failure:

1. *Criticism:* There will always be complaints in a relationship, but criticism is personal: "You always ... You never ...," along with questions that are not really questions, but more insults. The criticism is an attack on the personality or character of the partner.
2. *Contempt:* This conveys an ugliness in a relationship and is associated with cynicism, sarcasm, eye-rolling, hostile humor, and mockery. The contemptuous person assumes the higher ground. It's toxic and is virtually absent in happy relationships.

3. *Defensiveness:* While this can be understandable, it's blaming ("You're the problem") and rarely helps because the partner may turn up the heat in order to be heard.
4. *Stonewalling:* This involves tuning out or not hearing the partner. It's a protection against feeling flooded.

Can you identify the modes in these behaviors? Criticism and contempt are parent modes (the first more Demanding Parent and the second Punitive Parent), while defensiveness and stonewalling are coping modes. All are toxic and will potentially poison a relationship. Use the techniques in this chapter to address the parent modes.

Reflect: Punitive Parent mode in relationships costs on both sides. The person who suffers from the messages of Punitive Parent and has low self-esteem cannot assert their rights in the relationship. The person who expresses Punitive Parent to a loved one cannot allow that person to meet their normal needs. This is a balance of sorts, but thoroughly unhealthy.

According to Arntz, the general pattern of individual growth involves:

- helping the child modes develop and find safety through emotional processing of traumatic childhood experiences, acknowledging the original childhood needs, and finding corrective experiences
- eliminating punitive and demanding parental modes as much as possible and replacing them with healthy attitudes to needs and emotions, healthy standards, and moral principles
- letting the Healthy Adult side strengthen, with the result that the dysfunctional coping modes are less necessary (practice swimming, so you won't sink into your old life-traps—that is, your old coping behaviors).

Reflect: Gitta Jacob observed that some people suffer from "generalized dysfunctional parent modes," in which parent modes affect every area of their lives. She and her colleagues recommended carrying symbols, such as a small shell, to remind you to oppose the negative parental voices.

Summary

This chapter has discussed the internalized voice of the parental modes: Demanding Parent and Punitive Parent. It's important to be very clear when dealing with the parent modes. There's a lot of confusion between them and about what is healthy for an intimate relationship. This is further explored in the next couple of chapters.

To Read Further

• Patterns of growth in schema therapy: Arntz (2012)
• Behavioral experiments: Bennett-Levy et al. (2004)
• Using the mindfulness card with troubling thoughts: Cousineau (2012)
• Behavioral change ideas: Farrell and Shaw (2012)
• Parental modes and healthy ambition; expressing Punitive Parent in relationships: Jacob, van Genderen, and Seebauer (2015)
• Weakening typical triggers for schemas or modes: Parfy (2012)
• Mindfulness strategies to refocus attention: Roediger (2012)
• Shifting from "doing mode" to "being mode": Segal, Williams, and Teasdale (2001)
• John Gottman's work in an easy-to-read book: Gottman and Silver (1999)
• Mindfulness and schema therapy: van Vreeswijk, Broersen, and Schurink (2014).

References

Arntz, A. (2012). Schema therapy for cluster C personality disorders. In M. van Vreeswijk, J. Broersen, & M. Nadort (Eds.), *The Wiley-Blackwell handbook of schema therapy: Theory, research and practice* (pp. 397–414). Oxford, UK: Wiley-Blackwell.

Bennett-Levy, J., Butler, G., Fennell, M., Hackman, A., Mueller, M., & Westbrook, D. (Eds.) (2004). *Oxford guide to behavioral experiments in cognitive therapy.* Oxford, UK: Oxford University Press.

Cousineau, P. (2012). Mindfulness and ACT as strategies to enhance healthy adult mode: The use of the mindfulness flash card as an example. In M. van Vreeswijk, J. Broersen, & M. Nadort (Eds.), *The Wiley-Blackwell handbook of schema therapy: Theory, research and practice* (pp. 249–257). Oxford, UK: Wiley-Blackwell.

Farrell, J., & Shaw, I. (2012). *Group schema therapy for borderline personality disorder: A step-by-step treatment manual with patient workbook.* Oxford, UK: Wiley-Blackwell.

Gottman, J., & Silver, N. (1999). *The seven principles for making a marriage work.* New York, NY: Three Rivers Press.

Jacob, G., van Genderen, H., & Seebauer, L. (2015). *Breaking negative thought patterns: A schema therapy self-help and support book.* Malden, MA: Wiley-Blackwell.

Parfy, E. (2012). Schema therapy, mindfulness and ACT: Differences and points of contact. In M. van Vreeswijk, J. Broersen, & M. Nadort (Eds.), *The Wiley-Blackwell handbook of schema therapy: Theory, research and practice* (pp. 229–237). Oxford, UK: Wiley-Blackwell.

Roediger, E. (2012). Why are mindfulness and acceptance central elements for therapeutic change in ST too? An integrative perspective. In M. van Vreeswijk, J. Broersen, & M. Nadort (Eds.), *The Wiley-Blackwell handbook of schema therapy: Theory, research and practice* (pp. 239–247). Oxford, UK: Wiley-Blackwell.

Segal, Z., Williams, J., & Teasdale, J. (2001). *Mindfulness-based cognitive therapy for depression: A new approach to preventing relapses*. New York, NY: Guilford Press.

van Vreeswijk, M., Broersen, J., & Schurink, G. (2014). *Mindfulness and schema therapy: A practical guide*. Oxford, UK: Wiley-Blackwell.

9

The "Great Escape"
Understanding the Coping Modes

The coping modes obey one command: Do not feel! These modes are protective, and similar to what Freud called "defense mechanisms" or what Steven Hayes called "experiential avoidance." Coping modes avoid bad feelings, but they trap us in old life patterns and prevent us from learning new strategies for problem solving. The most common coping modes are explored in this chapter, along with some management strategies.

Reflect: Gitta Jacob noted that the coping modes confront a deficit with an excess.

Coping modes are not all specific to humans. You can see their primitive form among animals as well. They reflect instinct-based behavioral reactions between struggling species. Humans just apply them in more sophisticated ways. The following broad categorization of coping modes in terms of fight, flight, freeze, and surrender, as seen in animal behavior, has been suggested:

1. *Fight* in overcompensatory modes such as Self-aggrandizer, Over-controller, Bully and Attack, or other antisocial modes
2. *Flight* as active avoidance mode of Detached Self-soother
3. *Freeze* as passive avoidant Detached Protector mode
4. *Surrender* with Compliant Surrender (cf. Atkinson, 2012).

You can recognize these strategies in your social interactions. Inevitably, you'll be in one (or in between two of them). They describe a continuum between submission (to gain attachment) at one end and overcompensation striving for control or dominance at the other end.

Breaking Negative Relationship Patterns: A Schema Therapy Self-help and Support Book,
First Edition. Bruce A. Stevens and Eckhard Roediger.
© 2017 John Wiley & Sons, Ltd. Published 2017 by John Wiley & Sons, Ltd.

Submission makes sense. You lose, but you remain part of the flock and survive. This is why children usually have to surrender.

If submission leads to lasting pain and you're too weak to fight, the next option is avoidance. Active self-soothing is our modern way of flight—we escape into distracting action.

But if you can't escape, all that is left is to freeze. Remember: The freezing rabbit does not surrender, but it does not want to be seen. An abused child in dissociation does not surrender even if she's not defending herself. Her abuser might assume that her passive behavior is consent, but it's not: The child tries to escape internally.

We now go into the details of each of these modes.

Detached Protector Mode

Numbness. To be in Detached Protector mode is to be cut off from feelings, but in a passive way. This mode is common enough for most people: We daydream and detach, but to what degree? Or we work like a robot. Functioning like a machine might have been helpful to survive in childhood, but it becomes a problem when you or your partner withdraws and rejects any offer of meaningful connection. The subjective feelings include being "spacey," distracted, disconnected, empty, or bored. Sometimes a person will adopt a cynical or aloof stance to push others away. Although it's hard to detect, there's usually a certain underlay of disappointment or anger behind the wall of numbness. Usually, the critical parent voices won't allow that anger to emerge, and numbness is better than feeling anger with no way to express it. The unconscious rule is: "Swallow it and detach."

In the following session, the therapist used chair-dialogues to help to clarify Henrietta's relationship to a Detached Protector mode.

Henrietta would often come to sessions in the numbness of Detached Protector mode. Her therapist said to her, "I know that Detached Protector feels safest, but I'd like you to shift into another seat. You're now Detached Protector speaking to me. What's your purpose?" Henrietta said, as Detached Protector, "I keep Henrietta safe. I know that she can't cope with strong emotions. She's easily overwhelmed. I'm doing my best to protect her." After this interchange, Henrietta went to her normal chair and said, "I do understand that Detached Protector is protecting me. But then I don't feel anything. And since I'm like a zombie, does anyone ever get to know the real me?"

Another approach by the therapist was to highlight the choices Henrietta made to go into Detached Protector:

THERAPIST: "I want you to go back to a time today when you felt some-
             thing intensely."
HENRIETTA: "Yes, when I was driving here, a bus nearly ran into me."
THERAPIST: "What happened then?"
HENRIETTA: "I was startled. Then I was flooded by anger and I didn't want
             to come today. So I shut down."
THERAPIST: "So that was the point of choice. You went into Detached
             Protector?"

The therapist then continued with a somatic awareness exercise so that Henrietta could identify a place of tension in her body. This led to more awareness of emotion, leading her to access the Vulnerable Child beside the Angry Child, separate it into its own chair, and progress in the session.

Henrietta was also able to think about the impact of Detached Protector on her romantic relationship with Sally. She said, "Sally gets frustrated with me being so flat. She feels tempted to start a fight just to get a reaction and some kind of connection. I'd really like to be able to relate to her in a way that escapes the destructive cycle of heightened conflict."

Henrietta was able to look at the various domains of her life and see how much she was shut down in Detached Protector mode. This was costing her in areas that really mattered (such as in friendships). This self-examination led to a greater determination to change.

Reflect: How much time do you spend in Detached Protector mode? Do you have a sense of what you're avoiding? You might try a sentence completion: "When I'm in Detached Protector, I successfully avoid ..." Try this a number of times until you have a list.

This is not all bad. Detached Protector can be very useful (it can be as benign as thinking about what you want to do for your next holiday), but when it impoverishes your relationships, people impor-tant in your life will notice. What does your partner say? Do family members complain about how little you're available? Or not emotionally present?

Spencer would go through the motions when talking to his children. He would also do this when dutifully watching them play sports. He knew he was in Detached Protector mode because he hardly felt anything when something good or bad happened in the games. His children noticed when he wasn't as enthusiastic as other parents. Spencer began to monitor himself carefully and recorded the time he was emotionally detached. He became aware of some anxious and sad feelings, which tended to trigger his desire to retreat. He learned to recognize the triggers and, instead of going straight to being detached, he practiced being mindful of his emotions. He became more aware of his avoidance.

Consider: Detached Protector might feel rational and functional, like Healthy Adult. The difference is that Healthy Adult can act in a rational way while being connected with his feelings, even if he doesn't express them. Detached Protector feels cut off from needs and feelings, detached from others and rejecting of their help, withdrawn, spacey, distracted, disconnected, empty, and bored. Do you notice yourself being cynical, aloof, or pessimistic to avoid engaging with others?

Detached Self-soother Mode

The Detached Self-soother mode is more active, but with the same result: to reduce feeling or replace bad feelings by a surface or superficial sensation seeking. Usually, this mode needs to be powerfully distracting if you have intense negative feelings. Recreational drugs or very exciting activities can achieve this. David Bernstein noted that this mode can feel like a constant "buzz" or state of excitement. Looking for a kick could mean a slippery slope toward addiction of some kind.

> *Charley* was a workaholic. He put long hours into his business with the justification that "A lot of people depend on me to make it a success." But he worked 15-hour days and had not had a break in years. His new girlfriend was complaining after just four weeks of dating him.

> *Lolita* overeats. Her doctor has warned her and suggested surgery. She felt so unattractive that she despaired about ever finding a romantic relationship.

> *Ben* has a problem with gambling. He bets on anything—horses, dogs—but has a particular attraction to slot machines. His partner noticed when some money from their savings account "went missing."

> *Val* is a gym junkie. She spends hours every day getting fit at the gym and exercising at home with Jane Fonda DVDs.

In these cases, there's a source of powerful stimulus that acts as a distraction from negative feelings or pressing life problems.

Reflect: Have you ever "used for effect" binge eating, risky behavior, gambling, internet pornography, sexual acting out, or adventure sports? What was happening in your life at the time? It's normal to want to have some escape (after all, a holiday overseas is an "escape" from your normal routine), but an overreliance can lead to problems. The border between the two is not clear. How about people who come home and immediately start texting or making phone calls? Spending hours on the internet or playing computer games can be a Detached Self-soother behavior, too. Besides the behavior's impact on your daily duties, another important measure is its function. If you use any behavior as a pill, be careful that doesn't make you ill instead of making you better.

It's easy to see that Detached Self-soother mode can easily lead to overusing such escape mechanisms. In time, it can lead to addiction.

Addiction

Addiction is a huge field of research and practice. It has been understood in various ways. Schema therapy can add to this with an understanding of mode dynamics, especially Detached Self-soother. Twelve-step programs are very effective for dealing with addictions, but schema therapy provides another approach.

> *Nick* had a problem with internet gambling. His credit cards were maxed out and his finances were a mess. In some desperation, Nick went to Gamblers Anonymous. The members supported him through the stressful time and helped him in the recovery process. He was fortunate with his partner, who not only supported him but held him accountable for his promises to her.

To do: If you have identified an area of addiction, it's important that you take some steps toward change. Sometimes, there's a gap between wishful thinking and taking action. Small steps will close that gap. The steps have to be defined.

Try a self-experiment: Identify a possible area of addiction. Identify triggers, problematic behavior, and a series of steps to change. Try your plan. This usually works better if you go public and involve friends or your partner in your project. For example, if you have, say, a drinking problem, you can make a contract with your partner about your drinking conditions and commit yourself to enroll in a guided program if your reality check fails. If you cannot control your drinking, abstinence is the best goal (you might need professional help to understand the severity of your problem). Invest in your relationship, since it will be one of the strongest motivations for recovery. Once you gain control over your drinking problem, you have solid ground on which to continue working to improve your relationship.

Accessing the modes relating to addiction

In the mode model, we understand addictions in terms of Detached Self-soother. In this section, we use problem drinking as an example of addiction. However, what we say here also goes for other addictions, whether they're to substances or behaviors.

Most people with substance abuse problems simply have no better solution for coping with their emotional discomfort. If you're drinking in a problematic way, you'll need to consider the underlying triggers of the avoided emotions and try to address the needs of the child modes.

To do: In your journal, write from your drinking place. Take a seat as the Detached Self-soother (the part within you tending to drink or do other obsessive things). Try interviewing yourself and write down the answers:

1. When did you show up first?
2. What was this situation like?
3. In which way were you helpful?
4. What do you prevent?
5. What purpose do you serve?
6. What could happen if you disappear?

This inquiry will reveal the hidden emotions of the child modes—the vulnerable as well as the blocked anger—and the commandments of the internalized parent modes. There are probably as many reasons to drink as there are drinkers, but following the internal dynamic of the journal dialogue reveals typical internal mode cycles with flips between two or more coping modes. One of them is described in the following case vignette.

An extended example

Mary and Bob sought couples counseling. She accused Bob of drinking too much. He claimed that his drinking was normal among his friends, and said that Mary had become sexually withdrawn from him. The first step was to analyze the drinking. However, at the end of the first session, there was no agreement about how much Bob consumed, so the therapist assigned homework to both partners to separately monitor his drinking.

In the next session, the two protocols were compared. There was significant overlap, but some differences remained; for example, Mary smelled alcohol on Bob when he came home from work. Bob, however, denied drinking anything that day. Establishing "facts" is sometimes almost impossible, and the attempt should be avoided.

The therapist took the opportunity to establish a controlled drinking experiment for the future. Bob chose the drinking rules he wanted to follow, and the therapist made a protocol including an initial blood check followed by a second in the month after the end of the experiment. There was an agreement that if Bob failed the test he would immediately enroll in an outpatient alcohol addiction program. His wife stated that she had no choice but to ask him to leave if he didn't follow through. This was also written down. All three took a copy of the contract.

In the following session, a typical drinking situation was examined in terms of modes. One night, Bob had become very intoxicated. He drank alone in the living room after Mary went to bed. Tracking back, he could describe that he felt guilty because he broke the social drinking rules during the day, unobserved by Mary. His Punitive Parent voice said, "You can forget about passing the test! You'll fail and Mary will leave you anyway!" The Vulnerable Child felt hopeless and desperate, so he started drinking heavily.

Analyzing the steps that led to Bob breaking the drinking rules revealed that he had had a very successful day closing a big deal for his company. The voice in his head said, "All these bastards in my company don't acknowledge that I'm the number 1 seller!" He felt anger, which led him to drink a glass of wine with lunch. Later he felt guilty and couldn't enjoy his success. This feeling spoiled the rest of his day and he returned home sad, wanting to talk with Mary about his mistake. But Mary was watching TV and he didn't feel confident enough to interrupt her. After the program finished, she was tired and went to bed. Despite having said nothing, Bob felt rejected and his sadness turned into a kind of frustrated anger.

The therapist went beyond the successful sale to ask the parent modes what they expected from Bob in his job. This revealed that Bob had strong Demanding Parent voices pushing him to always be the best. He devoted an excessive amount of every week to his job (surrender). On the child chair, he admitted that he needed the approval of his boss so much that he would do almost anything to gain it. Mary's sexual withdrawal increased his need. This excessive work was an expression of Detached Self-soother mode. In the following days, this over-work resulted in a building tension. It was a vicious circle (Figure 9.1).

One trap is to only look at the drinking pattern. This case illustrates the need to acknowledge the underlying sadness of the Vulnerable Child. Bob needed support. His Angry Child wasn't obvious. He needed to approach Mary and express his need for more connection. His need for approval through his job undermined the emotional bond between the couple. The therapist coached Bob to express his needs to Mary openly and to find

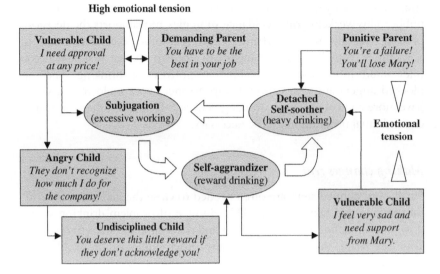

Figure 9.1 A drinking mode cycle

effective ways to combine sex with caresses (making sex more appealing to Mary). When he readjusted his work–life balance, his urge to drink diminished.

It's important to note the internal mode cycle. Usually, the hidden internal dynamic and conflicts within the drinker, between the hidden Angry Child and Demanding or Punitive Parent modes, have to be faced. If there's a relapse, try to identify the mode cycle preceding the drinking behavior by a chain analysis. The drinking is usually just the tip of the iceberg, and the chain starts much earlier. Return to the initial situation that led the drinker to feel uncomfortable.

The coping mode here is typically surrendering behavior. The involved child modes and parental voices should be recognized. The function of the coping mode should be acknowledged as possibly the best solution in the absence of any other solution, but now we can see that Detached Self-soother is a consequence of an exaggerated (surrender) coping style.

This helps to break the cycle by reducing feelings of guilt and shame. Also, explore the disadvantages of the drinking behavior for attachment (assertiveness is better than surrender; mutual understanding is preferred). Finally, share ideas for a better coping style.

There are many avenues of support. Think about the assistance of best friends, "wise minds," religious texts, a support group, an Alcoholics Anonymous 12-step program, or whatever might be helpful. All these strategies work by getting you out of your shell and making your problem public. This weakens your avoidance strategies and supports the decisions of your Healthy Adult to change. There are more eyes watching you! Sometimes, your life circumstances will need to change first. Once you understand more about your hidden motives for drinking (such as blocked anger) and you can find ways to meet your child needs, you'll have more control over your drinking behavior. If this fails, then a specialist or residential program might be necessary.

Making changes real

Small, well-defined steps are often needed to close the gap between wishful thinking and taking action. This example of problem drinking shows how you can define a set of behaviors and determine the steps to recovery. You can adapt the guidelines to any other addictive or problematic behavior.

Technical point: It may be important to distinguish between abusing a substance and being dependent on it. This also applies to addictive behavior not involving substances, such as gambling or other compulsive activities. Interestingly, the activations in the reward system in the brain stem don't differ much between substance and other addictions. Briefly, dependency includes a lack of control over the activity, even if you aren't physically dependent. If you lack control over alcohol or other drugs, you may need to get addiction treatment before you can make other behavior changes.

To do: To determine whether you have control over your drinking, do the social drinking experiment (adapted from Sobell & Sobell, 1973). The following list shows rules about drinking situations and drinking behavior:

Drinking situations
- Never drink alone.
- Do not drink with anonymous people.
- No drinking before 6 p.m.
- Drink only while having a meal.
- Not more than one glass of wine or beer with a meal.
- Do not drink when you are feeling bad.
- Two alcohol-free days each week.
- Do not drink alcohol when you are thirsty (drink a glass of water).

Drinking behavior

- One glass should last at least one hour.
- Sip at least 10 times from one glass.
- Not more than two glasses within one hour, even when you are celebrating.
- One alcohol-free drink between two glasses with alcohol.
- Do not "party" more than two times a week.
- Try to refuse when someone offers you a drink.

Choose the rules that you want to follow. If you're dealing with another self-defeating behavior, adapt the rules so they match with your problem. Be creative!

Write a contract that includes the rules and the consequences if the experiment fails and leave it with a friend or your partner. Inform close friends and your partner about your rules. Choose a person to review the outcome of your experiment, perhaps your physician or a priest. A month is an adequate time frame.

Now try to keep to the contract for the specified time:

- If you succeed, you're unlikely to be dependent. Try to continue sticking to your rules anyway.
- If you fail and your dependency is on alcohol or other drugs, that usually means that you need addiction treatment in a specialized unit.
- If you fail and your dependency is of another type, persist with schema therapy to gain control over your behavior.

How about self-help groups?

A self-help group can be very helpful to maintaining your recovery. The group can support you in a new pattern of life. Indeed, there are self-help groups for almost every problem. Some groups require abstinence; others don't. Talking to people suffering from similar problems also helps to normalize your difficulties, which can moderate the voices of the parent modes. Such a group can give emotional support to the child modes. The 12 steps of Alcoholics Anonymous are very useful as a new belief system. Such recovery programs have been used for a wide range of problematic behaviors, including eating, drug, internet, and sexual addictions.

However, there are limitations from a schema perspective. Without a clear strategy of becoming aware of your modes, the group can become a substitute soothing entity. It's possible to join an accepting group while continuing to avoid your underlying difficulties in life. Some programs, such as Alcoholics Anonymous, have helped countless people give up addictions and stay abstinent, but may not deal with the psychological difficulties associated with the addiction (for example, the "dry alcoholic").

This is not to diminish the very real gains made in such programs, but they're only the first step to a full psychological recovery. The goal is not only abstinence but personal growth in Healthy Adult.

Dependence and Avoidance in Relationships

It's easy to be overdependent in a relationship. To some degree, dependence is natural, but what is the dividing line? Gitta Jacob listed some markers of dependence in relationships:

- Dependent people look for a lot of advice and reassurance.
- They depend on others for the organization of important areas of living.
- They find it difficult to answer back or speak up for themselves.
- It is hard for them to try out new behavior.
- They tend to accept too much responsibility in an attempt to please others.
- When an important relationship ends, they are quickly in a new one.
- They have a fear of abandonment.

This can relate to patterns of avoidance. Jacob listed as methods of avoidance:

- in a narrow sense, staying away from things, including completing tasks
- the use of distraction, such as computer games, the internet, nonstop working, and so on
- stimulation from rich food, internet porn, gambling, and risky sports
- the use of alcohol and drugs
- monotonous complaining
- low expectations.

Reflect: Can you match these behaviors up with the various coping modes?

Bully and Attack with Other Anger-related Modes

Anger is one of the most distressing of emotions—for yourself and others.

> *Mary-Anne* said about her fiancé, "I have no doubt that Col wants our relationship to work. But his irritability has worn me down. And it's exhausting trying to deal with his unexpected explosions. He's a good person, and certainly genuine in his faith, but I can't take it anymore." It wasn't the first relationship Col had lost through anger.

Anger can spread like fire. This has been called the "kindling effect." Are you trying to deal with your anger? The following steps have been suggested:

1. *Ventilate.* Express anger fully—but do it when you're alone! Go out into the woods and shout out as loud and as long as you want to. How does that feel? Do any pictures come into your mind? Try to clarify what is at the core of your anger, but avoid being abusive or destructive, especially with family. Do this in your journal from Angry Child mode.
2. *Empathize.* Use your Healthy Adult to empathically sense the wound that was activated with an acknowledgment of the pain that was caused. Write from this perspective in your journal.
3. *Reality test.* Without being punitive or defensive, use your Healthy Adult to examine the situation in a realistic way, then look at what aspects have been schema or mode driven. What distortions can you recognize?
4. *Rehearse appropriate assertiveness.* After anger has abated, use your Healthy Adult to explore how your needs could have been expressed in an assertive rather than aggressive manner.

> *Nino* was easily enraged. His therapist encouraged him to scream into a pillow. She also engaged him in his Angry Child mode to play tug-of-war with a towel in a session. He worked through a work-related incident in his journal, writing from the various modes. They thought about how to better manage his anger in his home life.

Reflect: Bully and Attack mode is an overcompensation, usually for feeling weak and powerless. Bluster and bullying behavior derive from a hidden weakness, not strength.

A number of the modes are associated with anger:

- **Bully and Attack mode** is a coping mode. Anger is used to intimidate another person to meet your needs. While the anger of Bully and Attack is hot, in a **Predator mode** it's cold and more instrumental and calculated (see the discussion about antisocial modes below). Commonly, the threat from Bully and Attack has a physical dimension and leads to intense fear or sometimes reactive anger.
- **Angry Protector mode** has been suggested as a coping mode. In this state, an individual displays a diffuse generalized irritability against everyone and everything. It's a wall of anger. The anger power is used to keep people and potentially their demands at a safe distance. It wards off demands. Interestingly, the person to whom the anger is addressed usually does not feel attacked or frightened. The feeling is more some kind of helplessness combined with an impulse to help.
- **Punitive Parent mode** messages can have an angry or contemptuous tone, but serve to take the higher ground with righteous indignation. They're not emotional in their essence. The source of the anger is elsewhere (from the Angry Child mode) but the Punitive Parent directs it.
- **Angry and Enraged Child modes** are basically a "hissy fit"—an adult tantrum saying, "My needs haven't been met! I'll let you and everyone else know how angry I am!" In the pure form, this anger is not clearly directed toward somebody and seems less threatening. It just indicates that the need for assertiveness is challenged. However, sometimes people hurt themselves in a rage. Others feel irritated and withdraw.

Reflect: Do you think anger can become more threatening to others when combined with Punitive Parent appraisals? In this way, "permission" might be given to hurt another person.

Note: Sometimes it's easier to see these modes in others. Think about the effect of another's mode state on you. With Bully and Attack, you shrink and want to either withdraw or submit to unreasonable demands. With Angry Protector, you might feel frustration about being pushed away. The amount of distance in the relationship is noticed. Generally, with Angry or Enraged Child a part of you may feel caring and want to help the child get their needs met. With Punitive Parent, the feeling is of being judged and condemned—really being unreasonably punished.

A chair-dialogue exercise

How can you handle your anger better? Here's a chair-dialogue exercise that you can do on your own to modify the way you express it.

Facing your chair, place an empty chair representing your partner or any other person. Ventilate your anger towards the empty chair. Then stand up and look down on the scene between you and the other person. Watch the expressions of your overcompensatory mode. Find a name for it. Picture how the other person will feel and react in your current coping mode. Become aware of what basic emotion drives your coping mode.

Place the Angry Child mode on a chair behind the coping mode chair, as if it's pushing the coping mode. If you have noticed that people often withdraw and detach, turn the opposite chair away to express this distancing.

From the mode map, you know that there's not only an Angry Child expressing the need for assertiveness but also a Vulnerable Child beside it, standing in the shade when the anger bursts out, still longing for attachment. Put a chair for this unseen Vulnerable Child right beside the Angry Child chair behind the coping mode chair. Then take a seat and feel how the Vulnerable Child feels, looking at the turned-away chair. What does this child mode need now? Speak your desire out loud toward the turned-away chair of the other person.

Stand up again to shift back into the Healthy Adult perspective. Turn the chair for the withdrawing person back so it faces the coping mode chair. Put the coping mode chair aside to make way for a better solution. Be aware, standing on both your legs. What could you—or a wise person—do or say, acting in a way that the needs of both underlying emotional systems are met best? Speak out directly and in a balanced way to the chair for the other person, no longer withdrawing.

How does it feel talking and acting this way? Does the new solution satisfy both needs? Does it feel justified, moderate, and "healthy"? If not, try again. You can rewind the tape as often as you like, making your solution even better.

When you have done as well as you can, recognize your feelings and become aware of your body sensations and sense of power. Put a new chair for the Healthy Adult beside the Angry Child chair and take a seat so that the adult is in touch with both child modes (and not sitting in front of them like the coping mode chair, leaving them unseen behind). So finally the chairs are located as if the mode map is lying on the floor facing the opposite chair. Rewind the situation back to where you started deteriorating through your outburst of anger and rescript it from a Healthy Adult perspective, speaking up directly to the chair in front of you. How would this person react now? Is this OK? If not, give it another try until you're satisfied or until you have done the best you can.

Eventually, ask a friend or your partner what they would do, stepping into your shoes. Going for help is a very adult way of dealing with current problems. You're no longer alone in your difficulty!

To do: After you have been angry in a situation and when things have cooled down, ask the other person how they responded emotionally to your anger. This might give you a clue to which mode you were in. When we're overwhelmed by emotions, our self-reflection drops down to almost zero. Sometimes we cannot recall things we have said and done. These gaps are caused by an overflow of corticoids in the brain. Basically, this is a protection system preventing us from storing distressing memories. Our memory system shuts down. So your perceptions are not absolute! And, once you get a clearer picture, do not forget to ask for your behavior to be excused! This helps heal wounds to relationships.

If your anger is often overshooting, that's a road to hell for your relationship. It's imperative that you gain better control. Try using the advice in this chapter. If you fail to manage your anger, we suggest that you look for some professional help or enroll in an anger management program.

Try to go behind the screen of anger to discover what your hidden needs are. Unstable people are often highly avoidant of their own needs, since those needs were dangerous to them as a child in an abusive environment, but discovering them is the way Vulnerable Child changes and Healthy Adult can be built up.

> *William* lived with his partner, Barry. He was encouraged to ask Barry to listen when he was upset. They negotiated a plan that he would stop what he was doing and listen for a minimum of 5 minutes when William asked in a clear and assertive way, without any "attitude" or tone of aggression.

To do: Work out an anger scale to rate yourself from 1 to 10 (from mild irritation to out-of-control rage). Think about this as a volume control. Now think about how you speak to your partner. At what point do your words change to bullets? This is an important self-reflection. Avoid trying to resolve issues in your relationship when your anger has gone beyond that limit. This intervention is also useful in dealing with hostile modes, such as Enraged Child, Bully and Attack, and Punitive Parent.

Self-aggrandizer Mode

The Self-aggrandizer mode is "puffed up," and has been linked to narcissism. The Self-aggrandizer may feel special, powerful, and unique. They often have a sense of superiority and look down on others, sometimes with contempt, and see the world in terms of "above" and "below," which leads to dominating interactions. For them, it is more important to maintain a successful image than to relate to people. Tokens of status are important to them: prestige cars, a corner office, a trophy spouse, degrees or qualifications, name-dropping friends.

> *Stanley* was the chief executive of a finance company. He was also very grandiose and demanded deference from his staff and his young trophy wife.

It's important to get a sense of the childhood needs underlying this mode. It's an overcompensation for what may be deep feelings of inadequacy. Sometimes the sense of superiority or feeling special comes from parental messages, which can sound like Demanding Parent messages but have a different meaning ("You're better than everyone else!").

To do: Write in your journal from the various positions. If you recognize traces of Self-aggrandizer, start out in that mode, then move to Demanding Parent (listen to the voice about being special), and then perhaps try to write from Vulnerable Child. Finally, write from Healthy Adult and try to integrate the various modes you have explored. What does it tell you about yourself?

Reflect: Think about a recent time when you were feeling grandiose and almost too big for yourself. Identify your feelings and then think back to a childhood experience in which you felt the same way. Did you *need* to feel superior because someone was putting you down? What were the triggers then? What are the triggers now?

Overcontroller Mode

The Overcontroller mode is an attempt to protect oneself from a perceived threat by focusing attention, ruminating, and exercising control over others. It can be driven by parent mode messages such as "Nobody does it as good as I do!," but less in a narcissistic sense than in a sense such as "If *you* don't do it, it won't work (and you are responsible for a possible failure!)" There may be a somewhat paranoid feel to this, with excessive attention to any possible external threat and an obsessive use of order, repetition, and ritual.

> *Cindy* was a member of a religious cult that was preparing for the end of the world. She carefully monitored the news for any signs of international distress. This became problematic to her husband, who thought that the attitudes of the cult were "silly."

To do: In your journal, start with a sentence completion exercise: "I need to maintain control because ..." Try this a number of times until something feels right. Then recall times when you weren't fully in control but you had a very good outcome. This provides a different source of learning.

The Antisocial Modes

Some modes are antisocial. They are more common in prison populations than in the general community. The modes we discuss here are not limited to deviant groups but are simply more common among them. For example, Bully and Attack mode is often seen among the incarcerated, but is also familiar in the workplace and on occasion in intimate relationships.

> *Edward* was a natural bully. He would intimidate others for money. He spent most of his time settling drug-related debts for a local motorcycle gang.

> *Suzanne* had a reputation of downsizing the staff in areas she supervised. They were terrified of her coldly calculating manner. Her coldness became a problem to her partner at home.

The following additional modes have recently been suggested.

Overanalyzer mode is typical of some people in computing or academia. The Overanalyzer is usually a very intelligent person but highly ruminative, and never gets to a solution. This leads to a "stuckness" in intellectual abstraction.

> *Nat* was a computer engineer who overthought every problem. His conversations in therapy went around in circles. Eventually he complained, "We never seem to get anywhere. What am I doing wrong?"

Fantasy mode involves a person being lost in a world of endless daydreams or make-believe.

> *Vetta* was overinvolved in internet games. She would withdraw to her room, and her homework began to suffer.

Avoidant Protector is about avoiding everything. It's a state of mind in withdrawal. There's no engagement with people or even life.

> *Ned* was an older man who kept mainly to himself. He came to the attention of the pastor at a local church when he was unable to do his shopping and neighbors asked for help. He had a pattern of withdrawal, with no family or friends to assist.

Perhaps there's a temptation to multiply modes beyond those that are absolutely necessary to understand the dynamics of personality disorder. We think it's best to identify styles of thinking that can lead to a person being stuck in life or therapy. Naming a mode helps them to understand and then address their coping state in a healthy way.

Bernstein has identified some additional modes typical of antisocial people.

In **Conning-manipulative mode**, the person swindles others, lies, or manipulates to attain a specific goal. This can include taking advantage of others or escaping punishment.

> *Stella* engineered a complex fraud, which led to a number of investors being taken in. They lost thousands. Eventually, she fled the country using a false passport.

In **Predator mode**, the person acts to eliminate a rival or enemy in a cold and ruthless way. Usually the plan is calculated and callous.

> *Edward* hid his convictions for child-related sexual offences and carefully groomed a teenage boy who lived in the same apartment complex.

> *Michelle* spread vicious rumors about her ex-husband after a custody dispute.

This can be seen as a kind of survival mode in which the world is viewed in terms of the survival of the fittest.

These antisocial modes give a schema understanding of what is commonly known as the psychopathic personality. You can learn more about this through the work of Robert Hare, a leading researcher.

Reflect: Have you ever experienced what might be called "psychological vandalism" in a relationship? This might indicate some kind of involvement with a psychopath. Talk to someone who has had experience in forensic psychology or psychiatry. Read the book by Robert Hare in the reference list.

Note: Some of the overcompensating antisocial modes feel good and can be rewarding to some degree. The problem, as Gitta Jacob has noted, is that overcompensators are out of touch with themselves, and there can be negative effects on others.

Compliant Surrender Mode

Above, we have described detached or addictive behavior as avoidant coping and then described "externalizing" behavior, such as outbursts of anger. In this section, we look at the opposite: "internalizing" or submissive coping. Internalizing responses often go along with the basic emotions of fear, latent panic, or sadness.

Our needs are often in conflict with our partner's. In Compliant Surrender mode, one partner gives in to the wishes of the other.

> *Tania* was saving for a new car that she needed for her job in real estate. Her partner, Matt, wanted a few thousand to cover gambling debts. She gave him the money and felt disappointed in herself. She wanted the security of feeling connected, even though she knew it was a destructive relationship. She could not bear any conflict, so she sacrificed her needs for her partner's to maintain her attachment to him.

You might wonder why this might be regarded as a problem. At times, it's important to make sacrifices, but a pattern of neglecting personal needs creates a problem. In Tania's case, her attachment need was more activated than her assertiveness need. The price was a loss of autonomy and self-expression. She felt safe but unhappy.

If you spend too much time in Compliant Surrender mode, it will result in very passive, subservient, submissive, approval-seeking, and self-deprecating behavior. You'll often tolerate abuse or being treated badly. Inevitably, your self-esteem will deteriorate. Do you find yourself in relationships with people who are aggressive and controlling?

Look at your mode map. Do you find yourself trapped in the left part of the coping mode spectrum? It's inevitable that sooner or later your assertiveness need will become activated and you'll get angry. Usually, people tending to submission don't perceive anger. It leaks through in feelings of disappointment and sadness, and later in frustration or a latent tendency to slow down a little bit, which can grow into passive-aggressive behavior (such as sabotage or refusing to cooperate). This indicates that your assertiveness need has slowly woken up and that you're no longer willing to pay any price for attachment. The emotions slowly shift from fear over sadness to feeling annoyed. Thoughts that might occur in this state include "I've already paid my dues. Now it's their turn!"

That realization can signal your Healthy Adult to bring you to the awareness that you weren't treated fairly. It's much better to become aware of growing anger than to ignore it in a Detached or Angry Protector mode and eventually risk an outburst of anger, which might bring your

Punitive Parent mode into play, inducing feelings of guilt or shame and kicking you back into Compliant Surrender. Instead of staying in this ongoing loop, it is better to acknowledge your anger before it bursts out.

This is the main difference between the protector modes and the Healthy Adult: The Healthy Adult is aware of the coming thunderstorm when there's enough time to change your reaction. Channel it constructively by expressing it verbally and moderately. Being mindful of your current emotional undercurrents is crucial for swimming instead of sinking into old life-traps.

> *Eddie* was universally considered to be a nice person, but his doctor had warned him about his dangerous levels of stress and his high blood pressure. He worked for a mission agency, which loaded him up with work because he lacked the capacity to say no. Eventually, Eddie's doctor insisted he take time off. Fortunately, his boss was supportive and arranged for Eddie to have sessions with a personal coach. This led to him becoming more aware of his pattern and designing some strategies to become more assertive. While this change wasn't easy, Eddie felt he had to change "or I'll lose my ability to work effectively." What surprised him most was the new respect he found from colleagues at work, who almost welcomed the changes. He felt he was becoming more effective. His wife also noticed the changes. Although she had mixed feelings because he was less "malleable," she also recognized he was "more solid, less like a marshmallow."

You'll need gas in the tank. The gas is the power you feel when your assertiveness need is activated. You might perceive this as a feeling of strength in your body or even as "constructive anger" (so called by Les Greenberg). This is a matter of balance, which can only be achieved through Healthy Adult.

There's great value in visually rehearsing your new behavior.

> Eddie thought about common relationship situations, about how he would generally "just go along with her." Now he visualized the circumstances, such as choosing a film to see on the weekend. He saw himself expressing a preference for seeing a movie he was interested in. He saw his wife's face of disappointment, but he was able to stick to his preference. This provided an important halfway step until he was able to do it in real life.

Coping Modes and Relationships

The coping modes are crucial to understanding relationships. The intensity of our emotions and indirectly our needs tends to be expressed in the intimacy of family life, so each of the coping modes is a way to not be overwhelmed emotionally—or to sharpen the edge for emotional avoidance.

For example, avoiding conflict can be passive with Detached Protector or active with Compliant Surrender. All these strategies might have been helpful in your childhood, when you lacked the power you have today, but using childhood strategies for adult problems is maladaptive. Discovering that you're stuck in an old life-trap is the first step in getting out of it. There are so many more options today! Why keep flying on autopilot?

Even worse, the coping modes of a couple can interact in mode cycles. Some of them might appear adaptive at first glance, but can reinforce each other in a vicious circle.

These are the possible dyadic interactions:

1. *Fight–fight loop:* Both *Lee and Stacey* get into Punitive Parent to attack each other over an unexpected bill (highly unstable, one of them sooner or later has to shift into surrender or avoidance). There's sometimes considerable ugliness in intimate relationships, with Bully and Attack more often expressed than might be expected. Watch the movie *Who's Afraid of Virginia Woolf?* for a brilliant example of recurring fight–fight loops.

   Healthy Adult is essential to being able to relate to your partner in a more satisfying way.

2. *Fight–flight loop: Hetty* criticizes Paul for not talking to her over dinner; he withdraws to his study to play computer games (moderately unstable, tending to escalation because the more Paul withdraws, the more Hetty will pursue him).

3. *Fight–freeze loop: Marge* would switch off and daydream of a planned holiday. This helped her not to feel so overwhelmed by wanting to be closer emotionally to her partner. Or *Jane* criticizes Andrew for being late from work; he passively accepts the criticism while remaining emotionally detached (might be stable, but not satisfying for either partner).

4. *Flight–flight loop: Sandy and Cici* live parallel lives under the same roof (probably stable until one partner finds an alternative, but not satisfying) (cf. Atkinson, 2012)

5. *Fight–surrender loop:* This complementary cycle stabilizes a relationship unless the submissive partner resists (back to 3) or the dominant partner gets bored and leaves the relationship. *Solomon* would submit to the dictates of his wife. He joked about feeling henpecked, but a number of his friends saw that it was not really a joke.

Mike was always stressed and could be aggressive at work, but at home he was even worse, verbally attacking his children and barely containing violent feelings toward his wife. This intimidation tactic was rewarded when family members quietly submitted to his imperious will.

Couple exercise: With your partner, identify three recent incidents of conflict in your relationship. Then chart them in terms of mode interactions by:

1. identifying modes that were activated
2. classifying each in terms of fight, flight, freeze, and surrender
3. doing a chain analysis of the interactions leading to one of the loops.

Choice Points

Now that we've explained the coping modes, it's time to introduce a very important resource for you to manage dysfunctional modes. There comes a *choice point* when you're aware that you're in a mode. Based on that self-awareness, you can see yourself in the mode. Psychoanalysis called this an "observing ego."

The idea of choice has been explored in acceptance and commitment therapy, in which the idea is to decide to act in a way that's consistent with your committed values or to remain inconsistent.

> *Ned* had a stressful job in an accounting firm. He often found himself in Angry Protector mode, which he justified as giving him space to get his job done. However, he was also irritable and distancing with his wife and young children. He went on a Buddhist retreat, and he was challenged to live more fully, with intimacy to those he loved. He admitted to his wife that he needed help, but he was willing.
>
> Ned began with mode awareness and was better able to use some mindfulness techniques such as attention to his breathing to calm himself, but now he was able to identify choice points when he could say to himself, "I know I'm in Angry Protector mode. I need to stop and breathe. I have a choice to continue or to relax and be more present with people. I want to connect— that reflects my values. I can change gears and get where I want to be. I can drive; I'm not in the passenger's seat, being driven."

Choice points are important in a transition to a healthier mode. They open the possibility of more than management by allowing change. This can be a stepping-stone to Healthy Adult mode.

Reflect: When you become aware that you're in a coping mode, can you train yourself to stop in that moment, maybe pinch yourself, giving yourself space to make a choice? Ask yourself what value or values you want to guide you, then carefully make a choice.

Schema therapy recognizes that we aren't always in control. It doesn't set out a simplistic solution of "Try harder" or "Choose what is right or rational." Instead, it tries to maximize our choices based on an understanding of our automatic coping impulses and by recognizing those moments when we can claim a degree of freedom to act in a considered way.

Summary

In this chapter, we've looked at the shield that we use to try to protect our child modes. The strategy is simple: Do not feel. But that is to be less than human. We have emphasized the need to manage coping modes in romantic relationships, but also what changing might involve. Finally, we have considered choice points and how an awareness of them can help you to act in line with your values.

To Read Further

- Narcissism and the Self-aggrandizer: Behary (2012, 2013)
- The modes, especially patterns of interaction and the antisocial modes: Bernstein, Arntz, and de Vos (2007)
- An integrative approach to treating addiction and underlying personality difficulties: Ball (1998)
- Ideas to deal with anger: Farrell and Shaw (2012)
- Psychopathic personality: Hare (1993)
- Different ways to use chairs: Kellogg (2012)
- Using chair-dialogues and going beyond black/white thinking: Kellogg and Young (2006)
- Steps to dealing with anger: Kellogg and Young (2006)
- Coping modes and excess, and the way avoidance can keep Compliant Surrender going: Jacob, van Genderen, and Seebauer (2015)
- The social drinking experiment: Sobell and Sobell (1973)
- The kindling effect of anger: Solomon and Tatkin (2011, p. 108).

References

Atkinson, T. (2012). Schema therapy for couples: Healing partners in a relationship. In M. van Vreeswijk, J. Broersen, & M. Nadort (Eds.), *The Wiley-Blackwell handbook of schema therapy: Theory, research and practice* (pp. 323–335). Oxford, UK: Wiley-Blackwell.

Ball, S. A. (1998). Manualized treatment for substance abusers with personality disorders: Dual focus schema therapy. *Addictive Behaviors, 23*(6), 883–891.

Behary, W. (2012). Schema therapy for narcissism: A case study. In M. van Vreeswijk, J. Broersen and M. Nadort (Eds.), *The Wiley-Blackwell handbook of schema therapy: Theory, research and practice* (pp. 81–90). Oxford, UK: Wiley-Blackwell.

Behary, W. (2013). *Disarming the narcissist: Surviving and thriving with the self-absorbed*, 2nd ed. Oakland, CA: New Harbinger.

Bernstein, D., Arntz, A., & de Vos, M. (2007). Schema focused therapy in forensic settings: Theoretical model and recommendations for best clinical practice. *International Journal of Forensic Mental Health, 6*(2), 169–183.

Farrell, J., & Shaw, I. (2012). *Group schema therapy for borderline personality disorder: A step-by-step treatment manual with patient workbook*. Oxford, UK: Wiley-Blackwell.

Greenberg, L. S., & Goldman, R. N. (2008). *Emotion-focused couples therapy: The dynamics of emotion, love and power*. Washington, DC: American Psychological Association.

Hare, R. (1993). *Without conscience: The disturbing world of the psychopaths among us*. New York, NY: Guilford Press.

Hayes, S., Luoma, J., Bond, F., Masuda, A., & Lillis, J. (2006). Acceptance and commitment therapy: Model, processes and outcomes. *Behavior Research and Therapy, 44*(1), 1–25.

Jacob, G., van Genderen, H., & Seebauer, L. (2015). *Breaking negative thought patterns: A schema therapy self-help and support book*. Malden, MA: Wiley-Blackwell.

Kellogg, S. H. (2012). On speaking one's mind: Using chair-work dialogues in schema therapy. In M. van Vreeswijk, J. Broersen, & M. Nadort (Eds.), *The Wiley-Blackwell handbook of schema therapy: Theory, research and practice* (pp. 197–207). Oxford, UK: Wiley-Blackwell.

Kellogg, S. H., & Young, J. E. (2006). Schema therapy for borderline personality disorder. *Journal of Clinical Psychology, 62*(4), 445–458.

Sobell, M. B., & Sobell, L. C. (1973). Individualized behavior therapy for alcoholics. *Behavior Therapy, 4,* 49–72.

Solomon, M., & Tatkin, S. (2011). *Love and war in intimate relationships: Connection, disconnection and mutual regulation*. New York, NY: W. W. Norton.

10

Meeting the Needs of Your "Inner Child"

"The child is father of the man," as Wordsworth said in a poem. Childhood experiences not only influence us but shape the adults we become. We have a life cycle with important input from each stage, which is recognized and acknowledged in schema therapy.

Introduction to Child Modes

Begin with your emotional foundations of self. You'll need to get past your coping modes. Here are your emotional resources. Both your sensitivity and your power.

"Inner child" therapies have been popular in recent years, but they take a limited perspective. Schema therapy understands this dimension of experience, but the child modes are seen less as a stable person within and more as a complex experience that can become pervasive and even controlling for a moment. It describes more a transitory state of emotion-driven functioning than a persisting "subperson" within ourselves.

Here's the hope of change through schema therapy. Schemas were formed through the failure to meet childhood needs. As an adult, you can meet those needs. Reparenting involves becoming aware of this internal level of emotional functioning, acknowledging your core needs, and caring for them like good parents do. This can transform dysfunctional aspects of your schema legacy. This process is crucial for emotional healing and a huge step toward finding more happiness in life.

Breaking Negative Relationship Patterns: A Schema Therapy Self-help and Support Book, First Edition. Bruce A. Stevens and Eckhard Roediger.
© 2017 John Wiley & Sons, Ltd. Published 2017 by John Wiley & Sons, Ltd.

To do: The best way to appreciate your child modes is through a visualization. First think about a recent experience in which you felt lonely. Return to that experience, see it, feel it again. When you feel the emotions in a vivid way, allow your mind to travel back to any childhood event that felt the same. What images arise? It may be something you had forgotten, but now you're back there. Are you experiencing what you felt then? This is likely to be your Vulnerable Child mode.

The Importance of Keeping Your Vulnerable Child in Sight

Reflect: When do you notice that you're in Vulnerable Child mode? Identify a number of triggers and make a list. Think about how you react.

> *Morrie* noted that sad scenes on TV evoked an emotional reaction. He would initially feel sad but, to his surprise, found that rather than remaining in Vulnerable Child he would go into Angry Protector mode driven by beliefs about other people: "My irritability means no one feels safe enough to help meet my needs." This was a crucial turning point in his growth. He could clearly see how he pushed people away, influenced by the critical parent voices—often those who most wanted to help. So first he had to become aware of those voices, reappraise them, and cease believing them. After this obstacle was removed, he could be aware of his attachment needs and balance them better with his need for safety and control.

The first step is mode awareness. *See* (or, maybe better, *feel*) when you're shifting into Vulnerable Child mode. There may only be a moment before you flip into a coping mode, but try to catch yourself. Separate the child mode's basic emotions and body feelings from the entrenched toxic beliefs, then stay with your sense of vulnerability. Try to identify your need for attachment. It will usually be a simple child need for safety, nurturing, comfort, and love. It's nothing to be ashamed of. All of this is part of our nature.

Social Emotions

Some emotions are not as "pure" as the six basic emotions (sadness, fear, anger, disgust, surprise, and happiness). They include feeling misunderstood, defective, deprived, a failure, flooded by doubts, worried, victimized, worthless, unloved, unlovable, lost, fragile, weak, defeated, oppressed, powerless, left out, and hopeless. We weren't born with these emotions. They involve appraisals we had to learn. This is part of socialization. That is why these emotions are called social emotions. The inherent appraisal component is important to understand. There's a clear schema influence (mostly conditional schemas). Recognize the voices of internalized parent modes: Kick them out and care for the Vulnerable Child.

To do: Practice separating basic from social emotions. Since there are only six basic emotions (and some shades of them), all other emotions must be social emotions. Get a sense of the hidden message entrenched in them. Powerless can include "You're too weak to make it!" Worthless is easy to dismantle ("You're not worth being loved or respected"). Hopeless includes "This will never change" (what a child cannot know!). So social emotions include a nucleus of essential feelings (in the last examples, the basic emotions of sadness and fear) mixed with beliefs, making the emotions even stronger. This is why they're so toxic: Initially they appear like a genuine part of the emotion, but they're infusions of significant others. Instead of helping, they amplify the negative quality of the emotions and fix them in our psyche. This may sound complicated. Here is an example:

> *Nora* saw her alcoholic father repeatedly assault her mother. He often made promises that he failed to keep. This resulted in a Mistrust-Abuse schema. She often surrendered to this schema, but she felt guilty about not being able to protect her mother. First this belief had to be regarded as an unrealistic task from the Demanding Parent voice, to be evaluated and banished from her head. Now she could care for her own Vulnerable Child. Her trust was very tentative, and her Vulnerable Child needed frequent reassurance and protective measures to ensure a sense of safety.

Angry and Enraged Child Modes

Reflect: The Angry Child mode feels intensely angry, infuriated, frustrated, and impatient because the child's needs for assertiveness and autonomy haven't been met. Enraged Child feels the same, but more intensely, and is more likely to go into a tantrum and "lose it."

Anger in the child modes is perfectly natural. It's a reaction to our needs not being met. While this is a natural response, anger can be expressed in dysfunctional ways—or not, as we might choose. Try separating anger from directed aggression intended to hurt somebody. Pure anger is just expressing your natural need for being respected and not harmed. Small children don't hate anybody. They just try to get what they need. This is why Les

Greenberg called this pure anger "constructive." But, mixed with toxic beliefs, anger can turn destructive. This is an overcompensatory coping mode. So overcompensatory modes—while emotionally driven by anger power—always include the influence of some outside-directed beliefs justifying the damage done to others or at least controlling, bossing, or devaluing them.

> *Britta* felt insecure in her new position. She felt anxious at her first review of her work practices. The child in her wanted reassurance about her job performance. There was encouraging feedback but also some constructive criticism. She experienced this as overly critical, and it stung. She noticed that she was flooded with a kind of helpless anger. She then recognized her Angry Child. She practiced a mindful response: "It's just a feeling. The anger will pass and I'll get a better perspective later. I won't allow myself to blow up over this issue when my boss is just trying to do her job." Later, she talked with her partner over a special dinner that he made. It felt good to be understood.

To do: Try to detect the inherent messages when tending to overcompensate. Separate constructive anger from overshooting compensatory impulses. Sharpen your sense when your need for assertiveness and safety is threatened and when the voice in your head makes you hot, tending to make you overshoot. Let the voice in your head fade out or float away like leaves on a river in autumn.

Reflect: The Angry Child can be secondary. Gitta Jacob noted that if there are feelings of vulnerability, it's probably Vulnerable Child that's primary. If there's no sense of vulnerability, maybe the emotion is primarily anger.

Impulsive Child

Reflect: Impulsive Child feels impatient, frustrated, and easily angered.

The Impulsive Child acts on nonessential desires or impulses in a self-centered way. This state may appear "spoiled" but is often based on temperament.

Note that greed is also an expression of assertiveness needs. Seen this way, greed is another facet of anger but tends to incorporate things rather than push them away or be in control. Nevertheless, this can be a chronic problem for some people and may reflect a degree of inadequate parenting. Basically, children are needy, not greedy! But it's important to have limits, or preferably for the person with a strong Impulsive Child to set their own limits. There's a challenge to move toward greater maturity. Usually, this will be best met by strengthening Healthy Adult.

> *Brad* was in his first year of married life. He wanted to continue riding dirt bikes on both days of the weekend and be out with his friends a few nights during the week. He was surprised that Martina, his wife, thought he was "overdoing the going out." They saw a relationship counselor, and she helped him to see that he had not adapted to new responsibilities in married life. He tended to think that his impulsivity should have sway. But he grew in his Healthy Adult mode, and with his wife found some win–win strategies to balance his needs with hers.

What do you do with Impulsive Child? Basically, it's important to uncover the needs of the child and then find a way to meet those needs in a healthy way.

> Brad didn't want to lose Martina. He saw it was a risk. So they discussed times when Brad could meet his social needs one night a week. She agreed that she would not complain and would reward him with a meal of his choice on another night, one that they would share together. Brad also gradually learned when it was important to put Martina's needs first. This is a growth challenge in any relationship, but especially when there's a problem with Impulsive Child (or Undisciplined Child).

A person with too much Impulsive Child can find the cost in relationships. Most people will draw back from a person whom they find too self-centered or spoiled.

Undisciplined Child

Reflect: Undisciplined Child feels lazy and distracted, and "can't be bothered."

Nothing gets done in this mode. While it's normal to feel lazy and sleep in on weekends, if that state of mind dominates your life it will lead to difficulties. Relax, yes, but do what needs to be done. Undisciplined Child has trouble doing anything unpleasant. Again, the answer is to be able to shift into Healthy Adult when needed.

> *Nikki* found the first year of college difficult. She was soon behind in her studies: "Unlike when I was in high school, no one motivates me here." She began missing classes and couldn't even begin to do assignments.

Eventually, she had to see the student counseling service to develop a routine. This worked for her, and she felt she could better keep on top of things.

Sometimes Impulsive Child and Undisciplined Child modes show a child who was spoiled when their parents neglected to set reasonable challenges or limits. This is a form of neglect because it's not what a child really needs. Learning to deal with obstacles successfully is an important source of what is called "resilience": Solving problems and overcoming resistance makes us stronger.

Defiant Child Mode

Gitta Jacob also mentioned the Defiant or Obstinate Child mode. Both are highly resistant and can lead to profound difficulties in relationships.

Vince was encouraged by his couples therapist to list the advantages of his resistance to any suggestion Elaine made. He was surprised by how many he came up with! Then together they explored the cost for their relationship. Vince began the change process by setting out times in their relationship when he would listen carefully and try to give Elaine's viewpoint a priority.

What to Do in a Child Mode

Think about the following:

1. *List.* Make a list of things you would like to do, or what your best friend recommends that you do. Order them in a hierarchy, with the least challenging or anxiety provoking first. Make a plan for when to start with the easiest items. Remember to tell a friend about your plan. This increases your commitment.
2. *Clarify.* Become clear in your thinking. We often use what Arntz calls "emotional reasoning." This is like the belief that "If I'm afraid, it must be dangerous." So discuss or write about your fears in detail. Go with your story to its natural conclusion.
    Clarissa said to her best friend, "I'm afraid to leave my house because I might get attacked." Her friend asked, "Where would somebody attack you?" She answered, "Everywhere!" Then her friend encouraged her to be more precise: "Where are the most dangerous places and times to go there? What places and times are safer?" Clarissa found it helpful to make such distinctions.

It might also be helpful to estimate the risk of being attacked from a best-friend perspective (as a percentage). Don't let your emotions "drive your car"! Once you manage to separate objectively dangerous situations from those that only appear dangerous from an anxious child perspective, stop avoiding and do what every healthy person would do. How did it work out? In psychological treatment, this is called a behavior experiment.

3. *Accept.* Accept that fear, sadness, greed, or anger is part of being in your child mode. The feelings might be there, but do what you have planned anyway. In Healthy Adult mode we can act in the face of fear. The child mode may even feel overwhelmed by fear, but Healthy Adult can act differently. This is a definition of courage: It is not about being fearless but about doing something while tolerating fear.

    Tip: Making some small steps in the right direction can help enormously. Therapists call this "graduated exposure."

4. *Talk.* Talk to the child mode. If your fear or anger increases beyond what you can tolerate, keep talking your child mode down, like good parents do: "We'll make it. These are just old fears coming from old schemas. I'll just go ahead step by step." You might try describing what you see with "loud thinking." Count stairs while climbing them. Keep your mind busy so there's no space left for worrying.

5. *Write.* Compose a letter to your child mode. Writing activates your brain in a much more complex way than just talking, so deepen the impact of your intervention by writing it down. The *Healing Your Aloneness Workbook* from Erika Chopich and Margaret Paul (1990) provides a lot of suggestions for working this way.

6. *Revise.* If something doesn't work, revise your plans. Not every problem can be solved with a first attempt. Adjust. Discover and accept your limits. Find your own pace, but stay on track. Start with small problems and later continue with the more difficult ones. Be aware of your Demanding Parent modes and remain patient.

7. *Reward.* Don't forget to reward yourself. Children need rewards to be happy. And the Happy Child mode is often the reward needed.

This list outlines how to deal with fear or anger. You can apply the same steps to deal with sad mood states, worries, or somatic symptoms like vertigo or pain. It will work with any kind of thoughts or feelings that keep you from enjoying your life.

A metaphor: Put the fear on the seat beside you and remain in Healthy Adult in the driver's seat. It's not a problem to have fear alongside you, but don't allow it to take over the steering wheel. The Healthy Adult continues driving with fear at their side.

Remember: The bottom line is seeing thoughts and emotions as something different from *you* as the hidden observer within. Remember what was said about mindfulness: Thoughts and feelings will come and go, but you can choose to stay on track. If you find yourself in a maladaptive coping mode, try to change into Healthy Adult. Healthy Adult is free to act again and grow stronger. Do it for the sake of your Happy Child, who wants to be part of your life again. And they don't ask for too much (just to enjoy being).

Developing a Healthy Adult is important to your romantic and family relationships. This basic awareness can foster a solid and determined adult judgment on how to handle a relationship in a way that will best benefit all. Healthy Adult becomes the engine of healthy growth.

Reflect: Is there a part of you that you feel ashamed of? This might be Vulnerable Child or Angry Child. In Healthy Adult, you can write a compassionate letter to the mode: "Little Andrew, you're often hurt and feel completely alone. You feel full of frustration and flooded by anger. That's understandable, given the abuse you suffered from your stepfather and your mother's inability to fully protect you ..."

Reflective exercise: Look at your list of modes. Can you identify a theme song for each mode? Make this as fun and lighthearted as possible—for example, the Beatles song "I Want to Hold Your Hand" for Vulnerable Child.

To do: Use your Healthy Adult to compose a list of healthy parent messages to your Vulnerable Child.

> *Barb* to her Detached Self-soother: "My need is not to be intoxicated. It's for my Vulnerable Child to feel protected."
>
> *Salvi* to his Punitive Parent: "I know you're out for my blood and I don't need to listen to your messages."
>
> *Menoa* to her Vulnerable Child: "You'll be cared for, now and always."
>
> *Charles* to his Compliant Surrender: "You're a person with rights. You're brave enough to stand up for what's important."

Also: When you feel stuck in some way, stand up, move around, eventually get out of the room, do something different until you manage to shift to Healthy Adult. Then think again about the situation. Ask yourself what your best friend would do.

Happy Child Mode

Reflect: Happy Child feels loved, accepted, contented, connected, satisfied, fulfilled, protected, praised, worthwhile, nurtured, guided, understood, validated, self-confident, competent, self-reliant, safe, resilient, strong, in control, included, optimistic, and spontaneous.

It's easy to overlook the role of Happy Child in healthy development. Schore (2003) emphasized the importance of the mother and father in amplifying and regulating infant joy. And joy has a key role in wiring the social brain. Intergenerational playing together strengthens the parent–child bond. This can help to avoid or later transform maladaptive schemas.

> *Amanda* grew up with a harsh and critical single mother who was endlessly concerned about her daughter's weight. This became Amanda's focus through her adolescence, often bordering on an eating disorder. She found a therapist who was skilled in play therapy. This challenged her seriousness about body image. The idea of playing together, with delight in who she was—as she was—was ultimately transforming. Amanda said, "This was unexpected, and it helped a lot."

Think about how to integrate a sense of playful spontaneity into your life. Can you laugh in a spontaneous and healthy way? This includes seeing and enjoying the fun of a situation. Watch hostile or cutting humor, which can sabotage a healthy Happy Child. Naturally, Happy Child is best when it's a mutual experience.

> *Margie* had made good progress in therapy. There was a new, almost tangible, lightness in the room. The therapist raised the possibility of more Happy Child. An ice cream visualization was used (as recommended by Farrell & Shaw, 2012). At the end of the session, she assigned homework to eat ice cream sometime that week to nourish Happy Child. Margie also thought about how to enhance her experience of sex and add to the positives in her marriage.

There's a healthy mode cycle in a relationship when both partners can flexibly shift between Healthy Adult, Vulnerable Child, and Happy Child modes. This includes open communication, especially about individual and joint needs. The Healthy Adult mode can take risks, learn new ideas, and update models of the self and the world, with an enhanced ability to reflect on schemas.

Fill out the worksheet in Figure 10.1 with your partner.

Below are feelings or states we experience when we are in Happy Child Mode. Go through the list together and tick the feelings you already have in this relationship.

Partner 1	Partner 2	Happy Child feelings or states	Partner 1	Partner 2	Happy Child feelings or states
		Loved			Spontaneous
		Contented			Understood
		Connected			Validated
		Worthwhile			Self-confident
		Excited			Competent
		Playful			Being my own person
		Nurtured			Safe
		Guided			Resilient
		Strong			Satisfied
		Curious			Fulfilled
		Adaptable			Protected
		Included			Accepted
		Optimistic			Praised

Put a * next to three Happy Child feelings or qualities that you would like to grow in—either personally or as a couple. Write them below. Next to each quality write down some ideas of what your partner could do and say to help you experience that feeling or need being met. Decide on a plan to build those experiences—for example, you could send your partner a text message each day pointing out a way they have been strong or resilient, or plan a playful activity each week, or include in your goodbye in the morning a phrase that helps your partner feel safe.

Quality	How can my partner help me? What are we going to do as a couple?
_____	_____
_____	_____
_____	_____
_____	_____

Figure 10.1 Increasing Happy Child mode in your relationship. Source: Adapted from worksheet by Ruth Holt

To do: Can you make a representation of your modes in clay? This can engage the Happy Child in relating to dysfunctional modes. It can be very subversive of the seriousness of some modes, such as Demanding Parent and Punitive Parent.

Reflective exercise: This visualization is fun. See yourself as a young child, about age 4, playing in a sandbox. What toys would you want to have? What games would you play? Imagine the scene and share what you have "seen" with your partner.

Reflect: Often, our personal history feels like an accumulation of wrecked cars in a junkyard. How do we begin to make sense of everything? Therapists think in terms of case formulation. This brings together, into a coherent narrative, your problem, the history of the problem, previous therapies and attempted solutions, changes you have tried to bring about, any recent stressors or life changes, the prognosis, and the expected length of treatment, including an appropriate treatment plan. The whole is more than the parts, but it certainly includes such elements.

To do: If you're in therapy, you might ask your therapist for a case formulation. Can you contribute to this in terms of a mutual understanding?

Child Modes and Relationships

The presence of child modes in a relationship fuels intimacy, including erotic and sexual play (we come back to that in a later chapter). We hope to be our vulnerable self with those we love. Mutually encountering and accepting ourselves in our Vulnerable Child states glues us together and induces emotional bonding. This is a reasonable expectation of a committed relationship and family life. For most of us it's essential to a feeling of being loved. Something is wrong if we feel too unsafe to make this possible.

Remember your child needs. If they are not met, at least to some degree, then your intimate relationships cannot be satisfying.

Nathan and Cloe decided to both keep a journal about their deepest needs. Nathan said, "I am committed to recording what I need, just like you, but I don't expect you to meet *all* my needs. That would be impossible. Sometimes you'll provide what I want, but it's my responsibility to meet my own needs from Healthy Adult." Gradually, they developed a few agreed priorities to aim for in their relationship, and both had a sense of growing emotional intimacy and trust.

To do: Remember both that change is important and that small steps lead the way.

Progress Mapped Out

Exercise: You now have the resources to set out a personalized road map for progress in your relationship. Here's what you can do on your own behalf to cope better with your modes:

1. *List modes.* Start with your list of common modes. What three or four do you spend the most time in? Especially note any that cause you difficulties in intimate relationships, or at work or socially. Revising your mode map might help.
2. *Identify the core need that underlies each mode.* Be specific and concrete. Try to do this through Vulnerable Child (to feel) and Healthy Adult (for insight). Note that when you're in a child mode you're more likely to seek attachment, so you can make progress in reattaching or connecting emotionally with someone important to you. We never grow out of such needs. Discuss this with your partner.
3. *Devise a strategy.* Work out a specific strategy for each mode. Be realistic and try to be balanced in your reactions. What have you done in the past that helped when you were in that mode? The answer may be different for different kinds of modes, and it probably should be. Think about your response in terms of your language and appropriate behavior. If the need is for soothing, what works for you that is also healthy? The need can be for reassurance, protection, or nurturing. If you're in a child mode, then try to ask clearly for what you need. If someone you love is in a child mode, can you enlist Healthy Adult to try to meet their needs? Consider this a healthy transition, because the goal is to reach a stronger Healthy Adult. And Healthy Adults don't tend to be extreme but try to remain centered and to express this in their relationships.
4. *Test the strategy.* Have a strategy for when you have a conflict with your partner and neither of you is able to access Healthy Adult in the heat of the moment. The strategy should be practical and achievable. For example, mutually decide to separate for 30 minutes and then try to come back to discuss the issue in a more calm state. Intense emotions indicate that you're not in Healthy Adult mode.
5. *Healthy Adult.* Then try to remain in Healthy Adult mode to communicate and learn from what happened. Also shift when you can into your best self. Does this make a difference? What changes can you see in how your partner responds to you?

Your individualized mode strategy will be open-ended, and you can change it at any point. It's best considered as a work in progress. Indeed, it will only improve with experience (generally of getting something wrong and finding better ways to achieve what you want in the relationship). Make sure you do this with your partner if possible.

> *Sung-Lee* identified his main modes as Self-aggrandizer, Demanding Parent, Detached Self-soother, and Angry Child. He knew these by Self-aggrandizer "feeling puffed up"; Demanding Parent saying, "Nothing I'm doing is ever good enough"; Detached Self-Soother saying, "I get overinvolved in my work"; and Angry Child saying, "It just feels like I want to explode."
>
> Sung-Lee identified his childhood needs and reactions to the modes: to Self-aggrandizer, "I need to be looked at and told I'm OK how I am"; to Demanding Parent, "Remind myself that Demanding Parent asks too much of me on a regular basis"; Detached Self-soother, for someone to "say my work isn't everything"; and to Angry Child, "Ask my wife to listen for 5 minutes and let me run down. Tell me if I get aggressive."
>
> He added, "I think my Vulnerable Child is actually the motive behind all these modes that try to protect me." He was determined to go to a sauna daily and practice mindfulness while there, "dwelling in my body."
>
> *Mary*, his wife, identified Compliant Surrender ("I feel desperate to do anything to please my uncle"), Vulnerable Child ("lonely and lost"), Punitive Parent ("There's a harsh tone in my voice"), and Enraged Child ("It's like I hate everyone and want to lash out"). Mary identified her needs and individual responses: Compliant Surrender ("Remind myself to be assertive and say what I need in a clear way"), Vulnerable Child to Sung-Lee ("Just give me a hug and don't let go for 5 minutes; that will soothe me"), Punitive Parent ("Speak sharply to that voice and tell myself to have 'zero tolerance'. Throw it out of my head!"), and Enraged Child ("Go and do something very physical, such as long-distance running"). Mary wanted to become more mindful of the emotional needs of her Vulnerable Child. She developed a plan for self-care that involved a training course in self-compassion.
>
> Both took responsibility for their dysfunctional modes and, while their relationship remained volatile at times, there were also moments of "oasis" and more of a sense that they were both making progress.

Summary

With couples, 1 + 1 can equal 3. That *extra* is what draws people toward one another and keeps them united through experiences of disappointment and pain. Schema therapy is an opportunity to rework the mathematics of relationships. Modes have a lot of power, but the good news is that schema therapy provides resources to reduce their strength and introduce ways of regaining control.

In this chapter, the focus has been on the child modes. We noted the importance of writing a compassion letter to your Vulnerable Child mode. If you're to have a healthy relationship, at some point the needs of the child mode must be met.

You now know the main components of schema therapy for working with modes, including parent, coping, and child modes. The next chapter describes techniques for changing your modes.

To Read Further

- What the Healthy Adult mode can do: Atkinson (2012)
- Characteristics of the child modes: Bernstein, Arntz, and de Vos (2007)
- The ice cream visualization and early levels of emotional awareness: Farrell and Shaw (2012)
- More about emotion-focused therapy: Greenberg and Goldman (2008)
- Meeting the needs of the child: Jacob, van Genderen, and Seebauer (2015)
- The need to name modes: Kellogg and Young (2006, p. 449)
- Looking up at people with idealization: Ogden, Minton, and Pain (2006)
- Expressing your modes in clay: Simpson (2012)
- Early development: Stolorow and Atwood (1992)
- Developmental implications of schemas: Weertman (2012).

References

Atkinson, T. (2012). Schema therapy for couples: Healing partners in a relationship. In M. van Vreeswijk, J. Broersen, & M. Nadort (Eds.), *The Wiley-Blackwell handbook of schema therapy: Theory, research and practice* (pp. 323–335). Oxford, UK: Wiley-Blackwell.

Bernstein, D., Arntz, A., & de Vos, M. (2007). Schema focused therapy in forensic settings: Theoretical model and recommendations for best clinical practice. *International Journal of Forensic Mental Health*, 6(2), 169–183.

Chopich, E., & Paul, M. (1990). *Healing your aloneness workbook*. New York, NY: HarperCollins.

Farrell, J., & Shaw, I. (2012). *Group schema therapy for borderline personality disorder: A step-by-step treatment manual with patient workbook*. Oxford, UK: Wiley-Blackwell.

Greenberg, L. S., & Goldman, R. N. (2008). *Emotion-focused couples therapy: The dynamics of emotion, love and power*. Washington, DC: American Psychological Association.

Jacob, G., van Genderen, H., & Seebauer, L. (2015). *Breaking negative thought patterns: A schema therapy self-help and support book*. Malden, MA: Wiley-Blackwell.

Kellogg, S. H., & Young, J. E. (2006). Schema therapy for borderline personality disorder. *Journal of Clinical Psychology, 62*(4), 445–458.

Ogden, P., Minton, M., & Pain, C. (2006). *Trauma and the body: A sensorimotor approach to psychotherapy*. New York, NY: W. W. Norton.

Schore, A. N. (2003). *Affect regulation and the repair of the self*. New York, NY: W. W. Norton.

Simpson, S. (2012). Schema therapy for eating disorders: A case study illustration of the mode approach. In M. van Vreeswijk, J. Broersen, & M. Nadort (Eds.), *The Wiley-Blackwell handbook of schema therapy: Theory, research and practice* (pp. 145–171). Oxford, UK: Wiley-Blackwell.

Stolorow, R. D., & Atwood, G. E. (1992). *Contexts of being: The intersubjective foundations of psychological life*. Hillsdale, NJ: The Analytic Press.

Weertman, A. (2012). The use of experimental techniques for diagnostics. In M. van Vreeswijk, J. Broersen, & M. Nadort (Eds.), *The Wiley-Blackwell handbook of schema therapy: Theory, research and practice* (pp.101–109). Oxford, UK: Wiley-Blackwell.

11

Mode Change

Change counts. Growth takes us somewhere better—toward a safer, more intimate, and satisfying relationship. Schema therapy has developed creative ways to enable this. The general pattern is to begin with an *intellectual understanding*, what may be called insight, then *experience* something different, which leads to new *behavior* being put into practice. This chapter contains common schema interventions to work with modes, including visualization with limited reparenting, chair-work, and behavioral pattern breaking.

Cognitive Challenging

Exercise: Have you identified your modes? List those that cause difficulties. You can begin with some cognitive reviewing of the evidence. Then write out a healthy voice versus schema voice dialogue.

> *Gemma* had a Perfectionistic Overcontroller mode. She found it hard to express her feelings. She joined a theater group that put on skits to entertain a local aged care facility. She still felt very inhibited but decided to test whether she had made any improvement. She devised a 10-point visual scale from 0 (emotionally reserved) to 10 (emotionally expressive). She asked members of her group to rate her on the scale. She rated herself 2, even with her growing confidence, but was surprised to find that the others rated her between 5 and 6. She could see that she was now in the normal range. What was even more surprising was that she could now believe that she had made a dramatic improvement.

Breaking Negative Relationship Patterns: A Schema Therapy Self-help and Support Book, First Edition. Bruce A. Stevens and Eckhard Roediger.
© 2017 John Wiley & Sons, Ltd. Published 2017 by John Wiley & Sons, Ltd.

Michelle wrote down thoughts from her Punitive Parent mode voice. They came easily: "I'm boring," "No one will ever find me interesting," "People look at me and then look for someone more interesting." It took a lot of work to find her Healthy Adult voice: "I'm OK as I am. I can express how I feel and I have something to offer in friendship. I have friends and they're interested in me."

You don't have to accept the thoughts of your mode. Instead, find ways to actively challenge the negative self-feedback. If you feel trapped and regard the negative thought as the plain truth, picture your best friend beside you and step into their shoes. Imagine what they would say. Try changing the chair you're sitting in and closing your eyes. This may help to shift your perspective.

You already have the solution, but as long as you're trapped in a mode you cannot access it. Your brain is like a warehouse with many shelves. When in emotional activation, you can only access information matching with your current mood state. You have tunnel vision, and there are only a limited number of all the shelves in sight and reach. When you're in love, you deny any negative thoughts about your lover. When you're angry, you don't want to hear any excuses—you're just "ready to kill." This is how your brain works: It wants to remain in the state it's currently in, whatever that is! Once your emotions cool down and you're in Healthy Adult mode again, your mind broadens and you're able to access all shelves again.

This is why you have to use tricks and special techniques to reset the mind. This is also helpful when you're in conflict in your relationship. You can interrupt the clash and separate, and try stepping into somebody else's shoes. Sometimes simply standing up and walking around helps change the mood state. It's simple: different input, different output. Once you've shifted gears, thoughts stored on different shelves are accessible again.

To do: You can use the "downward arrow" technique from cognitive behavioral therapy to interrogate your modes. It's an uncovering technique to get to a core belief. Think about a mode and a typical thought. Keep asking yourself what it means if that thought is actually true. Record this in your journal. In this way, expand the core beliefs. Then do a "historical test" in which you write in your journal all the evidence you can find in both the past and the present that either supports or contradicts the schema. Draw a scale marked from 1 to 10 and place an X on it somewhere from 1 (true) to 10 (completely false) to show what your historical test revealed.

Why do we ask you to closely examine your thoughts and emotions? It's the only escape from your life-traps. Thoughts and feelings are just transitory activations in your brain. They constantly change depending on the input. Nothing is "real"—everything is relative. There's no "truth" in our perceptions, just opinions. Everything comes and goes.

But your *values* are different. They're not based on opinions or wants, but on basic or core needs of people. We come back to this theme later.

The next step is to try to look on your thoughts and emotions as separate from your core self. Your real self is your internal observer looking at the thoughts and emotions. So try to distance yourself from everything appearing on your mental stage and try relieving some of the emotional pressure. Whatever is worrying you is not a life-or-death matter! This is what Buddhist-influenced therapists call "desactualization." Transitory issues don't need to be so serious.

Using Visualization

Visualization can change memory. While events cause schemas, it's the memory that persists. Changing the substance of a memory and how you feel about it can provide an escape hatch for your mode states.

Exercise: Can you visualize a lemon? Bright yellow. Notice the texture of the skin. Now, in your imagination cut it in half. Can you smell the citrus? Run your tongue over the exposed fruit. Does it have a sour taste? Don't worry if you find it difficult to visualize (although most people find this visualization easy). Try another sensory perception such as touch, smell, or taste—is this more vivid than sight? This might be your favored sensory channel and easier to use.

Note: If you have difficulty with visualization, when you do the exercises below just try to *feel the presence* of the person you're thinking about. This is enough for the exercise to work.

Schema therapists encourage imagery work in therapy. This captures a visual memory of a past event. It's a very powerful technique for working with disturbing memories. Naturally, visualization should be used with caution. Once you can see a childhood incident, or even a recent distressing event, it can be very surprising how much you're "back there." You may feel completely overwhelmed. Perhaps alarmingly, you may find that you have only the resources you had as a child or when the event happened. It's easy to feel alone and very vulnerable. But visualization is a way of gaining access to and potentially changing childhood memories that profoundly affect your adult patterns of behavior.

Imagery work is now more common in short-term therapies such as cognitive behavioral therapy. It has been found to be highly effective in the treatment of trauma through exposure to an imaginative rescripting of the event. The technique of imagery combined with limited reparenting is an essential part of schema therapy.

Safe Place Visualization

One of the most basic and widely practiced visualizations is the "safe place." You can visually create a place that signifies safety. This won't be further discussed since it's so widely known and practiced (Google "safe place visualization" for lots of examples). Develop and use your safe place as a transition to working with a traumatic memory and as a way out when you need it. You may find it useful to have a doorway in and out. That might not make logical sense, especially if your safe place is a beach or a scene from nature, but visualization can be easily adapted to include what is psychologically useful. Doorways are helpful for ease of access as well as for keeping any disturbance from your safe place.

To do: Make sure you have mastered the safe place visualization. This is essential if you intend to do any of the following exercises with past memories. Find one on the internet that interests you. It will only take a few minutes to establish; with time, it can be more fully elaborated.

> *Ned* created a safe place visualization remembering a visit to the Kakadu nature park in Australia. He said, "It was the wet season and I could see the lakes full. I looked around to see the bird life and I could hear their mating calls. I could even see the crocodiles lurking under the water with just their noses and eyes showing. I pictured myself inside a boat and I didn't feel threatened in any way."

Exercise: Try visualizing a container. John Omaha (2001) offered some useful guidelines. The exercise can also be done as a couple together along these lines, but try as an individual first.

Visually design a container that is sufficient to hold "every disturbing thing" about something distressing in your life or relationship. You don't need to remember everything, just to visualize a container that is strong enough to hold it. Sometimes it helps to see yourself making it out of thick steel and welding it together.

Then create a hatch in the side of the container that allows you to agree to take out a single issue and work on it without releasing the other contents of the container. Material that is not fully processed or newly emerging can go back into the container through the same opening, which is locked when you're finished with it. The container also has a large sign on it, reading "Only to be opened when needed."

Take your time to elaborate this image, visualize every disturbing thing passing into the container, and then seal the container. There's no need to *see* everything going into the container—it's enough to *know* that it's all going in. If you have anything left over, then consider what percentage of every disturbing thing has gone in. Then you can ask, "What quality would I need to have to complete the containment?" You can see yourself receiving this quality and completing the containment exercise. You can use a visualized helper to get what remains into the container. This begins with the question "Who could help me to get that remaining percentage into the container?" Omaha called this an "alliance resource."

> *Xeng* thought about the emotional turmoil of being harassed at his previous workplace. In his imagination he built a concrete bunker with thick walls and a steel door. This was bolted with an iron bar and locked with a large padlock. He was able to stuff the turmoil into the bunker, with the aid of his closest friend, and lock the door. In therapy, he took out specific issues to work on, but he felt considerable relief between therapy sessions.

You may also feel some relief when this is done. It also helps to gain a sense of control over distress.

To do: As a couple, identify some hurtful experiences, or issues that upset you emotionally. List them. Then construct a visual container together, so you can both "see" it, and agree to put those experiences in the container. Agree that you both need to consent to take an experience or issue out and then you talk about it. Use the "connect talk" rules described in Chapter 13 to make the talk safe.

Now that you have the skill of visualizing, we can move on to its use in schema therapy.

Schema Therapy Visualization

The past is not past. Imagery makes significant past events present. Usually, a therapist would lead you through a visualization of a hurtful incident from your biography: "Recall that time when you were bullied in the school-yard. If you were holding a video camera, what would have been recorded? Describe the scene in as much detail as you can recall." A therapist would constantly check your Subjective Units of Distress Scale (SUDS) levels (1 to 100, with 100 being the most distress you can imagine) and try to keep you in a therapeutic window of about 40 to 70.

In visual work, SUDs are raised by asking you to close your eyes and describe what you see in the present tense: "I'm in the school-yard. They're coming toward me, looking angry. I'm confused—have I done something wrong?" If SUDs go too high, open your eyes and talk in the past tense. If it's too overwhelming, go back to your safe place. Or give up visual work and return to grounding: "What three things do you see now? What three things can you feel? What three sounds can you hear? What can you smell?"

The following are suggestions about how visualization can become a self-help exercise. There are a number of steps, but it's easy enough to follow them in practice.

1. *Visualize your safe place* with a door in and a door out to a therapeutic space where you recall the memory. You'll have more of a sense of being in control if you practice going in and out of your safe place visualization.

2. *Comfort figure.* Include an additional resource. Identify an adult you knew as a child who was there for you (this person might no longer be living, but you were safe and nurtured in their presence). It can be a parent, an uncle or aunt, a grandparent, or a teacher. Or perhaps a spiritual leader. Can you see them? Visualize having a supportive conversation with that support person. See, hear, and feel their emotional support.

   Warning: When you start visualizing you may find a sharp increase in your distress, as if you were back in the scene that you're remembering. This can be surprising and even scary.

3. *List memories.* If you have a number of distressing memories, list them, rate the SUDs on each, and start with the memory with the lowest score.

4. *Return.* Go to your safe place and, when you feel comfortable, open the door to one of the incidents from your list. Perhaps begin with a crack in the door to peer out. Open it fully only when you feel you can tolerate facing the scene. You can also stand back from the scene, say 20 yards away, and gradually approach what is happening.

5. *Journal.* Write down what you see in your journal. Expect some distress, but watch that it remains in the therapeutic range (40–70/100). If you notice yourself getting very upset or feeling emotionally overwhelmed, return to your safe place. Write out the memory as you recall it. There will be considerable overlap of visualization and writing, which is fine (do not try to distinguish the two, which are happening together).

6. *Read.* Then leave the visualization and read your written account. Do you have any negative self-beliefs, such as "I was all alone" or "No one cared for me"? You may find some details in your account to contradict such a memory and be able to reconsider the validity of the negative belief.

Rescript the Memory

Now you can try to rescript the memory. This is a very powerful technique from schema therapy.

To do: Identify one thing that you would have liked to hear from your mother or father. When you arrive at a single sentence, visualize being a child and seeing them say what you wanted to hear. Try to hear the words in their voice. See your parent looking at you and speaking the words in a soft and loving way.

> *Amanda* was a successful gymnast. Unfortunately, she lost her father before he saw her win the state championship. In her visualization, she told him what she had achieved and heard him say to her how proud he was of her achievement.

Once you have done the brief visualization above, you're more ready to do a full rescripting of an incident and its memory. Visualize it, perhaps as seen through a video recording.

1. *Change the ending.* Find the point when you felt you lost control in the incident and write a different ending. Stop the video first—you have the remote control in your hand. Nothing happens now. Become aware of your feelings. What are your body sensations? And now the core question: What do you need now as a child?
2. *Strong enough?* Do you consider yourself now to be a strong enough person to have dealt with that incident? If so, picture yourself entering as the adult you are now. If you're still feeling too weak, pump yourself up until you're 10 feet tall. If necessary, bring some powerful people to protect you. For example, if you are dealing with a memory of being bullied in the school-yard, you might have a teacher you felt close to or a police officer enter the scene to rebuke the bullies and later to comfort you.
3. *Rebuke your adversaries* in direct speech and action. You can do whatever you want to—it's just imagery. Become aware of how you feel.

Acknowledge your strength. You did the right thing. If you don't feel comfortable with the outcome, wind the video back and do another rescripting. Now take a look at your child self. How do you feel looking at it? If you feel compassion, you can go on. If not, stop the exercise.

4. *Visualize calming* and nurturing your vulnerable self with a hug, or explain what happened from an adult understanding of the situation. Keep rewriting until you have an ending that feels right to you.

5. *Acknowledge* how you feel now compared to when you first entered the image. Look at your body feelings, too!

6. *A confident phrase.* Put your new experience into a phrase expressing your new insight, such as "Today, I can protect myself" or "Today, I can go for help and get support."

Once you have rescripted an ending, it's important to practice the positive visualization again and again for reinforcement.

> *Deb* remembered when she was a child in first grade. She was rejected and bullied by her peers. She finally got the courage to tell her teacher, but the teacher responded, "Don't be silly. You're too sensitive!" Deb was devastated and felt that she was unprotected at school. Initially, she rated her SUDs at 50/100. She went back to the memory through her safe place and was surprised that her SUDs quickly went to over 80, so she abandoned the image and went back to her safe place again. She calmed down and asked her husband to be with her, holding her hand, while she tried again. She identified Ms. Smith, her second-grade teacher, as her support person.

> This time when she returned to her memory she tried to visualize it in black and white, rather than color, to reduce the intensity. The support of her partner was helpful, and she stayed in the 60–70 range. She saw Ms. Smith enter the scene and intervene on her behalf. Ms. Smith said to the first-grade teacher, "What Deb is saying is important. She's only 7 years old and it takes a lot of courage to tell you this. You need to believe her and act to protect her. Unless you do this, you're failing your responsibility as a teacher!" Deb's SUDs went down to 30. In this scene, Ms. Smith took a healthy parent role and did what was needed to meet Deb's childhood needs.

To do: If you plan to face a traumatic memory using schema therapy, you don't have to experience the whole incident. It's sufficient to go only to the point when you feel threatened. You'll feel some distress and that is enough. The most important thing is a good outcome. But be careful: This imagery exercise can release locked memory. Stop immediately if you don't have a sense of full control—shift to grounding exercises and look for professional support. If you feel safe, as a next step you can repeat the exercise, going deeper into the feelings. Then change the ending so that you feel safe and well at the end of the exercise. Make sure that you perceive that feeling fully in your body. This will help to anchor the emotional change associated with that memory.

There has been some misunderstanding about what the term *reparenting* means in schema therapy. The basic assumption is that people who have experienced deficits in parenting "must experience positive parenting before they can learn to do this for themselves ... the goal of schema therapy is autonomy, so this early focus on the therapist doing the reparenting is ultimately replaced by a developed and strengthened Healthy Adult mode where the patient performs these functions" (Farrell & Shaw, 2012).

Keep asking yourself: "What did I need as a child?" You may be surprised that changing the ending will often change how you feel. Memory is "plastic," which means it can change. The emotional meaning is relatively easy to change. So we basically change meaning—not the memory itself. But this changes the emotional loading of the memory. It has been said that a memory of a past event is actually only the memory *of the last memory* of the event, not the event itself. This is reassuring when it comes to traumatic or disturbing memories.

Reflect: Look through an album of your childhood photos. Talk to your partner about the memories brought back by this trip down memory lane. List any memories that are upsetting to work on later with visualization. You already have a visual image, so working visually is very natural.

Giving Positive Messages

To do: Identify some healthy parent messages for this case:

> *Mandy* was 14 years old when she saw her parents argue. Her mother was having an affair and her father confronted her mother about it. There were angry, even threatening, words, and she was very frightened. Her mother left the house, never to return. She was raised by her father in a single-parent family.

What healthy parent messages would Mandy need to hear? Think about her needs for understanding, being protected, not blaming herself, and identify what she needed as a 14-year-old. Try to use language suitable for someone that age.

Such positive messages, coming from a healthy part of you (the Healthy Adult), form the basis for rescripting a visual memory. Think about a new message: "They never had the right to treat me (as a child) this way. They just had the power to do so. But it wasn't right at any time!"

Illustration of a Therapist Working Visually

This is an example from a therapy session of how a therapist worked with a couple visually to increase empathy:

> *Matt* (age 47) was a senior consultant to large corporations. He was used to earning more in a month than many people earn in a year. He was a bit of a bully, irritable, easily offended, and quite grandiose. Needless to say, he had narcissistic traits, but he managed to function at a high level in his employment. He met *Angela* (age 22) through an ad for sexual services. Thus began a very turbulent and explosive relationship.
>
> Angela said that Matt was often "too big for his boots." The therapist remembered a time when Matt said that he brought home a report card. His father said, "Yes, you got five As and a B. Where did you go wrong in that subject?" This scene was visualized and Angela saw how he believed, from his father, that nothing he ever achieved was good enough. She could understand the demands he made on himself.

Reparenting or imagery rescripting describes a therapeutic process of corrective emotional experiences. Schema therapy traces adult difficulties to early childhood needs not being adequately met. The most effective way to introduce change in the adult is to meet childhood needs. As Farrell and Shaw (2012) noted, "The new experiences, interactions and implicit attitudes that make up the process of meeting core emotional needs become the building blocks for the Healthy Adult mode."

Chair-dialogues

Schema therapy emphasizes experiential learning. Some techniques can help to make inner states external and concrete. This is done with chair- or mode-dialogues (both introduced in earlier chapters) to deal with the modes. The therapist asks the person to sit in different chairs representing different parts of the self to identify with and talk from the mode.

Chair-dialogues are especially helpful with the dysfunctional parent modes. Do you find that your Demanding Parent voice demands too much of you? Perhaps appealing to ideals or widely accepted cultural values? Even more potentially damaging are the Punitive Parent voices, which mercilessly condemn you. This can lead to self-injury and even suicide. You'll need to identify and oppose such modes with great vigor by separating the voice into a Punitive Parent chair. In a therapy session, your therapist may sit beside you to address the Demanding Parent or Punitive Parent chair. Or you may be asked to literally stand up with your therapist. This gives a "floating above" perspective. Also, you can act jointly to "impeach" a destructive Punitive Parent mode and throw the chair out of the room. Then Healthy Adult can more easily enter and open up caring for Vulnerable Child or another child mode.

To do: If you recognize parent voices in your head, write them down first. It's important to catch and fix them. They come in a natural way and we're often not aware of how toxic the messages are, but we end up feeling low or depressed. So mindfully watch the thoughts running through your head and write them down without thinking about them.

Use an empty sheet of paper and draw a line in the middle so you have two halves. The voices usually speak in the first person (the "I," "me," "we," and "us" form), as in "I have to make it. I can't break down. I can't talk back to my boss." Just write them down on the left side of the page. This is what happens when you're sitting in your coping mode chair. Can you feel the urge inside of you going into a coping mode such as surrendering, withdrawing, or eventually reacting with an overcompensatory outburst? Resist it if possible. Instead, change the sentence into the second person (the "you" form): "You have to make it. You can't break down. You can't talk back to your boss."

Now place a chair for the parent mode voice on the left behind the coping chair, just like the modes are presented on the mode map. Put another chair on the right behind the coping chair, so the three chairs form a triangle. Take a seat on the parent mode chair and speak the sentences in the second person (in the "you" form) toward the child mode chair in a firm voice. Then move to the child mode chair and feel what the voices do to you. Now you get closer to your basic emotions. You probably feel sad or anxious, and eventually helpless and depressed. Can you feel the drive to move to the coping mode chair. Once more: Don't do it! Instead, stay with your feelings and try to find out what you need now. What every child in your place would need!

Now stand up and look down on the scene below. It's easier to get a clear mind when floating above the scene. It also helps you to distance yourself emotionally. Look what the parent voices do to the child. Are they helpful? Do they make the child feel better? What do you feel now, watching this scene? Do you feel a justified anger? OK, then you're in touch with the constructive anger deriving from your Angry Child mode!

If not, try to picture your own physical child or another child you like in that chair. Do you feel anger now? This is just right! If you still don't feel anger, you're trapped in your avoidant or submissive coping mode and not on the Healthy Adult level. Stop the exercise there and try to get some support from friends, your partner, or a therapist to get out of this trap.

If you feel a justified anger, stand up against the parent mode voices, impeach them, push them back, turn them away, and literally kick their chair out of the room. How does that feel? Can you sense the power in your body? Feel the upright position you're in. Now you're in the Healthy Adult mode. Take another chair for the Healthy Adult, place it close to the child mode chair, and take a seat in it. Can you keep your power at the chair level, too? Look toward where the parent mode chair used to be. Do you miss them? Be careful at that point. You might feel a bit uncomfortable with this empty space where the parent chair stood. But you don't need those parent voices any more. You're a Healthy Adult now! You know what is right and wrong. You have your own values, beliefs, and appraisals. And if you're in doubt, you can go and ask somebody for help. Take your time growing accustomed to that new feeling of responsibility and power.

Now finally turn to your right and tell or give the child mode what it needs. Imagine your own child sitting there. If it makes it easier for you, close your eyes. How does it feel caring for the child? Before we stop, move to the child chair, close your eyes, and feel how it "feels to be felt" by the Healthy Adult. Is there anything else you need or want to do now? For the last step, move back to the Healthy Adult chair. How do you feel now at the end of the exercise? Can you fulfill at least one of the wishes of the child now or later?

After the end of the exercise, write down the new appraisals of the Healthy Adult on the right side of your paper now that you have gained adequate responses. You won't find them while sitting trapped on your coping mode chair. Standing up doesn't only change your perspective. It helps with shifting into other neural networks of the brain. Remember the shelves in your mental warehouse? Changes of posture induce mental changes, so every time you feel trapped, stand up and take some steps—new thoughts will come up more easily.

Why Moving the Body Changes the Mind

You might have recognized while trying the chair-dialogue exercise that sitting in different chairs, each representing another mode, intensifies feelings. The action of shifting to a different seat seems to activate another memory network in the brain. Physical changes induce mental changes. Our mind is closely linked with our body.

To do: Try to smile and feel sad at the same time. It just doesn't work. Your body will block mismatching emotions.

You can use this to regulate your emotions. When you feel sad or bad, you might go into an intense body activation, and sooner or later this reflects and changes your mind. Because of the intensity of activation on the chairs, it isn't recommended that you sit in a chair representing either Punitive Parent or Bully and Attack (although you might want to write in your journal from those modes). Instead, have an empty chair represent them, while you stand up in the Healthy Adult mode and look for a healthy way to resolve the situation in a well-balanced way (when working with your partner, balanced between you and them and the two basic emotional needs inside of you). It's essential to remain safe in all the exercises you do from this book, so be cautious.

To do: Adopt a posture of strength. Stand straight and look directly ahead. Square your shoulders. Flex your muscles. Do you notice yourself feeling stronger? You can do this before assuming Healthy Adult.

At times, it's very helpful after externalizing the mode voices to physically stand up to gain a different perspective. You can also invite your best friend or partner in to join in and take a stand beside you (a so-called extension technique).

Reflect: Using already existing neural representations as resources is much easier than building them up. For example, you can replace your child mode with an image of your own child sitting in the child chair (a so-called substitution technique). This usually activates strong protective emotions because our children are part of our extended self, which we won't hesitate to fight for. You can rely on your biologically entrenched caregiving system. This will challenge any maladaptive beliefs more intensely than just thinking about the alternative.

Kellogg noted that chairs can be used to give two sides of the "truth" of a mode or to express ambivalence about wanting to change.

To do: If you're torn between two options, place two chairs facing each other. One is the *pro* chair and the other is the *con* chair. Sit down on each chair, trying to get fully into this perspective. It may work better when you close your eyes. Speak out spontaneously what comes into your mind. Just perceive how it feels going in this direction. Then change chairs and do the same for the opposite position. Finally, stand up, looking down. Do you see more clearly now? What chair attracts you more? Do you know why? What are the motives? Do they derive more from the parent or the child side? Are there any possible compromises? Is there a third option that you didn't see before?

Reflect: The next time you're somewhere you go on a regular basis, such as a committee meeting or a professional dinner or church, try sitting in a different place. Does this evoke different feelings? What if you sat closer to the most influential person, or farther away? Think about whether there are modes involved.

Note: It may seem silly to move between the chairs. However, it's surprising how this simple, concrete act activates a neural network. It will help you experience or "work hot" on an issue. If you feel too silly to try this on your own or even with a therapist, try using your imagination and visualize yourself sitting on different chairs. Or have a number of different cushions that represent your different modes (maybe pin a picture, such as one of you as a child, on a cushion to represent the mode).

To do: You can easily adapt chair-dialogues to journaling. Simply identify your modes and then write from, say, Demanding Parent, and answer back from Vulnerable Child, then from Healthy Adult. You can also use the journal to address the modes.

> *Charles* was exhausted by his Demanding Parent. He wrote this to speak back to Demanding Parent: "You always talk to me with such authority. I used to think you were like an Old Testament prophet telling me to obey. I now know that you are my Demanding Parent in a religious guise. But I have disrobed you and removed your religious authority. I no longer 'buy' your influence in my life. I am developing my Healthy Adult. In Healthy Adult, I can be realistic and balanced."

Reflect: How can you adapt your journaling to add this dimension?

Choice Points to Meet Your Vulnerable Child Needs

Identify the need of your Vulnerable Child, and then act to meet that need. Ultimately, this will establish a healthy pattern of you meeting your own needs (the only reliable way of getting your needs met). An example:

> *Nellie* found herself in Compliant Surrender (again!). She was able to think about how she would handle a family situation. Her husband, Cliff, was insisting on visiting his brother's family, but she found it stressful because her in-laws continually bickered. She was anxious because it reminded her of her parents fighting throughout her childhood. She wanted to make Cliff happy, but couldn't continue to put her own needs last. She recognized that her Vulnerable Child would be even more vulnerable with the proposed holiday, so she suggested, "I'm happy to visit your brother for a day or so,

but I would prefer some couple time at a beach so we can just relax. I'm sure it will be better for both of us in the long run. We've worked hard this year and both of us really need a relaxing break." Cliff was able to see the sense in this suggestion once Nellie talked from her Vulnerable Child perspective.

Reflect: How can you become more aware of the needs of your Vulnerable Child? Don't think that you'll create a spoiled child by giving this part attention—you'll be on the path to fuller psychological and spiritual health.

The Good-night Ritual

Usually, the child modes will want to keep with Healthy Adult. Here's an exercise that you can use as a good-night ritual. It guarantees that you look after your child part at least once a day and helps to strengthen your Healthy Adult.

After getting ready for bed, sit down in a chair that you label the Healthy Adult chair for this exercise. Take some deep breaths to calm yourself and let all tension go as much as you can. How do you feel? Have a look to your left. How did you deal with your parent modes over the day? No excuses, no accusations! Just notice. Then take a look to the right. How were you in touch with your core needs and your child modes today? Tell the child that you love them and that you'll try to care for them even better in future. But make no excuses and no unrealistic promises. Just be aware of this aspect of you. That is all.

Think about this as a secular good-night prayer. Try to do it as often as you can. Rituals gain their power from repetition, preferably on a daily basis.

Applying Mode Change to Couples

To do: Write out the following mindfulness card, keep it with you, and practice when you have troubling thoughts:

- Right now, in this moment, I feel ...
- Why do I have this reaction?
- Use sound judgment.
- Choose a behavior and act.

The idea of behavior change is based on the assumption that we're able to choose between alternative behaviors. But making choices doesn't happen in a vacuum. The context will often include activated schemas or being in a mode. To be able to get out of what Young called life-traps, we have to find a state of mind that allows us to distance ourselves from the pull of the emotional activation and shift gears. This counterforce can include mindfulness.

To do: Identify a coping mode that causes you problems in your relationship and then choose a behavior that opposes that mode.

> *Natalie* is a busy manager in a clothing store. She has a strong Unrelenting Standards schema and Self-aggrandizer mode. She identified an attitude of "I always know the right thing to do." The area manager challenged her in her annual review: "You need to be more open to suggestions from others." She realized that this was something she did with her partner as well. She asked his advice on an important work-related decision.

Reflect: When you notice that you're in a child mode, ask yourself what you really need. Can you think of healthy ways to invite your partner to meet such a need?

> *Kelly* noted a feeling of loneliness, of disconnection, and identified her Vulnerable Child. She asked her husband, Ron, "Can you spare a moment for a hug?"
>
> *William* felt numb inside. He thought, "I've felt this way all day since my partner spoke sharply to me over breakfast." He went out to the back porch and felt the sun on his face. He reconnected with a sensual Happy Child to escape spending more time in Detached Protector.

You may be troubled by your parent modes. You might think of such messages as the voice of an inner critic. These are internalized messages from the past. Often, there's a contradiction with child-related needs.

> *Samuel* had a strong Demanding Parent mode in which no success was ever enough. He said, "I've been a part-time student for years, maybe decades. I collect degrees like some people collect stamps. I know my studies cause stress at home, and Margie asks when the family will benefit from extra income."

Samuel has followed the dictates of Demanding Parent, but missed his child-related needs for self-care. This emotional tension between the child's needs and acquired rules can result in coping modes.

> Samuel found that he valued the degrees as evidence of his superior intelligence (Self-aggrandizer mode).

We can see the result of Samuel growing up with a strong parental message that his efforts were not good enough. His father was absent from home with a demanding job, and his mother saw him as fundamentally lazy. As a child, he found his best solution in excelling at school. He got a lot of affirmation, but he also stuck with that coping style into adulthood when it no longer served the same need.

Behavioral Pattern Breaking

Young understood behavioral pattern breaking as acting in a way to counter an underlying schema. This becomes an adaptive way to respond to a situation using adult resources. It's important to learn to act from the healthy part of the self and not simply trigger unhealthy schemas. This includes feeling and expressing important needs. When you notice the intensity of your schemas becoming more manageable, challenge yourself to act in healthy ways.

> *Henry* was unhappy about his belief that he would always fail in whatever task he attempted. He was encouraged to act against this Failure schema. He volunteered to help with tasks with his Rotary Club. He wrote down how he responsibly fulfilled the tasks and even the positive feedback for his contribution.

This will include a shift to healthy coping strategies rather than automatic schema-driven responses. Try to act differently and notice how you feel. Positive change can be self-reinforcing!

> *Lesley* noticed that she felt less negative about her husband. She had practiced assertiveness and was better able to negotiate getting some of her needs met with her family. With less perceived frustration and irritability, Lesley found that her husband was more relaxed and talked more openly to her.

Other therapy resources include behavioral techniques such as relaxation exercises, assertiveness training, anger management, self-control strategies (self-monitoring, goal setting, self-reinforcement), and graduated exposure to feared situations. Farrell and Shaw (2012) outlined the main behavioral pattern breaking interventions: emergency plans, schema and mode management plans, evidence logs, and role-play practice. Target the behaviors that you find most limiting.

To do: Can you identify the modes that affect you? Can you address them by acting from a well-balanced Healthy Adult perspective like a wise person would do? Develop a plan to implement behavior pattern breaking. Begin with some easy-to-achieve steps. Small is good. Discuss your progress with a close friend or your partner. Perhaps celebrate noticeable changes with some mutually enjoyable activity.

Once you notice emotional progress, change your focus to altering your behavior. If you haven't already done so, make a list of your modes and identify your characteristic responses. Then choose a new behavior, in opposition to what is natural for the mode, to practice. Get feedback. You might think about mode management strategies, establishing boundaries, and assertively asking for your needs to be met.

> *Mal* knew that he would often go into Compliant Surrender mode. It led to difficulties with his partner, who put excessive demands upon him while she was completing her thesis. He asked her to prioritize what was important to her: "I want to be supportive to you, but I can't do everything you ask or I feel bad ... well, used ... so I want you to put things in order of importance. Then we can discuss it and hopefully come to more of a win–win for both of us." He found that he could be flexible and more balanced, and that ultimately led to feeling better in the relationship.

> *Natalie* was a manager with a fearsome reputation. She knew that she had Self-aggrandizer and Bully and Attack modes. This led to many complaints from staff, and she was cautioned by her CEO. She was given a workplace coach to help her. She began to change her management style and was more appreciative of her employees.

Mal and Natalie began to practice different behaviors in opposition to the dictates of their schema vulnerability. This is behavior pattern breaking in schema therapy.

To do: You might try a behavioral experiment. This exercise is commonly used in cognitive behavior therapy. There are plenty of opportunities for behavioral experiments if you're in a romantic relationship. For example, to try to increase affectionate exchanges (without telling your partner), first make a prediction and rate its chances (she won't notice: 90% likely; she'll notice: 10%).

> *Ned* felt that his opinion wasn't taken seriously by his boss. He said to his best friend at church, "I don't think my supervisor takes me seriously. He hardly notices what I say." He decided to try to work out a thoughtful suggestion to improve the workplace and say something to his boss about it once a week, "just to see if he notices." He rated his chances of this making any difference as "slim," maybe 20%. When he started this experiment, he was surprised by his supervisor's response. At first his boss was cautious, but

then took on some aspects of what Ned suggested. Ned noted the better feedback in his mid-term evaluation. He later tried a behavioral experiment in his relationship with Sally, with similar results.

Summary

We have introduced some interventions from schema therapy in this chapter and adapted them for self-help application where possible. While much of the focus has been on you as an individual, being able to deal with your issues and better regulate your emotional needs is essential for developing a healthier relationship with your partner.

The chapter has covered cognitively challenging negative schema beliefs with a healthy voice, returning to memories of childhood events with visualization and rescripting, paying attention to your language in response to schema activation, and breaking behavioral patterns.

None of this is easy, but all things are possible if you're committed to trying something different for the sake of your future and your relationship.

To Read Further

- Stages of visualization: Arntz and van Genderen (2009)
- Example of visualization in treatment: Arntz and Weertman (1999)
- Exposure for trauma: Creamer, Forbes, Phelps, and Humphreys (2007)
- Different interventions in schema therapy: Farrell and Shaw (2012)
- Gridlocked problems: Gottman and Silver (1999)
- Visualization in cognitive behavior therapy: Hackmann, Bennett-Levy, and Holmes (2011)
- Therapy resources: Kellogg and Young (2006)
- Affect management skills training: Omaha (2001)
- Using a visual analog scale: van Vreeswijk, Broersen, Bloo, and Haeyen (2012)
- Young working with a couple (training DVD): Young (2012).

References

Arntz, A., & van Genderen, H. (2009). *Schema therapy for borderline personality disorder*. Oxford, UK: Wiley-Blackwell.

Arntz, A., & Weertman, A. (1999). Treatment of childhood memories: Theory and practice. *Behavior Research and Therapy, 37*, 715–740.

Creamer, M., Forbes, D., Phelps, A., & Humphreys, L. (2007). *Treating traumatic stress: Conducting imaginal exposure in PTSD*, 2nd ed. Melbourne: Australian Centre for Posttraumatic Mental Health.

Farrell, J., & Shaw, I. (2012). *Group schema therapy for borderline personality disorder: A step-by-step treatment manual with patient workbook*. Oxford, UK: Wiley-Blackwell.

Gottman, J., & Silver, N. (1999). *The seven principles for making a marriage work*. New York, NY: Three Rivers Press.

Hackmann, A., Bennett-Levy, J., & Holmes, E. (2011). *Imagery in cognitive therapy*. Oxford: Oxford University Press.

Kellogg, S. H. (2012). On speaking one's mind: Using chair-work dialogues in schema therapy. In M. van Vreeswijk, J. Broersen, & M. Nadort (Eds.), *The Wiley-Blackwell handbook of schema therapy: Theory, research and practice* (pp. 197–207). Oxford, UK: Wiley-Blackwell.

Kellogg, S. H., & Young, J. E. (2006). Schema therapy for borderline personality disorder. *Journal of Clinical Psychology*, *62*(4), 445–458.

Omaha, J. (2001). *Affect management skills training manual*. Chicago, IL: Chemotion Institute. www.johnomahaenterprises.com/http://www.johnomahaenterprises.com/

van Vreeswijk, M., Broersen, J. Bloo, J., & Haeyen, S. (2012). Techniques within schema therapy. In M. van Vreeswijk, J. Broersen, & M. Nadort (Eds.), *The Wiley-Blackwell handbook of schema therapy: Theory, research and practice* (pp. 186–195). Oxford, UK: Wiley-Blackwell.

Young, J. (2012). *Schema therapy with couples* [DVD]. (APA Series IV, Relationships, hosted with Jon Carlson). www.apa.org/pubs/videos/4310895.aspx.

12

Putting "Healthy" Back in Your Adult

The emphasis on maladaptive schemas and problematic modes in schema therapy is arguably somewhat negative. Perhaps this is puzzling, considering that schema therapy is a cognitive approach that might be expected to be alert to any negative bias. We try to give a balance in this chapter on Healthy Adult mode. This is the natural conclusion to the process we have emphasized of moving from mode awareness to mode management to mode change.

Reflect: When you're in Healthy Adult mode, you feel good and can deal with frustrations, minor disappointments, and small signs of disapproval without feeling overwhelmed. It feels like having your head above the emotional waves. You act responsibly, taking care of yourself and being considerate of others.

In this chapter, we see how the Healthy Adult mode provides a welcome solution, but it's possible to go only so far in trying to decrease the strength and influence of troublesome or maladaptive modes.

The Problem

The problem is that people with strong parent modes and dysfunctional child modes really need their Healthy Adult, but often it remains underdeveloped.

Addressing maladaptive modes at the beginning of the change process can sometimes seem overwhelming, so this chapter may be used as a primer, building courage and confidence to later face the maladaptive modes more

Breaking Negative Relationship Patterns: A Schema Therapy Self-help and Support Book,
First Edition. Bruce A. Stevens and Eckhard Roediger.
© 2017 John Wiley & Sons, Ltd. Published 2017 by John Wiley & Sons, Ltd.

directly. You can, if you like, start reading this book here, but for most readers this chapter will be used as a way of consolidating gains already made, both as individuals and perhaps in relationships. It can help you strengthen your healthy side to further your growth and to assist in preventing a relapse. Make sure you try some of the different techniques designed to strengthen your Healthy Adult.

To do: Think about how you might plan and implement strategies to explicitly *build* the Healthy Adult mode. Clearly, this is as important as weakening maladaptive modes.

It's time to take a detailed look at the Healthy Adult mode.

Defining the Healthy Adult Mode

The Healthy Adult mode is the state of mind that represents maturity and psychological health. It equates with sound judgment in making decisions, responsibility in relationships, and good self-care. It's probably located in the working memory of your forebrain. That's under the area on your forehead that you probably sometimes point to when trying to express to somebody else that you're not stupid. So you're actually pointing at the right place!

A healthy person has more independence and is less dominated by patterns of reactivity. This is why we recommend that you work hard to strengthen your Healthy Adult, instead of expecting your partner to be the Healthy Adult in your relationship (such an expectation might sometimes work if you have some flexibility with roles, but it isn't a long-term solution).

The encounter between two Healthy Adults is foundational to a healthy relationship. In this adaptive mental space, you're able to balance your personal needs with the needs of others. It's obvious how important this is for your relationship.

Gottman described the need for positive interactions between the two partners in a relationship. "Masters of relationship" have a ratio of five positive interactions to one negative. Among deteriorating couples, the ratio is usually overwhelmingly negative! This demonstrates how much a relationship can take, but it also clarifies what can and has to be done to nurture it:

- Initiate positive interactions whenever you can.
- Become aware of what your partner needs and provide it for them.
- If you cannot fulfill their needs, at least show your concern and understanding.
- Don't be miserly with compliments, and acknowledge your partner's efforts.

Debbie was supportive of Frank's new exercise plan. He frequently went for long runs and he was becoming more fit. She knew he was proud of losing weight and she said, "You're looking trim and very sexy!" Frank saw that Debbie was making an effort to cook more healthy meals and told her how much he appreciated her efforts.

In Healthy Adult mode, a couple can balance their needs and find good solutions to mutual problems.

The Executive Function

Kellogg noted that the Healthy Adult mode performs an "executive function" relative to the other modes. Noticing what your partner needs is a Healthy Adult function. The strengthening of the Healthy Adult is another way of describing psychological growth.

The Healthy Adult mode has three main tasks:

- Nurture, affirm, and protect the Vulnerable Child.
- Set limits for the Angry Child and Undisciplined Child, in accordance with principles of reciprocity and self-discipline.
- Reappraise and moderate the maladaptive coping and dysfunctional parent modes.

How might you behave in a healthy way? It's sometimes easier to think in terms of specific behaviors. For example, when you do self-care activities to comfort the needs of your inner child, then you become a good parent to yourself! Being aware of the needs of your romantic partner is similar. Both are an expression of Healthy Adult mode.

If you can stay in Healthy Adult mode, it helps you to function in many areas of life. This includes more effective communication, but also a mature understanding of limits, a moral compass, the ability to act on conviction versus pure emotion, the ability to remain calm but be persistent, and the mature integration of effective social skills. This description overlaps with the "four points of balance" described by David Schnarch.

Healthy Adult can assist in work and relationships, since it encourages problem solving. This involves "here and now" perceptions, the interruption of spontaneous, dysfunctional coping behavior, and emotionally detached reappraisals of internalized parent mode messages. This can be understood in terms of mindfulness or emotional defusion (from acceptance and commitment therapy).

From this position, the Healthy Adult mode is able to limit the criticism or demands from parent modes and provide supportive self-instructions to initiate and maintain functional coping. The child mode has to be guided and transformed into an empowered child, providing you with the strength you need to adjust your goals and fulfill your core needs (and perhaps your partner's).

The concept of a Healthy Adult mode may seem complex and overwhelming at first. Think about it in terms of a comprehensive set of skills. Everyone has *some* current capacity for Healthy Adult functioning, so this is a case of identifying and then building on what is already there but is perhaps overshadowed by problematic modes.

Most of us function quite well on a Healthy Adult level as long as we aren't overwhelmed by emotions. The higher the emotional activation, the more we're on automatic pilot and the coping modes take over. So remaining calm and keeping your head above water is essential if you want to avoid drowning! It's basically sink or swim, but you have a choice. Taking control of where you let your awareness go is the key.

Here's a formulation that hits the nail on its head: mind full or mindful? We'll say more about mindfulness shortly.

Reflect: Identify a person who represents psychological and emotional maturity to you. Some moral hero, like Martin Luther King or Mother Teresa. Visualize that person. What qualities do they have? Can you see Healthy Adult functioning?

The Healthy Adult is a Healthy and Adaptive Voice

To do: Clinical psychologist Ruth Holt developed the checklist below, which we have adapted. Try to respond to each point by writing down an example in your life.

Healthy Adult:

- nurtures, validates, and affirms the Vulnerable Child mode
- sets limits for the Angry and Impulsive Child modes
- promotes and supports the healthy child mode
- combats and eventually replaces the maladaptive coping modes
- neutralizes or moderates the dysfunctional parent modes.

This mode also performs appropriate adult functions, such as working, parenting, taking responsibility, and committing:

- It pursues pleasurable adult activities, such as sex and intellectual, aesthetic, and cultural interests.
- It pursues health maintenance and athletic activities.

Now think about the following:

- What is an area of strength from the above list?
- What is the area that you're weakest in?
- What would be different in your life if you operated in a Healthy Adult way more often?
- What would be different in relationships, work, and leisure time?
- Would there be people in your life who would resent you operating in a Healthy Adult way?

Tip: One way to find your Healthy Adult voice is to imagine what you would say to a small child in each of these instances. It's often easier to access that mode when it's not about you!

Strengthening Healthy Adult with Mindfulness

Mindfulness is awareness. This realization has helped to transform a number of therapies in the 21st century. Increasingly, mindfulness is making an impact on schema therapy—a valuable contribution that we acknowledge here.

You can use other evidence-based therapies and techniques to strengthen Healthy Adult. This is consistent with the integrative philosophy of schema therapy. In particular, many of the techniques developed from the so-called third wave of behavioral therapies, including acceptance and commitment therapy, compassion-focused therapy, and dialectical behavior therapy, have much to offer in terms of explicitly building our Healthy Adult self.

Theoretical note: Two recent studies by Brockman (2013) have investigated the relevance of third-wave constructs to schema modes and found that constructs such as mindfulness, acceptance, and self-compassion demonstrate high correlations with levels of Healthy Adult.

Christian spiritual practice can be an expression of mindfulness. This is similar to what is practiced in some Eastern spiritual approaches, because it's based on present awareness.

The practice of mindfulness can prove highly effective in schema therapy. It can act as a counterbalance to the powerful impact of your schema activations. This can help you to switch to a more distanced, self-reflective level of functioning. If you shift to a more mindful approach to schemas, your goal will be to interrupt maladaptive coping modes. You'll observe, not dispute, negative beliefs associated with schemas or modes.

If this approach is adopted more widely in schema therapy, then schema therapy will become like dialectical behavior therapy, which attempts to combine Eastern acceptance strategies with Western change strategies. Mindfulness techniques have been explored in mode management and can be used in mode change, but are also an effective way of strengthening Healthy Adult.

The role of the Healthy Adult in behavior change can be compared to shifting gears. This takes three steps:

1. *Become aware* that the current gear is not working and shift out of it (des-identification or defusion).
2. *Reappraise* the situation from a more distant perspective and choose a different gear (take a mindful perspective, connect with your values).
3. *Decide* on shifting into a new gear based upon your needs and values in this situation (behavior pattern breaking and committed action).

Reflect: Think about using mindfulness to help you shift gears. Begin with observing how you feel in a distressing mode. Simply observe your present experience without judging it or automatically reacting.

Van Vreeswijk noted that this could strengthen Healthy Adult— "allowing the presence of intense observations without behaving in an automatic fashion can lead to the realization that schemas and modes come and go, but that desperately trying to control or avoid this will only lead to tunnel vision, as opposed to having several options at hand."

> *Ned* felt that he needed to have a daily oasis of mindfulness in his regular routine. He began the day by walking his dog. He decided that he would discipline himself to make this a mindfulness experience. After a few days he found that he was more aware of the sun shining on him, the coolness of the breeze, the sounds of birds and wildlife. He began to "smell the roses." He noted, "That's what Fido does. I suppose I'm trying to be more like my dog, living in the moment, and I feel less caught up in my thoughts. I feel more alive."

> And his partner noticed a difference in how he related to her. She said, "Ned, you seem to pay more attention to me when you're home. It's like you're more present, less distracted."

Building mindfulness skills

Mindfulness is a behavioral skill just like any other. It's the skill of noticing your present-moment awareness. This kind of noticing allows you to unhook from problematic modes once you notice them and redirect your attention back toward the present moment. If you do not notice yourself doing these things, what chance do you have to intervene? This skill of mindful noticing promotes the first two stages in the shifting gears metaphor for activating your Healthy Adult (*become aware* and *reappraise*), allowing you to form a defused perspective. This opens up the possibility of selecting a new gear, if that is in fact what you decide.

Exercise: We started off building mindfulness by using a technique that can be practiced without doing formal meditation in everyday life. More exercises on mindfulness are described at the end of Chapter 8. However, there's a long tradition of building mindfulness skill through formal mindfulness mediation practice. The most common of such practices are various forms of *mindfulness of breath* exercises. Google a mindfulness of breath script, record it on your phone (or ask someone whose voice you like to record it), and practice the exercise. There's a free mindfulness recording on the website of Canberra Clinical and Forensic Psychology (http://www.ccfpsych.com.au/main/page_links_resources.html) that you can download.

Mindfulness practice helps you to focus your thoughts better. It provides practice in attentional discipline. This can help with scattered or ruminating thoughts. Think about it as a mind gym where you can build up your mental strength.

Practice tip: Rob Brockman suggests that, once you get good at mindful breathing, using the breath to anchor you into the present moment, you can apply an ultra-brief version of this task in your daily life. We call the brief version the *30-second breathing space*. In the face of life's stress and challenges, if you're feeling overwhelmed with things or distracted, take just 30 seconds to anchor yourself using your breath, focusing on your breath in this moment, in and out, just as you practiced above. Once you're a bit grounded, you can then ask yourself, "Now, how do I want to proceed in this moment?"

Note: It would be wise to practice this before you raise a hot topic with your partner.

Exercise: Once you get an idea of how a mindful state feels, you can strengthen your mindfulness skills by taking a mindful stance for a few minutes several times a day. But this needs a trigger point. You can use a door handle in your house or office for this purpose. Every time you push or turn the handle, shift into an observer state for a few seconds: "How is my tension level, how is my body moving, how am I breathing, how do I feel, what thoughts are currently running through my head?" Then take three deep breaths, slow down a bit, relax for a moment. Try taking a new, fresh look at the situation you're in.

Some final thoughts on building mindfulness

There are thousands of different techniques out there to assist you in building mindfulness. Simply Google the term "mindfulness" or "mindfulness techniques" to get access to a vast number of those resources. Try some and see what works for you. Are there any that your partner likes? Can you do the exercises together, to benefit each of you and your relationship?

To do: Try to do everyday things mindfully. Start small—for example, by eating a piece of fruit slowly and mindfully. Try jumping up and down on the spot, or waving your arms, and in this way practice a mindfulness of movement. Or slowly walk in a private space, noticing how your body takes each step.

> *Shayleen* has a very stressful job. When she drives home, she tries to notice something different each trip. This is a simple mindful activity.

To do: Try a listening exercise. Just sit down in a comfortable place, either at home or outdoors. If you are in a room, you might open a window to hear more sounds. Close your eyes and listen. Just realize what you hear, maybe identify what the sound is coming from, but stay nonjudgmental. Feel how the space around you grows in all directions. Feel how your attention goes with the sounds. Realize how a loud sound affects your feelings and your spatial experience.

Suggestion: Some of the exercises that follow can be read into a recorder, such as a smartphone, which you can then listen to in your practice.

To do: When you have difficulty getting to or returning to sleep, practice mindful breathing. Check your body tension with a quick body scan. Especially look for tension in your neck, shoulder, and fingers. Direct your attention to your stomach area or to your limbs and dim it down, as in a twilight, letting all thoughts in your head fade away. If you often have trouble sleeping, you'll get lots of time to practice this skill.

The Healthy Adult is Accepting

Sometimes changes are difficult to achieve. This is especially so when you lack money, are in poor physical condition, have a chronic disease, or are very old. Talking about change and how to achieve it may even evoke a cynical response: "What's left to do?"

Acceptance. It's one of the six core processes in acceptance and commitment therapy. Acceptance is taught as an alternative to emotional avoidance.

Belinda had a chronic pain condition that gradually led to a shrinking of her world as she became more and more housebound. At church, she was offered very little support or understanding, only prayers for miraculous healing, but there was no change in her condition. She found herself complaining more to her husband, Matt, who didn't offer much support or understanding.

In desperation, she saw an acceptance and commitment therapist. He encouraged her to experience and accept her pain. He led her in a series of mindfulness-of-pain meditations in which she focused on her pain, sensing its parameters and texture and eventually giving it a color. She was able to visualize changing its color, which she found helpful.

Belinda identified what was most important to her, reflecting her values, and that was to spend more time with her two grandchildren. She wanted to go to a local park and watch them play. She knew that walking a few hundred yards would cause her additional pain, but she said, "Yes, it will hurt, but it's worth it. I can accept this as a price for living more fully." As she became more active she joined her husband in some of his interests, and gradually he became more interested in supporting her.

Reflect: A useful word to substitute for acceptance is "willingness." The Healthy Adult mode is willing to have its emotions, to experience its vulnerable or angry side when it's activated, without trying to push it away or punish it. This is not the same as wanting or liking painful experiences; it's about being willing to have those feelings there as long as they are there, and having a compassionate stance toward them. You might find this difficult to even imagine. It's a fundamental shift for many people.

Chloe spent her life repressing negative feelings. She came to this realization in a meditation retreat. She said to her partner, "I know I have depression. I've tried medication and therapy, but so far there's been little change. Recently, I've been more accepting of my sudden drops in mood. It's sad and I wish I had an easier time of it, but I try not to fight it to the death. I can accept that my moods are often like the weather, with frequent changes!" Mary, her partner, was relieved that Chloe was able to talk about a greater range of topics, and they enjoyed more intimacy in their relationship.

Your emotions can be likened to a cork in water. It takes energy to keep a cork underwater. Think about all the good things you could use that energy for!

Reflection: Reflect on what it was like to drop your struggle with a feeling that you had been struggling with. What happened when you tried to accept the feeling and allow it to be present? Did that make it worse or improve it? Did it stay the same over time? How could relating to your feelings in this accepting, willing way improve things in your life? Would you be able to use this stance to manage feelings so that you can engage in more valued living?

Travis Atkinson recommended the following Healthy Adult responses to emotions:

1. *Soothe and calm* through deep, slow breathing, muscle relaxation, and meditation exercises.
2. *Empathize* with yourself. Describe what you're experiencing inside and how that makes sense considering the situation. How do your emotions relate to past experiences?
3. *Context.* Put the situation into context. Use your rational, objective voice to determine a realistic perspective based on actual evidence.
4. *Guidance.* What would your Healthy Adult advise you to do in the situation?
5. *Limit setting or confrontation.* When necessary, what are the healthy limits to set with yourself, based on the context?

Acceptance and commitment therapy aims to build up cognitive flexibility, which is important for remaining in Healthy Adult mode. It develops a model of what is psychologically wrong during psychological distress—what therapists call psychopathology—which it understands as cognitive *inflexibility.* This form of therapy provides a way to become more psychologically flexible that has a number of components, such as contact with the present moment (mindfulness), values, committed action, self as context, cognitive defusion, and acceptance. We have already outlined values, committed action, and acceptance. To fully appreciate what acceptance and commitment therapy has to offer, it would be best to look at the work of Steven Hayes and his colleagues (2006).

The Healthy Adult and Values

Acceptance and commitment therapy has emphasized the central role of values in guiding our life choices. It's about being aware of your core personal values and then choosing how you want to live. The Healthy Adult mode is both aware of core values and committed to using them to guide behavior (toward a lifestyle reflecting those values).

> *Bettina* felt little satisfaction with her studies in mathematics. She was enjoying helping distressed people as a volunteer with Lifeline (a crisis phone line for

suicidal people). She decided to do a counseling course: "I want to invest all my working time in helping young people. I now know how much it matters."

There are many possible personal values, but there's generally no right or wrong about which value might be preferable to another. This is because they're *your* values.

From a schema mode perspective, people with less Healthy Adult mode tend to be overinvolved in emotional modes and avoidant coping modes. This means that they're unaware of their own core values and needs. If you have never taken the time to really consider the things in life that matter the most to you, those things that deep down you really would like to experience in your life if you were free from fear, then you're leaving your well-being to chance. Values clarification exercises allow you the time to reflect on which values are most important to you, so that you can voluntarily *choose* your valued directions in life.

Reflect: If you don't know where you want to be, you're bound to end up where you're heading. The following section is designed to educate you about the nature and importance of values and stimulate a process of clarification and awareness of what it is that you most value in life.

Russ Harris likened values to one's taste in pizza. He listed 60 values, including acceptance, adventure, assertiveness, authenticity, beauty, caring, challenge, conformity, connection, to contribute, co-operation, courage, creativity, curiosity, encouragement, equality, excitement, fairness, fitness, flexibility, forgiveness, freedom, friendliness, fun, generosity, gratitude, honesty, humility, humor, independence, industry, intimacy, justice, kindness, love, mindfulness, open-mindedness, order, patience, persistence, pleasure, power, reciprocity, respect, responsibility, romance, safety, self-awareness, self-care, self-control, self-development, sensuality, sexuality, skillfulness, spirituality, supportiveness, and trust. Add your own to the list. Can you identify 10 from this list that are very important to you?

Exercise: Download a values questionnaire. Google the term and choose what appeals to you. Steven Hayes has a personal values questionnaire at www.contextualpsychology.org. Fill one out and discuss it with your partner. Can you develop a personal mission statement that reflects your deepest held values? Can you do this as a couple?

Stacey had a strong ideological commitment to living in an environmentally sensitive way. The local government planned a new road that would cut through an old-growth forest. She organized a petition to protest this action and led a community group in making representation to a state agency.

Also think about your identity. Ask the "Who am I?" question. Doing work to sharpen your sense of self will strengthen your Healthy Adult. Think about your peripheral self, the one that everyone can see, and about your deeper core self. Make this a couple exercise by asking the "Who are we?" question. What difference does that make?

Self-compassion

Thought experiment: Visualize. You have left your house. You get to your car and find you left your keys behind. What would you say to yourself? Write three words or phrases.

To do: Imagine a compassionate color. What is it? Share it with your partner. Now take a moment. Can you color both of you with that color? Can you color yourself?

The notion of self-compassion is directly counter to the messages of Punitive Parent mode and, to a lesser extent, those of Demanding Parent. Compassion involves being accepting of suffering, especially your own.

Kristin Neff is a leading researcher in this area (you can explore her findings at www.self-compassion.org). She has articulated three principles of self-compassion. You might consider them three doorways into putting self-compassion into practice:

1. *Self-kindness versus self-judgment.* Self-compassion encourages you to relate to yourself with kindness and understanding, not harsh judgment. Sometimes it seems natural to be tough on ourselves (ironically, more than we would ever be to others), but this leads to psychological bruises, at the least, and at worst to self-destructive urges.
2. *Feelings of common humanity versus isolation.* Why me? This is an isolating question. The alternative is to see our experience as part of the human experience. To be human is to err ... well, to be imperfect. Understanding this can help us to feel connected to imperfect humanity.
3. *Mindfulness versus overidentification.* In this case, mindfulness helps us get a balance with our emotionally hot thoughts. We don't overidentify or become overly distant or out of touch. What changes is the relationship to negative thoughts. Symptoms are secondary; acceptance comes first.

   An example from acceptance and commitment therapy is *thought defusion.* Pick a self-critical thought and visualize skywriting it (yes, out of a plane across the sky). Watch it dissipate. If the thought comes back, write it again. A thought is just a thought. It has no more substance than skywritten words.

Self-compassion encourages you to hold painful thoughts and feelings in mindful awareness, rather than avoiding or being overly fused with them.

To do: Try saying to yourself something like "Soften, soothe, allow."

Also: Using your understanding of schema therapy, write another letter from your nurturing side of Healthy Adult mode to your Vulnerable Child. It is a good idea to use this to move from self-condemnation to acceptance. It might help to remember a time when you were distressed as a child. Can you visualize yourself? What would you like to say that is compassionate? How would you meet the needs of the Vulnerable Child?

Relapse Prevention

Once you have made significant progress in your relationship, think about relapse prevention. This will help you to avoid the old patterns that led to problems in the first place. What are your early warning signs of relationship deterioration?

Think about this in terms of your relationship slipping away from the gains you have achieved. What are the signs that you're taking each other for granted? Or that your relationship has a lower priority? These are danger signs, and it's easier to readjust your priorities than to repair things later.

To do: As a couple, identify three red flags that indicate that things are going backwards in your relationship. These are danger signals and need to be heeded sooner rather than later.

Inge and Bobby had recovered a new sense of stability and connection in their relationship. They were able to articulate a narrative of what had taken their marriage off the rails. Bobby was a househusband who looked after their three young children. Inge's job as a medical registrar was taking up 80 hours a week.

She said, "I think a warning sign is when I feel overburdened and resentful. I tend to take the stress home and I have nothing to give Bobby. I tend to resent all demands and miss the importance of connection." Bobby responded, "Yes, it really is about a balance. We can handle a bad week, but when it becomes a bad month or two, then we're sacrificing too much for the hospital."

The next task was to develop a strategy for relapse prevention:

> They were able to problem-solve this together. Bobby said, "I think having a regular time, like date night, is important. This also provides a marker for us: If it keeps getting canceled we know something's wrong." Inge agreed, "This is important to recognize. Also, I need to listen to Bobby when he raises the 'us' in our relationship."

You might think about how you would, as a couple, articulate your relationship story. If you're seeing a therapist, this might be a very useful discussion. It will include an account of what went wrong. It's also a story of relationship recovery through therapy, what both learned and how a repeat of the original crisis might be avoided in the future. Some couples will want to have check-up sessions, perhaps every three to six months. Once the couple can recognize their mode vulnerability, revealed in schema clashes, it's possible to anticipate times of vulnerability and perhaps take extra precautions. Of course, all of this is part of relapse prevention. We would also advise a final agreement meeting for connect talk sessions once you get into a trouble zone.

> The therapist recommended to *Valerie and Bart* that they make a mutual agreement: "What I would suggest is that you agree that it only takes one of you to initiate a return to a connect talk session. For example, if at some point in the future, say, Bart thinks that things have become stuck again, he can ask that you both return to connect talk sessions. And because of today's agreement, Valerie will have already agreed to return for at least a single session. This allows you to talk about the problem. If that doesn't work, you might ask for some feedback from me or another therapist, and think about whether a few therapy sessions might be helpful. This is a mutual commitment: to return for a connect talk session at the request of either of you."

You can also make an agreement to see a therapist at either's request even if you aren't currently in therapy.

Especially for Couples

Spending more time in Healthy Adult mode is obviously essential for a growing intimacy and satisfaction in your relationship. Only this can provide a healthy foundation for you as a couple. Use the techniques in this chapter to more easily shift into Healthy Adult mode. It takes only one partner to start a more realistic conversation and then often the other can be drawn into the same level of functioning and more effective problem solving.

An intimate relationship is like a credit card. Just as you must make deposits into your account, you must keep your relationship in balance through couple interactions. One way to achieve this is by building friend-ship. John Gottman raised the importance of expressing caring in concrete ways and suggested useful couple activities. Simply having fun together can make payments in your relationship.

To do: Buy a copy of Gottman and Silver (1999): *The Seven Principles for Making a Marriage Work.* The book is easy to read and includes their extensive research about what makes a difference for couples. Look at the exercises for building friendship and try some that interest you.

Couple exercise: Think about forming a book club with your partner in which you agree to read and discuss significant relationship books. This is a way you can stimulate growth in your relationship. Start with Gottman and Silver. A few additional books to consider:

- David Schnarch (1998), *Passionate Marriage: Keeping Love and Intimacy Alive in Committed Relationships*, New York, NY: Owl (about enhancing sexual intimacy)
- Mort Fertel (2004), *Marriage Fitness: An Alternative to Counseling*, Baltimore, MA: MarriageMax (if you feel "counseled out" and just want a positive approach to relationships that ignores character-related difficulties)
- Gary Chapman (2010), *The Five Love Languages: The Secret to a Love That Lasts*, Chicago, IL: Northfield Publishing.

Build on the Positives

There's a long history of therapists encouraging positive activities for couples. Hendrix's "care behaviors" are often recommended.

Couple exercise: The care behavior exercise involves each of you making a list of five small things that your partner has done in the past that have helped you to feel loved. This might not be easy if you have a long history of being distressed as a couple. But try some positive interactions, even if that means simply remembering when you first dated.

Carly struggled to list five things *Mark* had done but eventually came up with the following:

- Brought home flowers.
- A kiss on the cheek before he left for work.
- Noticed when I wore something different.
- Went for a walk and chatted.
- Gave a compliment on a meal that I took extra time to prepare.

Mark was then given the homework of choosing one thing from the list to do at least five days a week. What makes this effective is that Carly has previously found the activity affirming. It's not based on what Mark believes to be loving (which may miss what she wants from him). Mark also made a list and gave it to Carly to respond to in a similar way. This is a simple behavioral strategy that helps to rebuild attachment.

We have talked about the ratio of good and negative interactions within a couple relationship. It isn't a good idea to try to avoid clashes, ruptures, or negative interactions. You would lose your spontaneity, which is not good for your Happy Child mode. It's better to constantly pay into your relationship account with small positive interactions.

To do: Say something positive about your partner at least once a day. For example: "That shirt suits you," "Thank you for the meal," "You're looking good today," "I enjoyed having dinner with you," "I like to come home to you after work."

This doesn't take much effort, but over time it makes a big difference in the atmosphere of your relationship. (By the way, it also works with children or work colleagues.)

Gary Chapman's idea of "love languages" has become popular. It can help one partner to convey their love in the way that will be heard by the other.

To do: We recommend that you have a date night to go out and simply enjoy being together. This is best scheduled once a week. Take turns to decide what to do.

A variation on care behaviors is "surprise behaviors," in which each partner thinks of something really nice to do for the other about once a month. Ideally, it's something different. This can add spice to the relationship.

Franco gave *Belinda* a four-hour beauty package at a spa. This was part of a romantic weekend away.

Belinda made a leather bookmark as a gift for Franco. It wasn't a birthday or anniversary gift—just an appreciation. It had a quote from the Bible that he found very meaningful.

Working Solo on Your Relationship

You may have a partner who wants to remain with you but has no interest in working to improve the relationship. Perhaps you want to stay in the relationship but are frustrated by their resistance. This is common enough because interest and motivation differ from person to person. Of course, this book can guide your discussions if your partner is willing to talk.

But what if there's no willingness even to talk about the relationship? Don't give up in despair, but remember that relationships are systemic. This means that a change in any part of the system will inevitably lead to changes elsewhere. We're not saying it's easy to predict such changes, or that all changes will be the sort that you'll welcome, but changes will eventuate.

> *Natalie* had been married for 20 years, and she now faced the prospect of an empty nest with some apprehension. The children's focus was with friends, although they were still home most nights. Her husband, Brad, was a good man and a dedicated provider and respected her wishes. But she wondered about the lack of intimacy in their relationship. Brad wasn't a talker and had no interest in improving their marriage: "If it isn't broken, why fix it?"
>
> Natalie started in a small way. She put extra effort into cooking regular meals but insisted that the TV be turned off while they ate. She did this basically because she liked to have a good meal for herself. Initially, she sat with Brad mostly in silence. She was friendly but asked him repeatedly about what happened during his day and was interested in seemingly irrelevant details. At first he was somewhat irritable about the pressure to speak, but gradually he relaxed and spoke more freely about his work. This led to better conversations.

We would recommend that you work hard, guided by this book, to make the changes that you see as most important and to be comfortable with yourself. It's important that you do not do anything that you don't want to do for yourself, too. Stay in balance first! Doing it only for your partner is submission and secretly puts pressure on the partner. That leads to a relationship that David Schnarch calls "functional": Your partner fulfills a function for you ("I need their approval to feel good"). This creates enmeshment and dependency in the relationship. Try to rely more on yourself. If you feel fine, your activity is no burden on the relationship, but always invite your partner to share what you're doing.

Then notice what effects happen in the relationship. The first reaction to any changes is likely to be a "change back" message, so don't be surprised. Remember that you're acting and observing; your partner will be reacting and hardly noticing. However, if it does you good it will make you look happy, and that usually attracts your partner. With time, you'll see patterns emerge. Caring for your own needs is the best way to not feel stuck in an unsatisfying relationship.

Note that working on the relationship by changing yourself is the only way you can guarantee that things will change. You're acting within your range of choices, not staying in dependency and doing nothing while waiting for your partner to change in a purely functional relationship.

Bring your Healthy Adult on board. This will set you on a journey of change, although it cannot guarantee a smooth road. However, even if your relationship breaks up you'll have gained personal growth, and your efforts might pay off in your next relationship.

Summary

In this chapter we identified a lot of ways to build up your Healthy Adult mode. That strengthening depends on mode awareness and being able to manage your modes. This is essential in understanding the potential of Healthy Adult to lead you to a healthier life. The chapter also included some important concepts, such as using mindfulness strategies, acceptance, cognitive flexibility, values, and self-compassion. But don't stop there. Being in Healthy Adult mode can enhance your couple relationship— especially when you're both in Healthy Adult!

To Read Further

- Using third-wave techniques to build Healthy Adult: Brockman (2013), Remond, Hough, and Brockman (2013)
- Love languages: Chapman (2010)
- Building friendship: Gottman and Silver (1999)
- Values: Harris (2010)
- Acceptance and commitment therapy: Hayes et al. (2006)
- Acceptance mediations in acceptance and commitment therapy: Harris (2008)
- Care behaviors: Hendrix (1988)
- An excellent table distinguishing Healthy Adult and dysfunctional modes: Jacob, van Genderen, and Seebauer (2015, pp. 102–103)
- More about dialectical behavior therapy: Linehan (1993)
- Healthy Adult's "executive" function: Kellogg and Young (2006)
- Self-compassion: Neff (2011), Germer (2009)
- Mindfulness and schema therapy: Roediger (2012), Bennett-Goleman (2001)
- Behavior change as shifting gears: Schore (2003)
- The healthy person: van Genderen, Rijkeboer, and Arntz (2012)
- Using observation to strengthen Healthy Adult: van Vreeswijk, Broersen, Bloo, and Haeyen (2012).

References

Atkinson, T. (2012). Schema therapy for couples: Healing partners in a relationship. In M. van Vreeswijk, J. Broersen, & M. Nadort (Eds.), *The Wiley-Blackwell handbook of schema therapy: Theory, research and practice* (pp. 323–335). Oxford, UK: Wiley-Blackwell.

Bennett-Goleman, T. (2001). *Emotional alchemy: How the mind can heal the heart.* New York, NY: Harmony Books.

Brockman, R. (2013). *Schema modes and psychological flexibility processes: An approach to functional integration and initial cross-sectional data.* Symposium presented at the 11th World Conference for the Association of Contextual Behavioral Science, Sydney, Australia, July 11.

Chapman, G. (2010). *The five love languages: The secret to a love that lasts.* Chicago, IL: Northfield Publishing.

Fertel, M. (2004). *Marriage fitness: An alternative to counseling.* Baltimore, MA: MarriageMax. www.marriagemax.com

Germer, C. K. (2009). *The mindful path to self-compassion: Freeing yourself from destructive thoughts and emotions.* New York, NY: Guilford Press.

Gottman, J., & Silver, N. (1999). *The seven principles for making a marriage work.* New York, NY: Three Rivers Press.

Harris, R. (2008). *The happiness trap: Stop struggling, start living.* Boston, MA: Shambhala Press.

Harris, R. (2010). www.thehappinesstrap.com

Hayes, S., Luoma, J., Bond, F., Masuda, A., & Lillis, J. (2006). Acceptance and commitment therapy: Model, processes and outcomes. *Behavior Research and Therapy, 44*(1), 1–25.

Hendrix, H. (1988). *Getting the love you want.* Melbourne, Australia: Schwartz & Wilkinson.

Jacob, G., van Genderen, H., & Seebauer, L. (2015). *Breaking negative thought patterns: A schema therapy self-help and support book.* Malden, MA: Wiley-Blackwell.

Kellogg, S. H., & Young, J. E. (2006). Schema therapy for borderline personality disorder. *Journal of Clinical Psychology, 62*(4), 445–458.

Linehan, M. M. (1993). *Cognitive-behavioral treatment of borderline personality disorder.* New York, NY: Guilford Press.

Neff, K. D. (2011). *Self-compassion: Stop beating yourself up and leave insecurity behind.* London, UK: Hodder, & Stoughton. www.self-compassion.org

Remond, A., Hough, M., & Brockman, R. (2013). *The role of self-compassion in the schema mode model.* Uunpublished manuscript.

Roediger, E. (2012). Why are mindfulness and acceptance central elements for therapeutic change in ST too? An integrative perspective. In M. van Vreeswijk, J. Broersen, & M. Nadort (Eds.), *The Wiley-Blackwell handbook of schema therapy: Theory, research and practice* (pp. 239–247). Oxford, UK: Wiley-Blackwell.

Schnarch, D. (1998). *Passionate marriage: Keeping love and intimacy alive in committed relationships.* New York, NY: Owl.

Schore, A. N. (2003). *Affect regulation and the repair of the self.* New York, NY: W. W. Norton.

van Genderen, H., Rijkeboer, M., & Arntz, A. (2012). Theoretical model: Schemas, coping styles and modes. In M. van Vreeswijk, J. Broersen, & M. Nadort (Eds.), *The Wiley-Blackwell handbook of schema therapy: Theory, research and practice* (pp. 27–40). Oxford, UK: Wiley-Blackwell.

van Vreeswijk, M., Broersen, J. Bloo, J., & Haeyen, S. (2012). Techniques within schema therapy. In M. van Vreeswijk, J. Broersen, & M. Nadort (Eds.), *The Wiley-Blackwell handbook of schema therapy: Theory, research and practice* (pp. 186–195). Oxford, UK: Wiley-Blackwell.

13

A Clear Path

Dealing with Conflicts, Communication,
and Decision Making

We have covered a lot of ground. We hope you have learned something about your and your partner's psychological makeup, biographical under-pinnings, schema chemistry, and schema triggering situations. We have provided tools to map your modes and identify strengths and weaknesses among your coping modes. Now you have a range of ways to manage and even change your modes.

Reclaiming Conflict

Conflict is actually essential to your growth as a couple. A couple without conflicts will find themselves either in a trap of complementary roles (one partner dominant and the other submissive) or stuck in avoiding each other emotionally. Conflict cannot be avoided. The real issue is how to use it to improve the relationship.

Think about the complementary dominant–submissive roles. There's a mutual fit, but you need each other in unhealthy ways. And for emotional stabilization, but not growth. Of course, maladaptive coping works to a degree, even in a couple relationship, but it restricts personal growth and autonomy. The relationship is fused or, in other words, symbiotic. It's what David Schnarch calls a "functional" relationship: If the submissive partner starts strengthening their autonomy, the dominant partner gets nervous and increases their control. Conflict arises.

Typically, an overcompensatory mode such as Bully and Attack or Overcontroller is matched with an avoidant mode, such as Detached

Breaking Negative Relationship Patterns: A Schema Therapy Self-help and Support Book,
First Edition. Bruce A. Stevens and Eckhard Roediger.
© 2017 John Wiley & Sons, Ltd. Published 2017 by John Wiley & Sons, Ltd.

Protector. The resulting fight–flight loop wears out goodwill in the relationship, which becomes fragile. This is conflict without progress.

However, this is a good time to make changes and not to return to the dysfunctional balance, which would result in stagnation, not growth. So push the frontiers and find the possibility of healthy change.

> *Nick and Claire* felt they were stuck in unhappiness. Nick had been a sports star at university, and Claire was the prom-queen pretty girl. They later married and had two children. Their central pattern was identified by a sche-ma therapist: Self-aggrandizer mode for Nick and Compliant Surrender mode for Claire. It's easy to see that these modes "match," but as long as they both remain in such coping styles there will be no progress, only unhealthy functioning.

By now the solution will be familiar: Strengthen both of your Healthy Adult modes. This will enable you to meet on a higher level of emotional functioning. Everybody is responsible for caring for their own emotional stabilization—there are no lifelines and everybody learns to swim—but this will lead to conflict of course. This is why there has been so much emphasis on skills in previous chapters. Consider some of the questions covered in Figure 13.1.

We'll give you some ideas about how to deal with conflict in a functional way. Only emotionally functioning people are able to have a healthy relationship. There's hope, but only if you find the high road to improve your relationship and leave the low road of just trying to tolerate it.

We become stronger by dealing with challenges. The problem is not the conflict but our lack of knowledge about how to deal with it in a constructive way.

A Practical Way Forward

What practical steps can you take to improve your relationship? The three essential ingredients for a different future are having the skills to resolve hot conflicts, communicating with greater sensitivity, and arriving at well-reasoned and fair decisions. Schema therapy gives us a language to understand all three processes.

Reflect: Think about your relationship. What is your usual pattern? Who typically fights or initiates conflict, possibly in an aggressive way? Who tries to ignore complaints or hopes things will quiet down? Now think about

What are some issues that you and your partner regularly disagree on? Money, in-laws, parenting, relaxation, work hours, something else?

1. Choose the topic

Together choose an area of conflict that you would like to work on (for your first try at this activity choose a mid-level topic, not your most heated).

2. Choose your roles

Give one person the chance to speak while the other listens. If you are the listener, your job is to work through the questions below and to stay in Healthy Adult mode. Be really curious about the other person; don't push your perspective or justify your own opinion. Try to ask with a generous spirit.

If you are the one talking, use this opportunity to talk from your heart about your position (don't talk about your partner—stick with your perspective). You can switch roles at the end of this process or choose another time to hear from your partner on this topic. Remember: Repeating the essence of your partner's message slows the process down and provides a sense of understanding.

Listener's questions
- Tell me what your perspective is on this topic?
- What are the feelings that it brings up for you?
- When we fight about this, what does that feel like for you?
- When we fight about this, what do you want to do?
- When we fight about this, what does that feel like in your body?
- Do those feelings and body sensations connect to your past?
- Are there other memories connected to this?

What did you need in those past experiences? (It could be things like safety, nurture, ability to choose, someone to step in, validation.)

What did you need to hear in those past experiences? (Write this down.)

Listener meets the needs: Take some time to say the words that your partner needed to hear and connect with them—they may need a hug, permission to cry, or other soothing. When your partner feels able, move to the last part of the process.

3. What would be one way to meet those needs when the conflict comes up today?

Talk together about what modes were triggered for each of you when you were listening and speaking. Then talk about one thing each of you could do to help deal with the conflict to address the need of the child modes (you can use the strategies in Chapter 10 or whatever feels right).

For example, *Narelle* realized that when her partner complains about her sister always calling, that triggers Vulnerable Child mode, connected to a history of not being allowed to invite any of her friends over to play (this built her Social Isolation schema), so when her partner complains she feels really alone and unloved by him. After this conversation they decide that when he feels that he needs to raise the topic he will say, "I want you to be free to connect with whoever you want to, but can we talk about me getting some time with you too?"

Figure 13.1 Couple's activity: What are the needs fueling your common conflicts? Source: Adapted from worksheet by Ruth Holt

your pattern together. Are you in fight–fight or fight–flight or flight–flight (where there's no apparent conflict)?

Conflict is your best opportunity for change. What is the pattern of your conflict? Take the opportunity for clarification and growth. Remember that conflict is essential and the only way to improve your relationship. Harmony means stagnation. But be warned: As soon as one of you tries to change, the relationship will become unstable.

How does this play out? The loss may be on the attachment side. Then the other partner is forced to react. Depending on their set of coping styles, the reaction varies between submission ("I'll do everything you want, but please don't leave me"), avoidance (ignoring the changes), or overcompensation (threatening). These kinds of coping will give a "change back" message and, if you agree, you'll waste the opportunity for growth in your relationship.

> *Claire* found it difficult to change her pattern of submission. She took small steps but even those were vigorously resisted by Nick. He couldn't see how grandiose and entitled in his expectations he was. Eventually, his best friend said to him, "You're going to lose Claire unless you begin to see that you expect too much of her. You can't keep putting her down and expect her to be happy." Nick got some individual therapy and began to see what his sense of superiority was costing him in his marriage. He even began to encourage Claire in her assertiveness.

Conflict signals different perceptions of a situation. If you're both standing on your assertiveness leg, a conflict is inevitable. Of course, this is normal, but it provides a chance to broaden your perspective instead of insisting that you're right. A broader perspective will give you more options to react, but will also increase flexibility and induce growth. This is the basic idea of positive psychology. Insisting on your perspective and defeating your partner means stagnation (or, at best, stability). A simple example: Imagine a mug with a handle. The handle is on your partner's side so you can't see it. From your perspective the mug has no handle, but to your partner it's obvious that the mug has a handle. You're both convinced that you're right because you *see* it clearly. The example is simple, but the core idea is important. Unless you shift from your assertiveness leg to your attachment leg and develop some interest about the view of your partner, this will lead to a conflict (and if two nations were involved, maybe to a war!). So moving to see another view, instead of fighting, is an important step to understanding more about your partner and the world. Remember that there are two sides to any mug!

Getting Practical

Don't shoot unless you know the target. If this is true with guns, it's equally true in dealing with conflict. It's better to carefully and patiently try to understand your partner's perspective and then mutually attempt a solution. This is what relationship communication is about.

Here's a rough road map showing how to deal with a conflict. Try these seven steps on the stairway to heaven instead staying on the highway to hell:

1. *Stop clashing*—whatever it takes. When you're clashing you're coping mode driven and not in the Healthy Adult mode.
2. *Separate* into two different rooms to eliminate all triggers and give your brain the chance to adjust to the Healthy Adult mode again.
3. *Perspective change:* Step into your partner's shoes, trying to get a realistic picture of what has happened and what kind of mode cycle you're in.
4. *Emotional needs:* Become aware of the emotional needs of both you and your partner, and look for a balanced solution to the current conflict. Both try standing on two legs again!
5. *Connect talk:* Slowly approach your partner again to discuss the issue.
6. *Establish safe places* where you will meet to solve problems coming up over the week.
7. *Find the positive:* Work continuously on positive interactions.

The Seven Steps

Now the seven steps in detail.

1. **Stop Clashing**
   It's normal to become emotionally driven in times of conflict. So forget about who is right or wrong and any or all justifications, and instead strengthen your reflex to stop clashing. Neither one of you is solely to blame. The mode cycle is the problem! So stop it, whatever it takes! Like in a war, when the killing has to cease before the negotiations can begin. A break doesn't mean peace, but nothing works until the shooting stops! And there cannot be any preconditions for the cease-fire.
2. **Separate**
   To stop mutual triggering by nonverbal expressions or cues, initially separate into different rooms. Once your partner is out of sight, your

self-assertiveness need will no longer get stimulated. The activation calms you down, and the silence around you gives way to your attachment need returning to the foreground. Now there's a chance of perceiving the full spectrum of your core needs again in a balanced way—not only your assertiveness needs. You're standing on two legs again.

3. **Perspective Change**

Remember: Neither you nor your partner is causing the conflict. You both contribute. You can't clap with just one hand (and it takes two to tango). Schema therapy can provide an analysis of the mental states in the communication process. What is your contribution to the conflict? With this information you can predict likely consequences. Try to get a realistic picture of what has happened and what kind of mode cycle you tumbled into. Fill out a conflict solving chart or a mode cycle clash-card (as described below in detail) to broaden your scope again.

When you're in a hot conflict, your scope narrows down to tunnel vision. We offer you two methods to guide you step by step to a broader view and help you out of the tunnel:

- the conflict solving chart
- the mode cycle clash-card.

We'll start with the conflict solving chart because it's a little bit easier to handle and come back to the mode cycle clash-card in a later section. We suggest the following steps: Take a white sheet of paper and draw a vertical line in the middle. The left side is for you, the right side for your partner. You can fill out such a chart for each serious conflict you have. You'll soon be able to identify your most frequent and important conflict patterns, along with possible solutions.

Become aware of your coping modes (you and your partner). Write the coping modes on the two sides of the chart. Think about the following situations. Can you identify the modes and whether any reasonable communication is likely to happen?

> *Margaret* returned a dress to an exclusive shop. She wanted a refund, but the salesperson was very defensive.

> *Nester* blamed another driver in the parking lot for a scratch on his car. He became hostile and had to be restrained by his partner.

Reflect: Watch a relationship movie and try to spot the modes the actors are in. Look at their communication. Be prepared to use the pause button after a tense interchange. Do you think that there's a match or mismatch of mode communication? Is the match healthy or unhealthy? Think about this in terms of mode cycles. How would you predict the relationship will be affected?

Reflect: Think about a mode clash in a recent conflict you had with your partner. What basic emotion were you both in? If in doubt, try a multiple choice with the four relevant emotions (fear/panic, sadness, disgust, anger). Write down your emotions on both sides of the line.

To do: Which underlying need (attachment or assertiveness) is mainly driving your emotions and coping modes, or have both needs been activated? Write the activated need on the chart.

4. **Emotional Needs**

Become aware of both poles of emotional needs and look for a balanced solution to the current conflict. Stand on both legs!

To do: What are the core emotional needs that are not fulfilled? Which need is more or less blocked and should be included for a more balanced solution? Add the information to the conflict solving chart.

Be sure you're looking at your basic needs and not at a specific wish. In our couples book for therapists, Chiara Simeone-DiFrancesco suggested separating real, basic needs from superficial wants. We all share the same universal needs because they are basically attachment and assertiveness. Needs are not negotiable. Everybody has them. Wishes are the specific strategy to fulfill a need at a given moment. Wishes are like clothes you wear. You can change your clothes but not your body.

Here's another metaphor for differentiating: Needs are like main roads we're taking. Sometimes, we end up in a side street. If it turns out to be a dead end, we have to go back to the main road to continue the journey.

Remaining flexible and focusing on the core need behind the want increases the chances that you'll get what you really need.

> *Marc* feels the "need" to have sex with Jenny, but that's really what he wants on the surface. Basically, the need behind it is for attachment, so a possible compromise could be to sharing some tenderness or affectionate touching. Both partners can decide how far down the road to sex they want to go.

The most important part for Marc and Jenny's relationship is *how* they talk about their needs and interests, starting with their wants (which might be different) and arriving in an overlapping zone of mutual needs that they can connect on. The way they perform in this process is what gives both of them a sense of being seen and respected by their partner, instead of feeling used by the partner. This enriches the emotional basis of the relationship and increases the chance that the less willing partner will become more motivated to go deeper into a sexual interaction. We come back to this topic in a later chapter. If you want to read more about the relationship between sex and emotions, we recommend the books of David Schnarch.

To do: What are your realistic wishes? What would a good solution for the current conflict look like, based on your basic needs? Write your wishes down on both sides of the line on the conflict solving chart. What can you and your partner contribute in detail, from your now more distanced perspective? Add this to the chart, too.

Express your contribution as precisely as possible. For example, instead of "I'll try my best to be on time," it's better to offer a concrete commitment, such as "I'll call you or send a text message if I'll be more than five minutes late."

Once you have the road map, you can "talk the walk," but the best plan won't help if you lack the skills to communicate to your partner what you expect. That's what the next section is about.

5. **Connect Talk**

There are manuals to guide effective communication. They can be helpful, but schema therapy brings a different perspective on communication skills. We have encouraged you to be more aware of your needs. This focuses you on what is important. You'll get further by analyzing your need perspective than by mechanically following a communication skills manual. It will also help you to fine-tune necessary changes. Once you have a less emotional and more comprehensive view of your current conflict, you're in a better place for problem solving.

Schema therapy adds to your potential for effective communication. The goal is to better meet the underlying needs of both you and your partner and try to create a win–win situation. It requires you to become aware of your needs and effectively convey them to each other.

In these guidelines, we set out a road map for mindful and compassionate communication that goes beyond a simple technique or strategy. It's a way of reconciliation based on a mutual perspective and a peaceful way for finding fair and lasting solutions. It isn't based on power but on mutual understanding.

Picture yourself and your partner sitting at two ends of a sandbox. Put your contributions in the middle of the sandbox—don't throw them to the other side. Take your time watching what you and your partner have put into the sandbox. Slow the process down. Acting slowly makes it easier for your Healthy Adult to keep the steering wheel in their hands, but speeding up strengthens your emotion-based autopilot. Always try to make sure that you're in Healthy Adult mode before starting to talk about serious issues.

Here are some further steps on the stairway. Use a token for the person who is speaking. The person holding the token in their hand has the microphone and the right to speak until they pass it over to the other partner. This makes the speaker feel safe.

The word "discussion" is derived from the Latin for "cutting apart." To underline the opposite intention of our way of talking in schema therapy for couples, Chiara DiFrancesco, in our 2015 book, called it "connect talk." It tries to connect people, not divide them. The steps to take are as follows:

1. *Decide what you want to talk about.* Find a precise focus. Start describing the situation first, but don't talk about feelings or assumptions. At best, start with a recent issue that you're aware of. Avoid overgeneralizations, such as "You always …"

2. *Talk about your experience.* The first partner, whom we'll assume to be you in this case, expresses their view and associated emotions on the issue and nothing else. Don't say more than two or three sentences. Your partner is encouraged to listen empathically. At the beginning, it's OK if your perspectives differ. Remember the example of the mug!

3. *Repeat.* Your partner repeats what they heard. They shouldn't repeat your words mechanically but try to grasp your meaning and put it into their own words. You have the chance to correct the message until it reaches your partner accurately, but don't fall back into discussion. You'll both find that this "echo-listening" will feel painful in the beginning, but it slows the pace down. And over time it creates a feeling of being heard and by that a basic sense of connection. Soon an atmosphere of acceptance will be the new normal in your relationship. This is a crucial turning point in your conflict culture.

4. *Reverse roles.* Switch roles, so that your partner expresses a view and you do the echo-listening. This process often involves extensive clarification until you both understand more deeply what the other means by their words. Listen carefully as you exchange your perspectives on the issue and arrive at a common understanding. This movement is like dancing the tango. Dancing creates connection! But don't move too fast or you'll get out of step. It might take

several turns until you're really able to put yourself into your partner's shoes, but this is what it takes to find solid ground for a well-working solution.

5. *Wishes.* You then make a wish. Your partner repeats the wish and adds their own one. Don't comment on each other's. Let them stand side by side in the middle of the sandbox. There doesn't have to be an agreement at this point. Diplomacy takes time! Try keeping up an atmosphere of understanding, acceptance, and goodwill.

6. *Suggestion.* Based on your different wishes, try to find out how you can take a step toward your partner. Take little steps, keeping the balance between your attachment and assertiveness needs. Don't surrender for the sake of a quick solution, but don't fight too hard. Go back and forth several times. You both need patience and a lot of goodwill at this point.

7. *Agreement.* Once you see a way forward, try to arrive at a solution to your problem. The agreement includes a precise description of the desired behavior of both partners. If your talk has been about an important issue, you might write out a contract. Looking at violations of the agreement can provide a starting point for your next connect talk. Remember: It's a good sign when you and your partner both feel you have offered too much, as a good compromise is painful for both parties. If only one party feels good, the solution is probably not well balanced.

To do: Can you identify any principles set out here that you don't currently practice? Target those steps in resolving an issue with your partner or a colleague at work.

To do: Think about a recent conflict with your partner. Can you do a mode chain-analysis of the shifting modes? Did you arrive at Healthy Adult or break off in one of the child or coping modes? Was there a sense of connection or just frustration?

To do: Try talking about an emotional issue with your partner, but this time with both of you trying to track any shifting mode states. Ask yourself, "What is the mode I am in? What mode am I talking to?" See whether you can adjust your communication style. Try to interest your partner in a connect talk experiment. If your partner is in a parent, coping, or child mode, what does that mean for how you approach them? What are the chances of your message getting through?

6. **Safe Places**

Connect talk requires a safe and calm environment. You cannot do it in the midst of crying children or ringing phones, so have a clear boundary protecting you and your mission of reconciliation or problem solving. At best make an appointment for about an hour a week (like a *jour fixe*) when you can discuss sensitive issues. Or, in the beginning, twice a week for half an hour at a time might be better. You don't have to reach a goal. Connect talk rounds are like gymnastics exercises: Repetition helps!

Once you and your partner get used to it, you'll realize that it clears the air between you even if you don't end with a significant result. Make it a healthy ritual in your partnership. A healing place. If you have a religious background, you can make it a bit of a sacred place, too—for example, by lighting a candle. When you have trained in this technique, you'll find a good solution in a reasonable amount of time. And you'll learn to talk in a healthy way in your everyday communication. Later, your *jour fixe* can become a place for a joyful encounter. You'll find it reassuring to know you have a reliable time for two and see it as an island in the sun, so keep the appointments up even if you fear the worst.

7. **Positive Interactions**

After you begin to communicate effectively, your relationship needs to be maintained. Remember Gottman's rule: A healthy relationship is based on ongoing positive interactions between the couple. Try saying something nice and approving to your partner whenever you can. Test the limits! Sometimes we're tempted to praise less, following another rule ("If I avoid criticizing you, that is enough approval!"), but that is wrong. How do parents react to their toddler's first steps? Right: They praise the child in a very exaggerated way, as if the child won't learn to walk without loads of support. Instinctively, the parents are doing the right thing: Children need our approval to enhance their motivation and strengthen their assertiveness. So we recommend that you give positive feedback to your partner until they give you a sign that "It's enough now." You now know the upper limit and can find an appropriate balance.

The Mode Cycle Clash-card

We now set out another plan to guide your reconnection with your partner. The mode cycle clash-card (Figure 13.2) is more formal than the conflict solving chart. Some people prefer it because it shows couple dynamics better and puts all the pieces together on one sheet of paper. The clash-card can illustrate your mode interactions based on a schema

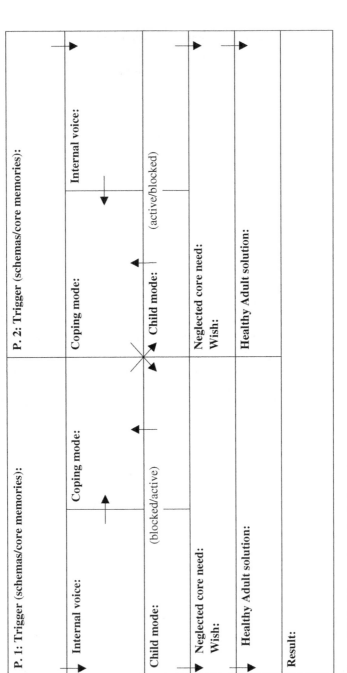

Figure 13.2 The mode cycle clash-card

therapy understanding and show the way to resolve conflict on one sheet of paper. The small arrows will guide you through the labyrinth.

Start with the triggering situation. There's one field for each partner because initially both probably have a different view on the starting point. Remember the mug! In the beginning you don't have to agree. Conflict solving is not a matter of right or wrong but of negotiating between two possible positions. Try to detect activated schemas and core memories if they're accessible, and write them on the card. This is where the schema model comes in.

Follow the downward arrows to the center part of the second row and add the coping mode that you're reacting with. Remember that there are only three basic options: fighting, withdrawing/avoiding, or surrendering. Even if it's a little bit challenging and painful, commit yourself to one of the three options, disregarding your reasons and goals. Don't be surprised at finding yourself in "fighting" mode. You might feel that you're the victim, but that's not the point. The task is just to label what you're *doing*—we're not concerned about the reasons but the effects. Your partner will be pleased to assist you!

If significant beliefs pop up (such as "Whatever I do, it doesn't change anything!" or "He's not interested in me at all!"), you can insert them in the "Internal voice" field. They contribute to the coping modes and might fuel them, but are not the central dynamic.

The next step, in the third row, is to assess the dominant affect (the child mode activation) fueling the coping mode on each side. Think in terms of the four basic emotions: fear/panic, grief, disgust, and anger. Identify which of them underlies your current feeling. The case is quite clear with fighting (Overcompensator), because it's usually fired by anger.

If you feel ambivalent emotions, such as a mix of disgust and fear, write the one that fuels the coping mode the most in the middle and the other one to the side. You'll need the more hidden one later. You might discover that withdrawal (Detached Protector) can be driven more by fear or more by disgust (or by some anger).

When you write the more prominent emotion in the center, decide whether it's more an anxious protector or an annoyed one. For a good solution, you'll need the more hidden emotion to balance out the more active emotion feeding the coping mode.

All this is initially challenging, but it's essential to reduce the complexity of your interaction and break it down into core processes. The limited choices help you focus. The arrows indicate how the cycle is perpetuated by the mutually evoked emotions driving the dominant coping behaviors.

Now comes the part that is crucial for finding a way out of the cycle: You'll find yourself more on one end of the emotional spectrum (or standing more on one leg—either assertiveness or disappointed attachment) and discover that not all the basic emotions are included in your coping behavior. This is the key to a better solution! Become aware of the emotions that you *don't* feel while coping, or that are more in the background. Which leg are you standing on less? The blocked emotions guide you to the need that is not involved in your current one-sided coping. You can get back to a balanced solution by unblocking the more hidden child mode, which is connected to unmet needs. Insert the neglected need (attachment or assertiveness) in the fourth row. In other words, add the missing leg.

For fighters this an easy task: Anger drags them onto the assertiveness leg but they have to get in touch with their vulnerable feelings connected with the attachment need again.

For avoiders, it depends: The angry or disgusted avoidance is stressing the assertiveness leg for self-protection, too, and has to shift to the attachment leg. But the anxious or sad avoider needs to strengthen the assertiveness leg and stand up to the overcompensating partner to set limits on them, but of course without losing their balance. This is an important detail of this model: The withdrawer takes himself or herself away from the partner. In the depths of their heart, the overcompensating partner is fighting for more connection, too (this is why they want the relationship). If their partner withdraws, that activates their underlying emotional or Abandonment schema that they coped with by overcontrolling. This is why they feel helpless and vulnerable behind their mask of aggression on the front stage. What they really want their partner to do is to face them and show strength. So, if you are that partner, instead of withdrawing be a brave knight and show your sword. (By the way, as a side effect, this makes you more sexually attractive too.)

In the fourth row, you both insert a wish based on your rediscovered core needs, not on wants. Try to be realistic. If you have difficulty finding out what you wish, close your eyes for a moment and picture your partner at the beginning of your relationship. What was attractive? What did you want them to do? What did you like doing together? Try to tell this wish to your partner while you look at each other's faces. How does that feel? How does it make your partner feel? Get in touch with your resources and find the spark for your fading love. Maybe you can reignite it by fanning the spark into a flame again.

In the fifth row, try to find a Healthy Adult strategy or a precise contribution you can both make to bridging the gap. Use the connect talk technique for a successful negotiation.

The bottom row is for recording the effects of your efforts. There's only one field for both of you because we expect you to have a shared view here.

This method may sound a bit abstract and artificial. For clarification, we have used the mode cycle clash-card for a typical conflict, between Bert and Cindy (Figure 13.3).

Bert's perspective. Bert had to stay longer than usual at his office because of some urgent work. He knew he had committed to an appointment with his wife, Cindy, at 8 p.m. He watched the time on the clock pass. The project turned out to be much more demanding than he expected. His anxiety grew. Soon it was already after 8 p.m. He knew from experience that if he called Cindy she would become angry and call him names, so he tried to finish as soon as possible. He arrived home an hour later. The prediction proved correct. After he arrived, Cindy started yelling, cursing him and hitting him in frustration. He escaped to his study and locked the door. Cindy continued shouting and hammering at the door. Bert became worried about what the neighbors might think. He turned on some music, waiting for the storm to pass.

Cindy's perspective. Cindy had canceled an appointment with her best friend, Joan, in order to have enough time to prepare dinner for Bert. She was aware of the effect of Bert's work on their marriage, but she enjoyed time with him and wanted the night to be special. Then Bert didn't come home. She had everything timed for 8 p.m. For a moment, she worried about what might have happened. She tried to call him, but he wasn't answering. She texted him but got no reply. She imagined him having fun with his colleagues and her anger grew. She started to drink the wine she had bought for dinner alone, and by 9 p.m. she was slightly intoxicated. When Bert finally showed up, she reacted in a rage. When he withdrew to his study, she felt worthless. After some desperate minutes, she went to their bedroom, crying herself to sleep.

First we focus on the triggers for both partners and reveal the underlying schemas and childhood memories we know from filling out the questionnaire or mode map of each partner. Next, we identify the voices in the head (deriving from the parent modes) that fuel the emotions. Then we label the coping modes and take a look at the child modes behind them. This allows some self-focus and enables a joint perspective on the problem. Both can agree, to some degree, that they're victims of past experiences and the schemas deriving from them! This helps them to move out of a blame position. The historical perspective helps calm them down. Both begin to understand that they're fighting ghosts from the past.

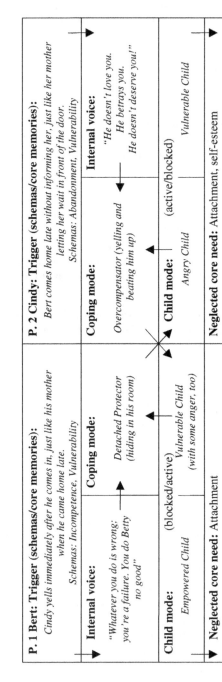

P. 1 Bert: Trigger (schemas/core memories):			**P. 2 Cindy: Trigger (schemas/core memories):**	
Cindy yells immediately after he comes in, just like his mother when he came home late. Schemas: Incompetence, Vulnerability			Bert comes home late without informing her, just like her mother letting her wait in front of the door. Schemas: Abandonment, Vulnerability	
Internal voice:	**Coping mode:**		**Coping mode:**	**Internal voice:**
"Whatever you do is wrong; you're a failure. You do Betty no good"	Detached Protector (hiding in his room)		Overcompensator (yelling and beating him up)	"He doesn't love you. He betrays you. He doesn't deserve you!"
Child mode: (blocked/active)			**Child mode:** (active/blocked)	
Empowered Child Vulnerable Child (with some anger, too)			Angry Child Vulnerable Child	
Neglected core need: Attachment			**Neglected core need:** Attachment, self-esteem	
Wish: Cindy gives him time to explain what happened and why he's under so much stress.			**Wish:** Bert should understand her feelings and care more about her vulnerabilities, showing that she means something to him.	
Healthy Adult solution:			**Healthy Adult solution:**	
Bert asks Cindy to give him 5 minutes when he comes home and not to explode when he starts explaining what happened.			Cindy asks Bert to send her a text message before the fixed time so she doesn't feel so abandoned.	
Result: Bert overcame his fears of Cindy, realizing she is not his mother and that if he uses the anger power of his Empowered Child he can overcome his fears, get out of his shell, and face Cindy's disappointment when he's late. Cindy trains to hold her anger back, realizing that now she can soothe herself if Bert informs her that he'll be late. She's no longer trapped.				

Figure 13.3   The clash-card of Cindy and Bert

We identify a pattern in which both are stuck, which is not simply the result of victimizing behavior by one of them.

This background understanding opens the way to a better solution. The first step is to rediscover the neglected child mode. For Cindy, this was the Vulnerable Child mode and the attachment system behind it. As soon as she got in touch with her Vulnerable Child, she could feel her neglected core needs and was able to ask Bert for what she needed. Bert had to get in touch with an Empowered Child as the agent of the assertiveness system behind it to overcome his fears and tell Cindy what he needed and what his inevitable work obligations were.

When the avoiding partner deprives the other partner of what's needed, it's like trying to lean on somebody who moves aside: You drop! As described here, most overcompensating individuals hope for someone in a relationship who is strong enough to resist, confront, and tame their anger. Their deepest need is for someone they can trust and rely on. So, too, for Cindy. She doesn't really hate Bert—she basically needs him!

The mode cycle clash-card helps you to go through this process step by step until you're both able to express your needs and wishes in a modest and solution-oriented way. It helps to be able to shift into Healthy Adult informed behavior to mutually fulfill each other's core needs.

In the beginning, you'll have to interrupt frequently when one of you is re-engaging in clashing. Think about ways you can slow down the pace by interrupting automatic reactions and giving time to build up new neuronal pathways leading to better solutions. Try applying the mode cycle clash-card to a simple conflict first, to grow accustomed to using it. Once you have practiced a bit, move on to more complex or hot issues. Every skill takes time to learn (sports, playing the piano, or solving conflicts!), but you'll soon realize that the patterns are very repetitive and remain the same.

The A-team

Bring your A-team to conflict resolution. This is your best capacity to communicate, negotiate, compromise, and resolve conflict in a win–win way. Couples who are in distress, especially those with a long history of unresolved conflict, often forget this and go into automatic reactions. Typically, it's dysfunction reacting to dysfunction. Instead, encourage yourselves to slow down, be mindful, and respond in a respectful way to each other. Remember: You have a choice! You decide which team you bring on. This can help to bring hope and goodwill back into play.

Couple exercise: Have a discussion about what strengths you can bring to your relationship when you have a hot issue to deal with. Think about this as your A-team. Be specific about what qualities you have, both individually and as a couple, and how you can remember to make them second nature or a habit in your relationship.

A Note About Decision Making

Your decisions are important. They shape your future. Schema therapy brings a unique perspective to the decision-making process, but doesn't provide answers. You need to consider what mode you're in when making a decision.

> *Claire* had a volatile relationship with Brad. On an impulse, she had an affair. This might be Angry Child or Impulsive Child acting out, or perhaps both. Once she has returned to Healthy Adult, she might regret this thoughtless action.

> *Ned* was growing increasingly dissatisfied with his graduate studies. He wasn't meeting deadlines. He said, "I just don't care about anything." He decided to quit and take a job as a research assistant. It was a decision made in Detached Protector mode.

> *Zella* decided that her car didn't have good enough fuel economy. She bought an expensive car that had excellent gas mileage, but it cost far more overall than running the first car. She justified this with an argument about climate change. Her Demanding Parent had the final say.

Some of the above decisions may have been the right choice. While it's almost never a solution to have an affair, it's possible to quit studying or to change cars and for that to be a good choice. The difference is making the decision in Healthy Adult mode. As a ground rule, we suggest that you never make important decisions when in a child or coping mode.

> *Ellen* inherited $200,000 when she was in a new relationship with Bradley. He suggested going on a holiday to Venice and staying on the Grand Canal. There were lots of such decisions in what amounted to a spending spree. It was a wonderful few months, but when the money went so did Bradley.

Think carefully about the long-term consequences for you, your partner, and your children or family. Think about the issue from the healthiest part of you. Consult people whose opinions you most value. It's easy to rationalize what amounts to selfish behavior, but you're assured of a better decision in Healthy Adult mode. And it will generally prevent later regret.

Good decisions, especially those with long-term consequences, are best made in Healthy Adult mode. It's equally obvious that in other modes we can make impulsive decisions that sometimes work out, but they're unlikely to be well considered and may lead to lasting regret.

So if you have to make a decision that's important, difficult, or both, try to separate schema-driven inclinations from the objective options in the situation. Schema-driven patterns recur over your lifetime: They're repetitive. Try to find out if you have ever before felt like you feel now. What kind of situation was that? Use imagery: Close your eyes, dive into the feelings, and let yourself float back in time. Do any images from childhood pop up, shedding light on the background of your inclinations?

What would your best friends suggest you do if they were in your shoes? Open up and actually ask them. You're no longer a left-alone child who has to decide on its own. Include your friends' views on the decision. Collect different perspectives—as many as you can get. Make a preliminary decision and try out how you feel with it over some days. Use a time-projection technique and imagine yourself taking the opposite option: How would you feel one year later (or on your 80th birthday)? Don't make it a life-or-death question. Play with different options. Life will go on anyway and most things can be corrected to a certain extent. However, even if you get it wrong you'll have learned something from the experience.

To do: If you're in a time of transition or facing a life-changing decision, you might find it helpful to record your dreams. Sometimes your dreams, once you understand the metaphorical or symbolic language, will suggest a way forward.

Summary

There's nothing more practical than good communication and making sensible decisions. If you get them wrong, the fabric of your life can quickly unravel. Both are of central importance in making your romantic relationship well-grounded and avoiding flights of romantic fantasy. In this chapter, we have brought a schema therapy perspective to a set of skills that we usually practice daily. As a personal experiment, take the time to make some changes and see if the results support you continuing to develop in these areas.

To Read Further

- Chiara DiFrancesco has made a very useful distinction between needs and wants (see her website, www.healinginternational.org)
- She also developed the concept of connect talk, which has informed our approach to communication. See the book we wrote with her: *Schema Therapy for Couples: A Practitioner's Guide for Healing Relationships* (DiFrancesco, Roediger, and Stevens, 2015)
- Susan Johnson used the metaphor of a dance in communication in the second edition of her book *The Practice of Emotionally Focused Couple Therapy: Creating Connection* (2004).

References

DiFrancesco, C., Roediger, E., & Stevens, B. (2015). *Schema therapy for couples: A practitioner's guide to healing relationships.* Malden, MA: Wiley-Blackwell.

Gottman, J., & Silver, N. (1999). *The seven principles for making a marriage work.* New York, NY: Three Rivers Press.

Johnson, S. M. (2004). *The practice of emotionally focused couple therapy: Creating connection* (2nd ed.). New York, NY: Brunner-Routledge.

Schnarch, D. (2009). *Intimacy and desire—awaken the passion in your relationship.* New York, NY: Beaufort Books.

14

Looking at Sex Through the Eyes of the Modes

The topic of sex has a way of getting the reader's attention. And although writing about it isn't an easy task, a book about relationship issues would be incomplete if this topic were missing. We hope to contribute a different perspective: looking at sex through the eyes of the modes.

The Place of Sex in a Relationship

Erotic and sexual encounters are an important part of an intimate relationship. If we look at the modified "Sternberg triangle" (Sternberg, 1986; see Figure 14.1) they're one of three major themes in life and partnership, perhaps more so in the beginning of a relationship (or an affair). Our goal here is to give you some ideas about how that part of your relationship can remain alive in the long term, so our focus is on sex as part of a relationship, rather than on sex itself.

Erotic and sexual encounters contribute to a satisfying partnership. In many ways, the resonance of lovers resembles a playful mother-and-child interaction. From a biological viewpoint, sex releases the feel-good hormone oxytocin in the brain, and oxytocin glues us together. The absence of this kind of contact can erode an intimate relationship and open doors to looking for sexual adventures somewhere else. Only having sex with yourself is less satisfying. Remember that masturbation, despite being a normal behavior, from a mode perspective can be seen as a Self-soother and—if it's related to withdrawal from the partner—as a Detached Protector undermining the connection.

Breaking Negative Relationship Patterns: A Schema Therapy Self-help and Support Book,
First Edition. Bruce A. Stevens and Eckhard Roediger.

Figure 14.1   The relationship triangle. Source: Modified from Sternberg (1986)

Sex is important and for most people rewarding, but it carries a cost. We're also very vulnerable in sexual encounters. Shortcomings in our sexual performance hit the core of our self-esteem. Playing safe (using experiential avoidance) may draw us into a slightly boring comfort zone of sexual activities that contributes to a decreasing interest in having sex. It's easy to repeat what is familiar because it's what promises to work best, but at some level sex has to have some novel elements to maintain excitement.

Reflect: Think about your previous relationship. Was it initially sexually exciting, when everything was new? But did you then settle into a routine? Did you try to make changes? Did that seem risky? Could you talk to your lover about the tension between novelty and a safe routine? Now ask yourself the same questions about your current relationship.

Child Modes are Involved

If we think about this in terms of modes, then both child modes and core needs are involved: the greedy part looking for stimulation, self-centered feelings, and approval, and the vulnerable, softer part enjoying the sense of connection, intimacy, and play. The latter part needs a safe atmosphere as a prerequisite for becoming sexually stimulated. When you're under severe stress and more or less in a fight-or-flight state of mind, your sympathetic nervous system is dominantly activated and shuts down the circuits required for sexual activities. Sexual play needs a safe environment to allow your autonomous nervous system to shift into a parasympathetic state. So sex brings our social and recreational lives together, allowing for relaxing, grooming, and sweet-talking. In general, women need this as a precursor for sexual stimulation, and that should be considered when trying to reignite the sexual fire. "Quickies" in a long-lasting relationship only work when the couple are well connected and can immediately shift from everyday hassles to the intimate atmosphere required for sexual stimulation.

So sexual activities involve the child modes within us: The Vulnerable Child mode needs to feel safe, and the assertiveness-related child modes want to be stimulated. It doesn't make sense to talk about the Angry Child mode in sexual activities because the emotion of anger only pops up when our need for assertiveness (and, in this case, satisfaction) is not met. But that happens, of course, when our sexual advance gets blocked by our partner. That could lead to intense frustration and sometimes an angry outburst, although probably more among men than women because males are more driven by testosterone, which is related to aggressive action and territorial protection. From a biological point of view, the woman is part of the "territory" or possession; jealousy is based on these biologically entrenched pathways. The potential anger reaction reveals that the assertiveness system is intensely involved in sexual activities, together with sympathetic activations once the sexual act has started.

Setting the Stage

So there's a triphasic curve of sexual activation. The starting point requires a parasympathetic state that then changes into a more sympathetic, excited state, which shifts into a relaxing parasympathetic state after orgasm. This intensive up-and-down movement is probably what makes sex so stimulating and rewarding. Our limbic dopaminergic reward systems show strong activation during sex, and orgasm leads to a great release of dopamine, oxytocin, and opioids. This is why sex can become a self-soothing drug.

If the self-assertive part dominates in sex, it can become aggressive and abusive in an overcompensatory way. While this can be stimulating, it carries risk and may cross the line. Interestingly, pure sex is not always connected with attachment needs. For the biological purpose of self-reproduction, attachment is not required, but it's important for allowing the offspring to survive. Interestingly, intimate partners' oxytocin levels fall three to four years after the birth of a child and, according to Helen Fisher, their relationship can become more unstable at that time. Perhaps this coincides with the time necessary for children to become less needy of parental protection.

A good balance between stimulation and intimacy is necessary. This provides our Happy Child mode with a playground of joyful activities that are safe and stimulating at the same time in a flexible, balanced way. Unfortunately, after a few years most couples find themselves on the safe side and the stimulating side has faded. So how can we bring back some of the excitement of the early years into our mature relationships?

Well, as you might have already guessed, if you find yourself resting on your attachment and safety leg you have to strengthen your assertiveness leg and take some risks. Being nice all the time won't work. It might strengthen the companionate and friendship corner of Sternberg's triangle, but it blunts the compassionate corner. To bring in a medieval metaphor: Courtly ladies may like the supportiveness of the servants but are attracted by the brave knights. So strengthen the assertiveness part in your relationship and reclaim exciting sex as a part of the relationship.

To do: Don't be too submissive or too avoidant. In preparing the ground for a satisfying sex life, show some presence, pay attention, make regular payments into the relationship account to satisfy the attachment needs of your partner, but also take a stance.

Adding Spice to Sexual Activity

Once your relationship has become dull and predictable, there's no easy way out. Be prepared to make an effort.

Start with a clarifying talk about your sexual dissatisfaction. This can be a very sensitive issue, so we strongly recommend starting the mission under connect talk conditions (as outlined in the previous chapter), but it will still take a lot of courage to put your sex life on the agenda. Although there might be an initial resistance from your partner's avoidant coping modes, you should persist. This is how knights are: not impatient, but enduring.

As recommended in the connect talk rules, don't become offensive or blaming. Balance assertiveness with attachment and speak from your vulnerable and sad part about your disappointment and pain, referring to the better times you once shared. Connect your expectations with a validating picture of the good phases in your relationship. This increases the chances that your partner won't react defensively based on the protective side of the assertiveness need, but will also feel their attachment need teased. Even as you read about this and picture yourself doing it, you might feel some weakness in your knees. So be aware: While this calls for a lot of courage, at the end of the day your partner is likely to approve.

To do: Look at the "Connect talk" section in the previous chapter. Become familiar with the principles of communication.

Let's go a bit deeper into how to apply the connect talk technique to the issue of having better sex. You both start by describing your experience and feelings about the situation. Remember to talk from your side of the fence; don't lean over it by making accusing or downputting comments. Follow the connect talk rules. Choose a very slow pace, don't forget the token and the repetition, and wait until both perspectives are standing beside each other in the sandbox between the two of you. Accepting your differences is solid ground for building up something new. Be aware of critical parent mode voices popping up from inside you and gently push them aside. Social conduct rules or do's and don'ts won't help much when it comes to finding your own rules about having sex. The possible variety is endless and it takes two Healthy Adults to negotiate constructively.

With a good balance of assertiveness and attachment needs, each of you can make your wishes known based on a sense of what the other might accept. Once the wishes are expressed from both sides, show a good deal of functional submission toward your partner when naming your contribution. Don't act too much out of fear or negative expectations driven by your inner critics. Give the process a chance (no risk, no fun), but clarify your limits and claim the right to stop the action immediately if you feel bad.

Feeling safe while trying something new needs a good balance of devotion and courage. For that reason, both of you need your assertiveness leg, not just the one who initiates the reboot of your sexual activities. Don't feel ashamed going into some detail about what you accept—your preferred times and places for sex, and what's OK or not.

If you like, you can both make lists of your preferences and share them step by step. Then you could put both sides together on a sheet of paper showing the comfort zone of what has worked or still works and what could work for you both. Figure 14.2 shows such a "sexual landscape."

We're well aware that this suggestion may sound artificial and not very romantic, but this kind of negotiation can lay the foundation for a better relationship. It's a foundation built in Healthy Adult mode (hopefully, the Healthy Adult of both of you). Remember: Sexual activities need a safe place to get started. Negotiating your rules of engagement helps you to improve your relationship while maintaining an observer stance.

Now the next hurdle. Make a start. Take your chances, and don't hesitate too long! Bring your Casanova or Mae West mode to the fore and give it a try. Try approaching your partner in the morning while preparing breakfast. Some people are much more amenable in the morning than in the evening. And even if there's some initial resistance, keep going, at least a little bit. Avoid becoming abusive, of course, but a hint of aggression is part of the sexual game. Once more the assertiveness part is required.

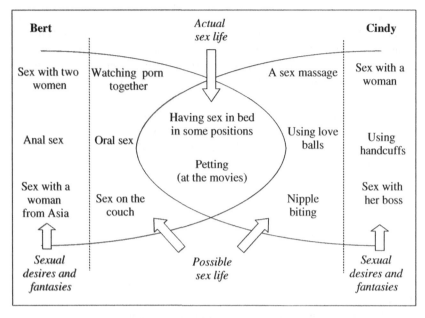

Figure 14.2 Bert and Cindy's sexual landscape

Avoid falling into anger when your partner is definitely not willing. Maybe you'll get a promise to try later in the day. That's not the worst possible result. It's kind of a teasing game. But you can rely on your partner's Demanding Parent mode to remind them that promises should be kept!

Being courageous and persistent, combined with some flexibility, brings rewards. Remember that being flexible is one of the core features of the Healthy Adult mode. If you show Healthy Adult behavior when your attempts are refused, that inclines your partner to be more trusting and strengthens the attachment bond between you, allowing greater flexibility. So finally it's like a dance movement: going back and forth and not directly going somewhere. But it can be fun and bring more intimacy.

This is why dance classes are a helpful way to prepare for sexual reignition. Music activates your emotional system, you're encouraged to touch each other, the teacher cares for the course of the lesson, you can shift more into a childlike, playful mode, and the moves bring you closer to each other. If your inner critic carps that you must learn and perform well, kick them out of the door and bring your Happy Child to the center of the dance floor! Learning to dance better might be a benefit, but the underlying agenda is somewhat different. And restarting sex is a bit like that: Move casually around the thick wall of the city that you want to conquer, and then take your chances if a crack in the wall appears ...

Some Tips

We'll get a bit more precise.

First create a safe environment and eliminate disturbing influences like children, ringing phones, and so on.

A reminder to men: Pay attention to your grooming. The female nose can be extremely sensitive and smelling bad is a turn-off. However, most women already know that there are ways to stimulate men by wearing particular things in particular ways.

Start softly and begin with the things that worked in the past. This is usually gentle foreplay, with more caressing and less genital focus. This helps to satisfy the attachment needs of your partner and encourages further sexual activities.

David Schnarch described some good exercises to reboot the system:

1. *Hug until you relax.* This strengthens the sense of being held by the partner and feeling safe. This creates a physical bedrock of belonging together.
2. *Heads on the pillow.* Softly touching your partner's face while you look into each other's eyes creates an intense sense of being seen and approved. It's close to what a child experiences when they're mirrored by their mother or father.
3. *Feel and touch.* Doing so without direct sexual intentions gives your partner a sense of being recognized, liked, and feeling felt as a person, not just as an object of desire and satisfaction.
4. *Have soft and youth-like sex.* Remember your sexual encounters when you were an adolescent? They were, we hope, very respectful and gentle and carried out with a good portion of feeling insecure. Wasn't that a nice way to explore new territory? Try getting back into that kind of beginner's state. Mindfulness supports this. Experience your partner's body, recalling the beginning of your relationship. Take your time and don't target the sexual organs too quickly. Once you're both able to relax into having sex, you can begin to move into more exciting or special sexual activities drawn from your common sexual landscape.

Exercise: As a starting point for your negotiation to improve your sex life, the more active partner writes out their minimal wish (taken from your agreed sexual landscape) and brings it into your next connect talk meeting. The more passive partner writes down the minimum contribution that they're willing to agree to on a sheet of paper, too. Then you both reveal the contents in the connect talk session and try agreeing on something.

Having sex includes a wonderful balance of being self-centered and feeling connected with your partner. Have you tried to look into each other's eyes while approaching orgasm? This creates a very special sense of connectedness, although diving into your own sensual feelings while having a climax is great, too. So try both, but always care for your sense of connectedness as the basis of your sexual activities. According to David Schnarch, desire is based on a sense of intimacy.

When you come to the core of sexual activities, remember that the curve of sexual excitement differs between men and women. Especially in the early phase of a sexual reconnection, the slower partner should set the pace and give a sign when they're ready for penetration if this is desired.

David Schnarch has recommended that it might be interesting to change your sexual strategies, but on the other hand too much variation can lead to a sense of "sexual gymnastics" that can bring the inner critic on stage, with the effect of reducing stimulation. Not everybody is fond of all the positions in the *Kama Sutra*! Once more: Sexual enactment is a sensitive issue, and too much of a good thing can spoil the party. The sense of feeling safe and comfortable is the bottom line for a successful sexual reconnection.

So why not give the less aroused partner the chance to manually self-stimulate during foreplay? Or use sex toys? Your lover will know best what they like. This calms down a partner's parent mode and allows them to relax a bit more. And participating in your partner's growing excitement is usually stimulating for you, too. This is part of what is called "emotional contagion."

What finally counts is the good, shared, loving, lustful experience that connects two Happy Child modes, sheltered by two Healthy Adults. This gives your relationship a new push, making it more vital and resilient for dealing with the everyday challenges. This gain is worth the risk you take by getting out of your comfort zone.

To Read Further

- Schnarch (2009)
- Fisher (1992).

References

Fisher, H. (1992). *Anatomy of love: The natural history of monogamy, adultery and divorce*. New York, NY: W. W. Norton.

Schnarch, D. (2009). *Intimacy and desire—awaken the passion in your relationship*. New York, NY: Beaufort Books.

Sternberg, R. J. (1986). A triangular theory of love. *Psychological Review, 93*, 119–135.

15

Affairs

A relationship can suddenly shatter, like a dropped porcelain vase. An affair can be the cause, but can also be the turning point in a failing relationship. There is opportunity, but sadly it seems that few people seem wiser after the event.

This is a common relationship problem, for which we offer a perspective from schema therapy. This will also draw together some of the threads in other chapters about communication and decision making in schema therapy.

Introduction to the Problem

The statistics indicate that almost half of marriages break down. One interesting trend is that younger wives are now more unfaithful than their husbands: Two-thirds of women and half of men who are having affairs are in the first five years of marriage. Until a couple of decades ago, men were more likely to have an affair, but now the genders are about equal. However, if a man is unfaithful he's more likely to have more partners. If a woman has an affair it's more frequently an exit strategy. There are many factors that contribute to the current crisis in romantic relationships: higher expectations of emotional fulfillment, a general lack of communication skills, changes in what is acceptable in society, and a greater proportion of married women in employment, making them more financially independent.

Breaking Negative Relationship Patterns: A Schema Therapy Self-help and Support Book,
First Edition. Bruce A. Stevens and Eckhard Roediger.
© 2017 John Wiley & Sons, Ltd. Published 2017 by John Wiley & Sons, Ltd.

Andy and Margo were an attractive young couple who seemed to have everything going for them. Andy was a high school teacher, and he had an infatuation with Kirsty, another teacher in his school. Kirsty had recently separated from her husband and Andy was "being supportive." Margo was in a state of near panic, and she acutely felt the threat of Kirsty to their marriage.

Almost all people enter a romantic relationship, whether marriage or living together, with a conscious intention of remaining sexually faithful. So an affair is inevitably a falling from an initial ideal, whether a religious or a personal value. It's usually secretive, guilt inducing for the person involved, and anywhere from infuriating to shattering for their partner when the partner finds out. In any case, it means a severe crisis for the couple, but sometimes a chance for growth and reconnection on a more mature level.

Reflect: One of the difficulties in talking about affairs is defining the term. What do you think qualifies as an affair? Long talks with a friend of the opposite sex? Sharing emotionally important events with an intimate friend? Watching internet porn? Seeing a sex worker? A one-night stand with a colleague after the office Christmas party?

A Symptom

While affairs may be erotic and intensely sexual, there's a sense in which they have little to do with sex. The real dynamics are often unexplored conflict, anger, fear, emptiness, and attention- or sensation-seeking. Such is the pain of an unhappy relationship that an affair tries to keep at bay. Mostly it's the symptom of a deeper malaise.

Will and Marg have been married eight years. There hasn't been much sparkle in their relationship for a few years. Will became attracted to a colleague, and what began as a few drinks after work ended up with sexual involvement. Will is now less troubled by Marg's emotional coldness, so the affair has drained away some of the tension from the marriage. This is a false calm before the emotional storm when Marg finds out about the relationship.

An affair almost always represents an externalization of an unhealthy process in the original relationship. In this way, it may help to keep the real issues, such as unresolved conflict over differing wants, safely underground.

An affair is often in a fairyland of unreality. The relationship begins with excitement, compelling attraction, and the thrill of forbidden fruit. But it's a protected relationship and somehow illusory. Brown noted:

> It does not have the everyday worries and chores of marriage or the pressures of living intimately with another person over time. It is a hidden relationship, shared only with one or two confidants who are chosen for their ability to be supportive and to keep the secret. The secrecy provides a shell against outside pressures.

The marriage still impinges on the affair: The spouse still comes first in finances, family crises, and celebrations, and in public. So the unfaithful partner becomes torn between competing demands, especially as their lover becomes more impatient.

If we're to understand the dynamics of an affair, the larger picture of the family is important. This includes the children, the respective families of origin, the behavior patterns of near relatives, and what's considered permissible in the wider ethnic group. The family of origin, for example, can leave an adult with unfinished business. There may be patterns of avoidance, seduction, secrecy, and betrayal. The precedent for turning away from relationship difficulties and escaping into an affair may be set over the generations as a behavioral model. It becomes natural as the pattern repeats.

The family is a primary place of belonging. It's where we long for attention and need to be needed. This is the place where we hope that the person we love will love us back in the same way. An affair threatens the glue that holds everything together. It arouses and fuels the fear of abandonment. No wonder emotions run hot!

The Nature of the Affair

The couple will tend to respond in very different ways, according to Brown:

> For the spouse, the betrayal seems unbearable. Yet for the unfaithful partner the affair is an aphrodisiac. The aura of romance and intrigue is compelling, especially when reality feels barren or boring. Affairs promise so much: an opportunity to pursue dreams that have been dormant, to come alive again, to find someone who truly understands. Their hidden promise is pain.

Involvement in an affair can be sexual, emotional, or both. Women are more likely to be emotionally involved. The combination of sexual and emotional elements represents more of a threat to the marriage than either alone. A generalization might be made about gender in marital dissatisfaction: Women tend to see sex as flowing from intimacy, whereas men see it as a path to intimacy. Therefore, it's natural that women's dissatisfaction will most often come from emotional issues, while men will complain about a lack of sex. While such distinctions seem to be breaking down, our clinical experience suggests that when the woman has an affair it's usually more ominous for the future of the relationship.

Gottman described a "distance and isolation cascade" that's characterized by flooding (of emotions), seeing problems as severe, believing that it's best to work out problems alone, leading parallel lives, and loneliness. From a schema perspective, this is likely to be surrendering to schemas like Abandonment or Emotional Deprivation. If there's no family history showing that problems can be overcome or solved by working through them with significant others, it's hardly surprising that as someone descends this cascade they'll be more open to having an affair. However, while an affair is an option, it's never a solution.

Depression may be a factor, and this should be carefully considered. Midlife issues can add another dimension of potential complications. So often, after yet another unresolved fight, one partner reaches a conclusion: "This is not where I belong!" There are also a number of ways that schema vulnerability, hidden behind coping modes, can contribute to an affair. But first we'll look at Brown's model of affairs (the first five types in Table 15.1) and add another with the same-sex affair.

Table 15.1 The six kinds of affair

Kind of affair	Characteristics
Conflict avoidance affair	"Peace at any price" leads to problems with the avoidance of relationship issues.
Intimacy avoidance affair	Hurt and difficulties with emotional intimacy lead to seeking it elsewhere.
Sexual addiction affair	The affair is part of a pattern of repeated infidelity.
Empty nest affair	Children have left. This is an affair to fill the emptiness of home life after raising children.
Out-the-door affair	The decision to leave has been made. This is the transition.
Same-sex affair	Perhaps sexual orientation has been long denied, but now it's acknowledged.

Conflict avoidance affairs

In a conflict avoidance affair, there's a shout, "I'll make you pay attention to me!" Sometimes a couple will have a "nice" relationship, like a pond with hardly a surface ripple. Every difference of viewpoint is avoided, and eventually this peace becomes suffocating. Usually, the more dissatisfied spouse gets into the affair and then manages to get quickly discovered. This takes the covers off problems in the relationship. It's a relief to have things out in the open.

> *Rob* confessed the next day to *Marlene*, "I have no idea what happened. I have no particular feelings for Sally. We were both at the conference, and after-dinner drinks led to ... well, you know. I feel so guilty—and I promise never to see her again. Can you just forgive me? I want to make things right." Marlene was certainly prepared to forgive Rob, but she realized that something was wrong in their marriage.

> The therapist saw them a week later. Rob and Marlene had only a vague sense of dissatisfaction in their relationship. It was puzzling: why the affair? But they soon began to realize that underneath the avoiding of hot issues, and even just warm ones, there was deep dissatisfaction. After the violation of the relationship, Marlene found it easier to be angry. Rob was obsessed with his guilt, but gradually he, too, was able to express resentment, especially about Marlene's frequent unwillingness for sex.

In this type of affair, the threat to the relationship is more in the avoidance of conflict than the affair. There's hope for the relationship if the couple is willing to face underlying issues. This is what connect talk is made for. Ending their relationship or forgiving too quickly are both cop-outs (see our comments about forgiving below).

Intimacy avoidance affairs

All affairs reveal problems in intimacy, but in this kind of affair the avoidance of intimacy is central. The outside relationship is a shield against hurt and disappointment, sending a barely conscious message: "I don't want to need you so much, so I'll get some of my needs met elsewhere." It's easier to argue than to be vulnerable and risk intimacy.

Intimacy avoiders appear to be very skilled at fighting but not at resolving conflict. Whether it's hot or icy, conflict is endless. Exchanges are filled with criticism, sarcasm, and blame. The mutual hostility may provide a justification for turning to someone else. The affair then becomes a weapon in the fight and the partner may counter with another affair.

The way the couple stays in contact is through conflict, but paradoxically the anger gives the safety of distance as well. It's easy to justify the affair when there may be quite abusive conflict. Expressions of guilt are rare, even after the discovery of the affair. Under the surface there's a great deal of pain and fear. It's a dance in which both want the assurance of the other's love.

> *Val* called her therapist early in the morning, asking for an emergency session. She asked, "Can I see you first? I've just found out that Paul's been seeing prostitutes when he's overseas." There was high tension in their relationship. It was hard to get the story straight, but eventually it came out that her husband had caught a venereal disease when he was last in the Philippines.
>
> The relationship was entangled and surprisingly strong for all the mutual blame. Neither raised the issue of leaving and both quickly engaged in the counseling process. They talked about experiences growing up. In Val's home, her parents were continually in an uproar. In contrast, Paul's parents seldom spoke to each other. There was a constant tension between two people who appeared to be strangers. Gradually, Paul and Val realized that they had no experience of healthy communication in family life.
>
> After about 10 sessions, they had made such good progress doing connect talk that they wanted to see if they could make it on their own. They had managed to get behind the wall of conflict and found a new reward in getting to know each other.

If vulnerability and dependency are not addressed, affairs can become a way of life. The "open marriage" is a variation on this theme of intimacy avoidance.

Sexual addiction affairs

The "womanizer" or "temptress" is a special case. This kind of person avoids dealing with personal needs by making conquests, perhaps with the expressed hope of finding "true love." Such individuals usually come from a deprived past, sometimes involving abuse or neglect, and experience themselves as empty—nothing fills them up in a lasting way. They always look for the sparkle in their mother's eyes that they probably never got.

So the affair's really about approval, not about sex. The conquests compensate for feelings of isolation, shame, and low self-esteem. It's addictive behavior, compulsive and seemingly out of control, so it usually continues despite the cost.

This can also be a pattern with people who have a personality disorder or strong traits. Sometimes, they express an adolescent quality by bragging about conquests. Risk may be something of a narcotic "hit" for them. Perhaps the only hope of change is through reparenting, with extended psychotherapy as well as the partner applying leverage of abandonment if this behavior continues. Schema therapy is well suited to this challenge.

In this type of affair, the lover is usually of little significance, although there may be surface qualities such as attractive looks or power of position. It's safe to predict that there'll be many lovers over time, but never enough. Such affairs tend to happen throughout the marriage. Often there's a defiance, a sort of "Catch me if you can!" attitude.

> *Nicholas* came to therapy after his new wife, *Bess*, threatened to leave him. She found out that he'd made a pass at one of her close friends. He was in his late twenties, tall, with an athletic build. He was very engaging and quite charming.
>
> In the next three months, Nicholas proved to be very motivated. His mother was an alcoholic who had never married, and he came to realize that his emptiness was related to a lack of nurturing when he was a child. He felt empty and tried to fill that intense need with the excitement of a hidden sexual relationship. Bess was very helpful in the process, holding him accountable and keeping lines of communication open.

Matthew Kelly encouraged people to become "the best version of yourself." This is the principle of mode work, where we ally with the person to help them change to a healthier coping mode or Healthy Adult.

> THERAPIST: "So, as I understand it, you like the excitement of the chase and the novelty of different partners. But you have found some heavy costs as well. What do you see as the main disadvantages?"
> NICHOLAS: "I think it's the Alfie syndrome, I always end up alone and full of regrets."
> THERAPIST: "And?"
> NICHOLAS: "I end up losing my self-respect. I want to build something lasting in terms of a relationship ..."

Empty nest affairs

The empty nest affair signals a marriage that has been held together by a belief in family rather than a strong emotional bond. It is the typical family man, married for 20 years, who will now admit that he has never really loved his wife. Or he'll say that he had doubts since the beginning but went ahead anyway. On the surface, it appears that he tried to make a go of it by doing his duty. (Of course, there are an equal number of wives who have filled the same role for a decade or two and now look elsewhere for intimacy.)

If a couple pays too little attention to their relationship and focuses on family and work too much, an initially promising relationship can become blunted. This underlines why it's important for a couple to spend at least a few hours a week together without the kids. This helps keep their relationship alive.

While the children are still at home, the focus is on them. When it becomes obvious that the marriage is empty, one partner may be tempted to seek fulfillment elsewhere. It's the relationship rather than the individual that is empty. Communication may be limited to purely practical matters.

The affair tends to be a serious matter and may last for years. The partner having the affair then idealizes the lover (because the lover's appearance isn't shaded by everyday hassles), and devalues the spouse (because life's boredom is blamed on them). The participants tend to be discrete and don't invite discovery. However, when the affair is revealed it can be deeply wounding to the betrayed partner, especially if they remain committed to the relationship. The long-lasting affair has been called a "tripod" because of the apparent stability it offers.

> *James* saw a therapist only at the demand of his wife, *Fiona*. He explained to the therapist, "I really have no energy to work on the marriage. It's pointless. Fiona has finally found out about my relationship with Michelle, and I suppose that clarifies things for me. I want to move to LA so I can be with Michelle. Our son Mike has nearly finished law school, and he can come to see me on the odd weekend."

Sadly, a typical motive for seeking counseling is to leave the abandoned partner in the care of a therapist.

Out-the-door affairs

In an out-the-door affair, the erring partner is seriously thinking about ending their relationship. So this affair is an attempt to answer such questions as "Can I make it on my own?" "Am I still attractive?" "Can I be happy in another relationship?" and, most importantly, "Can I get you to kick me out?" The purpose has two aspects. There's usually a quest for self-validation, but less consciously there may also be a desire to avoid taking responsibility for ending the partnership. The affair is a distraction from the difficulties and the pain of ending the relationship.

The other person in the affair is usually portrayed as "understanding." The affair may have been built on a close friendship. The lover is someone to talk with about marital dissatisfactions and hopes for the future. The affair confirms that the betrayed relationship is unsatisfactory, and this justifies the impending separation. The unfaithful partner will usually ensure that they are found out, and sometimes they're disappointed that even then their partner won't leave. The task of counseling is difficult, since the unfaithful partner may only be coming to therapy to self-justify ("I did everything that I could"). Usually, the person being left is more willing to face issues such as the loss of the relationship and adjusting to a different life. There may be some need to improve communication between them if they have parenting responsibilities.

> *Trudi* had married *Clarence*, a successful medical specialist about 15 years older than her. They had two children together. She was initially very reluctant to tell her husband about her affair with Frank. In therapy she made the decision.
>
> Trudi said to her therapist: "Yes I'll leave, but it's more to leave Clarence. I'm not really in love with Frank. I may see how it goes with him for a little while, but I really want to get on with my own life."

Generally, the prognosis for the marriage gets worse, moving from conflict avoidance to an out-the-door affair. It's helpful when both partners can accept responsibility for creating the unhappiness in the relationship. Rebuilding takes time, whether it's focused on the relationship or on the future after separation. Sometimes forgiveness is possible, and it has a healing effect.

Same-sex affairs

The same-sex affair is another category to add to Brown's five types of affairs. It's an affair with a gay lover. There are some similarities with the out-the-door affair, because the prognosis is usually poor for the original relationship, but it also has elements of the empty nest affair in that there may be a deep attachment to the lover.

There are differences with the apparent change in orientation. Some people are aware of attraction to someone of the same sex in their teens but hold back to avoid personal, family, or social disapproval. The social stigma may lead to them trying to make a heterosexual relationship work, and the expectations of family and peers as well as their moral values or religious beliefs might add to their determination. This resolve can later break down and raise doubts in their sexual orientation. (By the way, a quick way to detect an underlying homosexuality is to look honestly at your masturbation fantasies. If the genitals of your gender feature close to orgasm, there's probably a trait of hidden homosexual attraction.)

> *Bennie* experimented with some homosexual encounters when he was a teenager. He tried to dismiss this as sexual exploration, until he found the urge to visit gay bars irresistible. He had a troubled marriage, and when his wife found out about his homosexual activity she left him and refused to speak to him except through her lawyer. He was confused and somewhat ashamed of his desires: "I can't understand it. I still only want to have a steady relationship with a woman, but I go for casual sex with men I meet in bars."

In some cases there's a more recent attraction, and this can be confusing.

> *Mark* rang his schema therapist in a state of panic. He had found out that his wife, *Gabrielle*, had a female lover. On the phone he poured out, "Damn it! We have four children, all teenagers. How the hell could this have happened?" He sent Gabrielle for the first session. Mark was hoping that therapy would change her back.
>
> Gabrielle: "I met Angie at the gym. We both relaxed in the sauna after the workout. We began with being good friends."
>
> But Gabrielle had no interest in reconciling with Mark: "The thought of Mark touching me disgusts me. I can no longer sleep in the same room, and I think it's hopeless staying together for our children. This sounds like I've made up my mind to leave, doesn't it?"

The rejection of the partner is possibly the hardest to bear in this kind of affair. As Mark later said, "It's not just me personally. I could understand it if she went with another man, but a woman? She's so turned off that she's rejecting my gender as well. How could I fail her like that?"

Schema Vulnerability with Affairs

Some schemas may indicate a vulnerability to having an affair. Abandonment, Emotional Deprivation, and Approval Seeking reveal deep unmet needs.

> Angela said that she needed more than Barry could give, "and I found it with Hank at work."

An affair involving schemas such as Entitlement and Insufficient Self-control will be very different.

> Nick said with self-justifying anger, "I believe that I'm due recreational sex! What's the big deal?"

Some schemas indicate a lack in the self: Defectiveness-Shame, Social Isolation, Dependence-Incompetence, Vulnerability, Enmeshment, Failure, and Emotional Inhibition.

> Amie was very dependent in her relationship with Brad. She lacked any sense of autonomy. She was getting more and more frustrated at his lack of availability for her to lean on, but found a work colleague who began to show an interest in her.

Mode Work with Affairs

You may want to think about the mode, or state of mind, in which an affair is attractive. While a schema-based conceptualization looks at the underlying personality traits, a mode perspective focuses on the here-and-now reaction and leaves the history aside.

Think about the following cases:

> *Natalie* talked about her affair: "I just needed the comfort of being with him." (Detached Self-soother)

> *Val* said defiantly, "I just wanted to get back at her. Stick it to her and rub her face in it—the worthless bitch she is!" (Bully and Attack)

> *Desmond* said, with a sad tone, "I felt totally alone. I needed comfort. My wife was no longer talking to me." (Vulnerable Child)

> *Nerrida* spat out, "I hate Ben. I was glad that his younger brother was interested in me. I know it hurt Ben that I screwed his brother, but I deserved to get some attention!" (Angry or Enraged Child).

An affair might "feel right" when the person is in a child or coping mode. Naturally, it's important to recognize a mode cycle and introduce some circuit breakers to bring in choice. Perhaps mindfulness can be used to gain some distance. Then behavior pattern breaking can target choices to continue or stop the affair.

Mode work sets apart this therapy from other therapies. It's different in conceptualizing what caused the affair and how the healing process unfolds. It's important in understanding the mode cycle to lead to a foundation of insight, reduction of blame, taking of responsibility, and a layer of hope.

If your relationship has been challenged by an affair, try to understand which modes were involved and which needs haven't been met before. Then look for a path of healing for such modes.

> *Minh* had an affair with her work colleague. Her partner, *Barry*, was prepared to go to counseling with her: "I don't want our relationship to end. I want to fix things." In therapy, they found that the affair had come from Minh's Detached Self-soother mode, and they made progress in weakening that mode and discovering what it was detaching from.
>
> Minh also had a self-directed parental voice telling her that she was defective, and in individual sessions traced the origins of the voice to her mother. Then she started to unlearn it, block it, and ignore it. Memories were readily at hand of abusive messages in that Punitive Parent voice, and imagery work allowed her to reparent her Vulnerable Child and impeach the parental voice.
>
> Further couple work to identify the triggers for the parental voice involved looking at the mode cycle between Minh and Barry. Paying attention to the cycle didn't let Minh off the hook, but it was less blaming and allowed more of a redistribution of responsibility for the state of the relationship when the affair began.

Schema therapy aims to make both partners in the couple relationship fully responsible for more effectively meeting their own needs. Often, understanding where your feelings and needs come from allows you to be more effective in Healthy Adult mode.

Having a loving partner doesn't prevent affairs, but a good relationship is a barrier. So, to a certain extent, both partners are involved in the hidden onset of the affair, which is often just the tip of the iceberg. Both partners need to look at the part under water if they're to make the affair a turning point in the relationship. But this also means that both have to contribute to repairing the damage. The unfaithful partner carries the symptoms of a dying relationship, but both partners are infected by the disease. Maybe it will take an intensive care unit to reanimate the partnership, but that could be worth the price.

Schema therapy defines a "good" relationship as one in which the partners shift from maladaptive coping modes to healthier coping, led by the Healthy Adult mode. It's possible to trace a mode clash or an activated schema to the occurrence of an affair. The idea of schema therapy is to support a couple to move from getting stuck in dysfunctional modes or flipping between mode cycles to an encounter of two more or less Healthy Adults who are aware of their full spectrum of needs and are able to negotiate their mutual fulfillment.

Note: When there's been an affair, watch for the risk of a parent mode that demands the complete disclosure of all past betrayals. Satisfying that demand can be unrealistic or even impossible, no matter how much effort is made. As an illustration, the task of raking leaves in the backyard can never be complete; instead, aim for a "good enough" disclosure.

Reconciliation must always be between two equal partners, even if there are differences in understanding the affair. If your partner has had an affair and you're both trying to work through it, don't be tempted to make adverse judgments about their character. After all, most of us engage in bad behavior at times.

What Can Be Done to Prevent an Affair?

There's no assurance that covers all risks that you or your partner will have an affair, but here's some advice. Because most affairs start at workplaces or other places where the same people meet frequently, think about the following:

1. Put a picture of your partner or your family on your desk at work. If there's a chance to include your partner in business events, do so. This sends a clear signal that you belong together.
2. Show connectedness in public by holding hands, hugging, or gently kissing each other.
3. When you're at a party together, don't spend too much time with another attractive guest without checking back with your partner. Introduce your partner to that person.
4. If you meet a seductive person, let them know that you're in a relationship and give some details about it. This tears the curtain of secrecy apart, cools down your Impulsive Child mode, and helps your Healthy Adult mode keep you on track.
5. Disclose to your partner when you feel you're in danger. Affairs breathe the spirit of being secret. Reveal to your partner that you met

a seductive colleague. This acts like turning the lights on in a red-light bar: The emotions flatten. This needs a lot of courage, but it's another example of how vulnerability has to be balanced with assertiveness to overcome avoidance. Try being the brave knight! Use a connect talk session for this purpose to feel safer.

When Do You Forgive?

If you or your partner has had an affair and you both want to continue your relationship, you should understand that forgiveness has a precondition. It's never possible without fully experiencing the injury. Know what you're forgiving. Usually a betrayed partner has a journey to eventual acceptance. Make sure that it isn't pseudo-forgiveness, offered just to maintain the relationship.

> *Alice* had a one-night stand at a conference. She was so paralyzed by guilt that she returned home and confessed immediately to her partner. *Bob* was shocked and confused, and only came to some clarity about how he felt when he felt surges of anger. But this was an unfamiliar emotion to him, since anger was a taboo emotion in the very rigid family he was raised in.
>
> He went to see his parish priest, who encouraged him to forgive Alice. He was ready to forgive because he wanted to wipe the slate clean. Two months later, his family doctor encouraged him to enter therapy because he was waking up every morning at 2 a.m. In therapy, he realized that he still had plenty of feelings about the affair.

A Compliant Surrender mode will sometimes motivate a person to "forgive," but this has little to do with real forgiveness, no matter how sincerely that's desired. It can be a type of avoidance driven from a fear of disconnection. Such "forgiveness" may further undermine the relationship, especially when persistent feelings of revenge remain undercover.

Full recovery from an affair requires that all issues be laid out on the table. A very important ground rule is that an affair always involves, and is to a certain extent caused by, both partners. This might sound strange at first, but our clinical experience tells us that it's true. Thinking in terms of offender and victim won't get you far. It's better to look at an affair as a very hot mode cycle with a withdrawing (betraying) partner and a reactively overcompensating betrayed partner.

Use a connect talk session as a safety net to carry out the following steps, which uses some chair-dialogues:

1. The betrayed partner is given the chance to vent their anger, which comes from their wounded assertiveness side. They might take some minutes to speak the anger out to an empty chair standing next to the accused partner. Talking to this empty chair and not directly into the partner's face makes it easier for the accused partner to stand the anger outburst.
2. The betrayer is asked to repeat what they understood, acknowledge their partner's hurt, and apologize from their chair representing their own attachment need. It might take some additional rounds until most of the anger of the betrayed person is vented. It helps to separate the betraying (self-assertiveness-oriented) part on the empty chair while the formerly betraying partner now takes the stance of the attachment-seeking part on their current chair. So there's room to express the anger toward the "untrue" chair while the partner now represents the "willing" side.
3. The betrayed partner is asked to repeat the words, move to a second chair representing their attachment need, and say what they still expect or hope to get from the betrayer.
4. The betrayer repeats the expectations and, once the initial emotions have cooled down, moves to the assertiveness chair and says what they think might have left them unsatisfied with the relationship. This is the chance for the betrayer to stand up for their own needs in a healthy, assertive way.
5. The betrayed person repeats that. It might take some turns until everything has been said and understood. Stop if the talk becomes too emotional and start again at the very beginning.
6. Both partners stand up (leaving the betrayed and betrayer positions below) and float above the scene. They try to reconnect in a joint perspective on a Healthy Adult level. Then they can both make suggestions about what the couple down below might do to improve their relationship. If they managed to reconnect, they can sit down on two chairs for the Healthy Adult modes again.
7. The former betrayer can ask for forgiveness and name their contribution into the relationship account.
8. The formerly betrayed partner can forgive, with the promise that they won't come up with the betrayal again to strengthen their position. They can name their own contribution to the account.

Even though things will never be like they were before the affair, they may be better—at least at some points. Overcoming a crisis increases your resistance capacity as a couple and makes you stronger, but you both have to draw a line, face the future, and stop looking back.

> *Bob* had a number of sessions to explore how injured he felt about Alice's affair. He told his therapist, "Both Alice and I saved sex until our wedding night. It was something we had together, and now this uniqueness is lost." In couple sessions, Bob was able to say how he felt. Alice was relieved that he was moving out of a role of subjugation: "I can relate to you as more of an adult I respect. I know I've hurt you ... well, us ... terribly, but your strength is attractive to me."

Forgiveness can and must be given freely, as a gift. It comes from the Healthy Adult mode. In that mode, you can make a personal choice to not exact revenge, to not go into Punitive Parent mode towards your partner, and to seek a new beginning in the relationship. Trusting your partner again despite the pain means making another choice (remember: We often make choices based on goodwill and not on the odds).

This is a positive way of emotional reasoning:

> "I deliberately choose to trust because it makes me feel better. When we got married, we probably had some idea of the current divorce rate, but we felt much better in romantically seeing ourselves on the surviving side. We could know the rates of betrayal but still decide to trust, because staying in a skeptical position undermines the relationship."

Being safe and assertive can disconnect us from others: We decide to stand on our attachment leg more than on our assertiveness (or safety) leg. This is what human relationships are all about. When Lenin said, "Trust is good, but control is better," he took the stance of an insecurely attached child. That's not a good starting point for a flourishing relationship. Good relationships are built on trust: within a family, among friends, in a sports team, and in a good business company.

Healing the Affair with a Ritual

Farrell and Shaw have written about group exercises or rituals in group schema therapy, where "us" has a corporate identity. So, too, with couples.

The marriage ceremony is full of symbolism. Why not mark relationship recovery with some suitable symbols?

> *Scott and Diana* had repaired their relationship after Scott had a brief affair. Diana said, "I know I've forgiven Scott, and I need to work toward trying to forget. The difficulty is that our marriage was damaged. I wonder if we might renew our marriage vows? That would help me to get a sense of a new beginning based on a renewed commitment." Scott was happy to make a fresh start in this way. They arranged for a civil ceremony in which they repeated their vows.

Of course, you and your partner don't have to be married to restate some of those promises you made to one another when your relationship was young!

There are many other potential rituals of relationship renewal. Perhaps the richest resource is the creativity of the couple and their knowing what feels right for them.

To do: Can you develop a ritual to mark how you have grown as a couple? It might be a weekend away to a favorite resort to celebrate the relationship. It might be associated with an anniversary—or not. Healthy rituals are effective because rituals *repeat*. So build this into your relationship.

Couple exercise: You might think about rewriting your marriage vows or, if you're not married, finding some words of commitment for your relationship. This exercise was suggested by Sarah Calleja, a psychologist and sex therapist in Melbourne.

After the Affair

Affairs are painfully common. Often, an affair is the reason a couple comes to a therapist for help. Perhaps surprisingly, however, an affair isn't the most common reason for a relationship ending. Some research indicates that close to 80% of people leaving a marriage say that the reason for getting divorced is that they and their spouse were "gradually growing apart." In other research, affairs were cited by about 20–27% as the reason (Gigy & Kelly, cited in Gottman & Silver, 1999). Usually, the affair is a symptom and not the true cause of the breakdown in the relationship.

Schema therapy can help a couple to understand when one of them goes outside their relationship to meet emotional needs. This holds the most promise for healing both parties and the relationship itself after an affair. Janis Spring noted in *After the Affair*:

> In the end an affair may not be completely destructive. Sometimes the relationship survives and grows stronger—though usually both partners hurt terribly, the affair may indicate that they want something more in the relationship. The perfect dream for the relationship may feel shattered, but reality can yet be satisfying, rewarding, and may even wind up being better than the "untested love" of the "perfect dream." And even then, in the wake of a broken relationship, there's the possibility of insight and being wiser the next time around.

To Leave or Stay?

To leave or to stay; that is the question. Not every couple recovers from a crisis. Some relationships are built on chemistry, and time reveals that they're a poor fit. Some couples pass a point of no return and their relationship becomes blunted and burns out. Sometimes a person starts a change process in their relationship (with or without therapy) and grows apart from their partner, who doesn't want to follow them (this is one reason schema therapists began to include partners in therapy, even when only one partner came initially). Of course, this growing apart can occur at any point in a relationship: from an early "Are we compatible?" to a midterm "Can we survive this crisis?" to a later "Is this all there is?"

Schema therapy brings a perspective to our headline question, but not an answer. If you have a strong inclination to leave, then it's important to consider which mode you might be in.

> *Clarissa* had a volatile relationship with Bart. On an impulse, she walked out, taking almost nothing. This might be Angry Child or Impulsive Child acting out, or perhaps both.
>
> *Nick* was normally withdrawn in his relationship with Sun Li. He announced, "This is over." It was a decision in Detached Protector mode.
>
> *Zandra* decided that Gary's parenting wasn't attentive enough. She said as she left, "Our son deserves more than you give!" This was Demanding Parent.

You should make a decision to leave or stay, along with any other important life-changing decisions, in Healthy Adult mode. Try standing on both legs. Carefully think about the consequences for you, your partner, and, if you have any, your children. Think about your relationship from the healthiest part of you. Consult people whose opinions you value most. It's easy to rationalize what amounts to selfish behavior, but you're assured of a better decision in Healthy Adult mode. And you will usually avoid the regret of a hasty decision.

Therapy doesn't have to work in terms of the couple arriving at "happy ever after." You may have worked hard on your relationship, either in therapy or through this book. But you might decide that it isn't workable for a variety of reasons. Staying together at any price isn't necessarily the best solution. Separating and doing better with another partner based on a Healthy Adult can be a more promising option than getting stuck in endless mode cycles. You may have become more aware of dysfunctional schemas. Sometimes this leads to a less reactive relationship between two people after they separate, and better engagement in parenting. It's also possible to gain insight into your own schema chemistry or dynamics of attraction and potentially find a better matching partner in a subsequent relationship.

David Schnarch adds another layer to this issue by asking each partner whether they still "want" the other: Would they still choose them? A good point indeed! Such a question can help to wake you up when you feel trapped in a dying relationship and lack an intervention point.

It can be likened to an old maxim. If you place a live frog in a pot of cold water and then heat the water slowly, it won't try to jump out of the pot until the water's so hot that it's too weak to jump out and so it gets killed.

A crisis in your relationship, such as an affair, can be an intervention point for a real reconsideration and a clear decision for or against the relationship. In schema therapy, the therapist would usually have you do some chair-dialogues using two separate chairs: one for each perspective.

To do: You can try this decision-making exercise on your own by sitting on the *pro* chair first and bringing to mind all the aspects that support continuing the relationship. Take a little time to fully develop a positive picture of all that is good in the relationship and how it has the potential to grow. How do you feel—right down in your body? Then move to the *con* chair and you dredge up all the negative aspects. Imagine 10 years from now (or getting old) in the relationship. How do you feel now? Move back and forth several times until you get a clearer feeling. Decisions are often made on an emotional level, not by thinking about things over and over again. Standing up and looking down on both chairs might provide you with a more distanced observer stance and make a decision easier.

To do: Note your dreams while you're struggling consciously with your decision. Dreams include associations from the right brain, while our rational thinking is mostly done in left brain circuits. What's the first thought you have when you wake up in the middle of the night or in the morning? These observations give you additional input that you can acknowledge in your decision making.

Living Apart Together

But don't think only of black or white, yes or no. There are other potential outcomes. You might consider the option of "living apart together." At first glance, this might not be very appealing, but it's possible to look at it in a positive way. Especially if you've been together for years, your relationship is more than an emotional and romantic connection. You're embedded in social and economic structures as well. You'll lose this social bedrock if you separate. This has to be taken into consideration. A major concern might be children, since there is no good time to deprive them of a family unit. Or separation might not work in financial terms, especially if you're inclined to legal conflict about the custody of children.

Maybe you have difficulty with some behaviors of your partner but like others. You'll lose those positive parts, too. This is why a moderate degree of separation, such as moving into separate rooms in the same apartment or house and following some interests separately while sharing others, could be a good compromise. Why not take the best out of two worlds and skip what doesn't match? For some couples, this can also include separate sexual activities. But this is a very delicate solution, requires a lot of Healthy Adult functioning, and can't work while you're in an overcontrolling coping mode. It requires emotional distance and not asking questions (which might lead to hurtful answers). So it's better to not ask, look away, and bury your head in the sand. This could be called a helpful protector mode.

This is definitely not the desired outcome when you start a relationship, but it acknowledges what can be a painful reality and at the very least it's another option. There are also long-term consequences.

When older couples separate, the most common outcome is that the male partner quickly finds himself in a new relationship, often with a younger woman with lower social status, and probably with more submissive characteristics than his former partner.

And the women? They often stay alone. There's a simple reason: Once you've found your way out of an unpleasant relationship you don't want to go from the frying pan into the fire. Most of the available partners are probably not much better than the one you left. And when you've stopped submitting, it doesn't make much sense finding yourself chained again. Sadly, there are not so many potential partners left.

And there's another, not very appealing, aspect. We hope you permit us to be frank in speaking about something we've heard from many women beyond the age of about 50. They talk about tending to disappear in some kind of social invisibility. Finding a good partner isn't impossible, of course, but it's against the odds. This is another reason why we wrote this book and encourage couples to work out their relationships.

Reflect: If you and your partner learn to distance yourselves in a functional way, respect each other, and share your remaining overlapping interests, living apart together might be a good outcome. Some couples learn to refresh their relationship and start a new phase of growing together. This is the best result, of course, but not always achievable.

How About Ending the Relationship?

If you and your partner do your best to work on your relationship in Healthy Adult mode but find it's no longer working, we hope you'll be able to deal with the sensitive issue of a separation in a responsible way. There are some steps you can take to find out whether separating is better for you than continuing:

1. Make a *pro* and *con* list about your relationship. Eventually, use two different chairs for each position, as mentioned above. Look at the cons and what the first steps might be to weaken them. Look at the pros and think what might strengthen them.
2. Both of you should start working on your agendas and make an appointment for a connect talk in about a month to consider your attempts at trying to do better.
3. After the talk, reassess. What could be changed? Is there a chance to improve the process? What could help? Are there some structural issues to be solved (for example, moving to another place)? Could a couples therapist be helpful?
4. If it isn't working, maybe try separating for a month. Perhaps there's a chance to house sit or find temporary accommodation. It's sometimes helpful to separate physically to find out what you'll miss about your partner, giving the attachment need a chance to get stronger. If that doesn't happen and you feel better alone than with your partner, that might ease the decision.
5. Once you're clear about your decision, share it in another connect talk session. Try to find fair solutions for the practical issues. If necessary, include a mediator for legal aspects and make a separation contract.

Maybe there's still something left to share or do together, especially if kids are involved.

6. If you both have a strong enough Healthy Adult mode, you might end the relationship in a separation ritual acknowledging what each of you both gained from the other over the course of the relationship, and what you'll keep as good memories. Thank your now former partner for all of that!

Summary

Affairs are normally destructive in a relationship. Naturally. This chapter has outlined six kinds of affairs and brought a unique perspective to this relationship problem. We have explored ways that the relationship can survive an affair, along with some other options, including living apart together and formally separating. However, it's also important to note that sometimes a relationship does more than survive infidelity: Sometimes it grows.

To Read Further

- The five kinds of affairs: Brown (1991)
- More on forgiveness: Gordon and Baucom (1988)
- Research of L. Gigy and J. Kelly: Gottman and Silver (1999)
- The distance and isolation cascade: Gottman and Silver (1999)
- Affairs in the first five years of marriage: Lawson (1988)
- A self-help book on affairs: Spring (2012).

References

Brown, E. M. (1991). *Patterns of infidelity and their treatment*. New York, NY: Brunner/Mazel.

Gordon, K. C., & Baucom, D. H. (1988). Understanding betrayal in marriage: A synthesized model of forgiveness. *Family Process, 37*(4), 425–449.

Gottman, J., & Silver, N. (1999). *The seven principles for making a marriage work*. New York, NY: Three Rivers Press.

Lawson, A. (1988). *Adultery: An analysis of love and betrayal*. New York, NY: Basic Books.

Spring, J. A. (2012). *After the affair: Healing the pain and rebuilding trust when a partner has been unfaithful* (2nd ed.). New York: William Morrow.

16

Emotional Learning

Nobody believes in ghosts. At least, not until you think about your intimate relationship. Suddenly there's a sense of relationships not fully over, problems that seem bigger than your joint resources, and despair about a future with an endless repetition of dysfunction. If you know this, then you know about ghosts and having a haunted relationship.

In-depth Focus

In this chapter, the focus is on emotional learning. This is important because, unlike physical injuries, emotional injuries don't automatically heal with time. Bruce Ecker has noted that they're "peculiarly timeless." So we store our injuries as emotional learning. This can provide a powerful explanation of why we act as we do—often in surprising and puzzling ways! We might act before understanding our conscious convictions or beliefs, and sometimes in contradiction to them. As Joseph LeDoux pointed out, we're driven more by our "lower (emotional) pathways" than by our cognitions. So understanding the processes of emotional learning and schema-driven behavior helps us deal with such inconsistencies.

Schema therapy takes emotional learning seriously. The 18 schemas are essentially domains of emotional learning. This learning usually happens in childhood and is endlessly reinforced by life experiences. Schemas endure because of the emotional learning associated with our formative experiences. Understanding this helps us along the road to recovery, but in some cases not all the way.

Breaking Negative Relationship Patterns: A Schema Therapy Self-help and Support Book, First Edition. Bruce A. Stevens and Eckhard Roediger.
© 2017 John Wiley & Sons, Ltd. Published 2017 by John Wiley & Sons, Ltd.

Uncovering Themes of Emotional Learning

Not all problems are expressed in psychological symptoms. This is especially true in relationships. You may be distressed but not depressed.

> *Nancy* is frustrated that she keeps meeting men who refuse to commit to her. She wants a stable relationship, can become distressed when alone, and resorts to comfort eating. If she's to understand the emotional learning that drives this, she needs to discover an area of meaning that might currently be outside her awareness.

> Fast-forward six months: Nancy has developed an eating disorder as a result of her frustration about relationships. She's puzzled about why she can't control her eating, even though she feels upset before an episode of overeating. She hates that she overeats: "I feel out of control and then I'm filled with regret—even self-loathing—if I stuff myself."

This reaction to the symptom is what Ecker has called the *anti-symptom position*. This is usually in awareness. In schema therapy, it's part of the Healthy Adult functioning. What's more difficult to understand is the nonconscious *pro-symptom position* that maintains the symptom. In schema therapy, we see this as the automatic coping behavior learned in childhood. The process of discovery involves moving from the anti-symptom to the pro-symptom. For Nancy, this would be discovering and understanding why she needs to overeat. Her old coping mode wasn't essentially wrong but was the best solution available in her childhood.

Such problems occur when we try to solve current problems using outdated solutions. Or, in other words, we continue acting like we used to do in childhood, but do it as an adult. The time shift is the problem. Because the problem-solving procedure has remained unconscious, we've never questioned it. If we do so now, there's a chance to update our problem-solving skills.

Ecker gave the example of a couple who came to therapy with their "communication problem." The wife complained that her husband viewed everything she said to him as a criticism and would then counterattack and behave as if they were enemies. This is simply what he learned in childhood. The therapist saw that, indeed, the husband did react strongly to even moderate comments by his wife and treat her as an adversary. The therapist coached them in more restrained sharing of different views and then she asked the couple how they felt. The wife said "relieved," but the husband said "defenseless." He was quiet for a while and then said, "All I can tell you is, now, I feel unjustified in sticking up for myself." They came to understand that he had an emotional learning that he was "bad and selfish" if he expressed his own needs, but that it was legitimate to do that if he was *under attack*; hence his need to see that his wife was attacking him. In schema therapy this is an internalized message of the parents showing up as a parent mode voice. In this example you can see how the aggressive style of the husband was emotionally necessary if he were to ever express his needs in a relationship. He simply had no other option in his behavior repertoire.

Ecker has observed that there are three elements that comprise emotional learning:

1. *Emotional wounds.* The husband in his example had an emotional wound from childhood (we call it a schema) in the area of autonomy, in that he couldn't easily express his needs.
2. *Presupposition.* He had a presupposition about when autonomy was legitimate, in his case only with an adversary. (In schema terms, this is part of his internalized belief system.)
3. *Protective action.* He construed criticism as an attack in order to be deprived of his autonomy (as the formerly most promising coping mode).

Aspects of Emotional Learning

These terms can now be explored more for their general importance:

1. *Emotional wounds* carry emotional meanings. In our terms, these are the schema-creating situations in childhood. It's natural to have thoughts about what caused the experience and intentions to avoid such vulnerability in the future by using the coping styles you once learned. This can be nonconscious. Usually, the schema background is nonconscious. Just the applied coping modes used today are visible onstage. The emotional learning can be a re-experiencing of the original emotional state, commonly seen in trauma survivors, but equally from other negative experiences, such as a painful separation.
2. *Presuppositions* are nonconscious, unquestioned assumptions about "how things are." Often, they're influenced by internalized appraisals deriving from parental messages. All this is elaborated by what events mean and what possible choices there are in the situation (for example, "Whatever you do, it won't work"). Unless we go backstage and become aware of our nonconscious schema and coping activations, we can't access or modify our emotional reasoning. For example,

an infant who witnesses violence from an alcoholic father against his mother, who is beaten into submission, doesn't have a developed capacity for thought or even language but has already learned something about the roles of a male and a female in a family. This includes the use of favorite coping modes and the neglect of others. Of course this learning is unhealthy, but there's no doubt that the young child *knows* something from early experience. He just does the best he can. This is how imbalances in the spectrum of the applied coping modes arise between individuals.

3. *Protective action* is any rationale or behavior to avoid a recurrence of the pain. This can include, of course, any re-experiencing of emotions associated with the original injury. Protective actions include the whole range of behaviors leading to difficulties in a relationship, including withdrawal, obsessing, anger, blaming, shame, and low self-esteem. It can include behaviors such as using substances, binge eating, workaholism, manic activity, even violence. This serves to avoid feeling the pain or ever again being vulnerable. This is expressed in maladaptive coping modes.

Understanding the problem at this level comprises the pro-symptom position, or what maintains either the relationship problem or a symptom from an individual's perspective. The pro-symptom position is the emotionally governing one. It's the automatic pilot processing. So the goal is to help us discover why having the relationship problem is absolutely necessary as a road to discover its origins in childhood, offering a chance to make a change for further development. No pain, no gain.

Ecker called this a "naming into awareness" (Ecker & Hulley, 1996). One example of this is the person with low self-esteem who had abusive parents. It's easier to blame the self, with hypercritical messages to the self, rather than question an unrealistically positive view of the parents. It's impossible to hold both in awareness, so one remains out of sight, but the legacy of low self-esteem continues. And that can damage a relationship.

Reflect: Think about the three clues to pro-symptoms: *wounds* (schemas), *presupposition* (from the voice in your head), and *protective action* (coping modes). How can you use such clues? Think about what causes you distress in your relationship.

Here's an example of conflict being used in a relationship to maintain emotional distance:

> *Amanda and Matt* came for couples therapy. They were able to see how conflict kept them from feeling close. The therapist wanted them to discover

why it was necessary to have fights. This was the couple's pro-symptom agenda. Why was unresolved conflict the best solution to a deeper problem? The therapist led them to see, in their imagination, how they might feel after a long period of no conflict. Matt said, "I would feel powerless, like I'd lost myself and I was being controlled." His coping mode was a Detached Self-soother. Amanda thought, "I wouldn't be able to say no to Matt's sexual advances. I'd have no excuse to say no." This is a Detached Protector. So, for different reasons, they had been seeking conflict—the more intense, the better.

Understanding this can lead to better understanding of the relationship process. The anti-symptom *pain* and the pro-symptom *gain* of having the problem. Having the conflict is worth the benefits. Only if the pain exceeds the gain are Amanda and Matt ready for a change.

Once the two sides of a problem are understood, both positions could be placed on separate chairs, making it easier to find a better way forward to meet underlying needs, rather than self-destructing through conflict and the loss of goodwill in the relationship.

To do: Can you take a relationship difficulty and, through an analysis of both anti-symptom and pro-symptom discovery, arrive at a deeper understanding of its necessity for your relationship? Then write this down in a sentence and share it with your partner? Ideally, they will do the same. Use your sentence to say something directly: "The reason I need to have this (problem) in our relationship is ..." How does this feel? Notice how it's *I* focused. You might be tempted to offer your diagnosis of your relationship problem in terms of "The reason you have to contribute this problem to our relationship is ..." Stop. That won't work!

More About Emotional Truth

Ecker has outlined categories of emotional knowing based on internalized messages and beliefs:

1. *Ends.* "My wife will get obese; all women do, like my mother, and she'll care about food more than me."
2. *Roles.* "If my husband becomes irritable, it's my job to protect the children."
3. *Causes.* "It's my fault if my husband doesn't come home for dinner. I must be more attractive, to draw him home."
4. *Nature of self, others, and the world.* "There are two kinds of people: those who are creative and chaotic, and those who are boring but organized."

5. *How to know.* "The way I know I'm a good person is to get promoted and earn more money."
6. *Values.* "Doing what God wants is good; doing what I want is bad. I must sacrifice myself for the church."

Such underlying assumptions powerfully structure how we see reality. This is endlessly played out in relationships. Unless we reveal and question them, they keep us in our life-traps.

What can lead to revolutionary change is to become aware of how much such *knowing* is ever-present and determines your responses. It's not out there but inside. It usually orders our interactions with others.

Radical Self-inquiry

Now we want to offer you some techniques derived from Ecker's repertoire for strengthening your Healthy Adult mode. Let's start with better understanding the background of your coping modes. There are many ways you can explore your underlying assumptions about self and relationships. You might think that this detective task will be difficult, but there's a surprising reality that such *truths* want to be expressed. If you give your mind a chance to speak openly, you'll be surprised at the messages from within. This is why schema therapists place these voices onto separate chairs to encourage them to speak up without holding anything back. These messages are what you have constructed and maintained backstage, however unexpressed they are—so they're ever-present, waiting, as it were, to talk to you! In many cases, the internal voices deriving from our parent modes comment on us all the time!

Exercise: Consider a firmly held view of a family member. Think of something controversial, something that your friends have questioned. Then visualize that person, who may be your father or mother or a sibling, and say to them in your imagination the *opposite* of what you have always believed to be true. How do you react? How do they react? This helps to impeach the parent modes inside your head.

> Cindy thought her father was very supportive of her. Her father had left her mother when Cindy was 8 years old, although he had continued to see her for part of her summer vacation. She always thought he was generous to her, making time in his busy schedule and occasionally taking her on trips. So she visualized him and said, "Dad, you were selfish, just as my friends thought and my mother always said." Surprisingly, this felt true when she said it. She began to question assumptions she had long held about her family.

Think of a relational difficulty and then ask the *hard question*: What understanding must I have to make that difficulty more important to have than not have? The following questions from Ecker may help:

1. What does that difficulty do for you or the relationship? What does it prevent you from having to do? Is an important need or priority validated or pursued? What would it mean for your relationship if this difficulty never went away?
2. How is that difficulty a *success* rather than a *failure*? Is the problem in some way a solution to an unacknowledged problem? Who does it matter to, perhaps in some way more than to you?
3. What are the unwelcome or dreaded consequences that would result from living without that relationship difficulty? This is the price you'll have to pay for a change.

These questions aren't easy to ask and especially not easy to answer. Approach this task with a "beginner's mind" (Ecker & Hulley, 1996). Don't assume you have the answers, just start with questions that uncover layers of meaning—like a curious archaeologist digging at a promising site.

To do: If you were to teach me to have your relationship problem, how would you do that? How would you justify that it would be a good idea for me to have the same difficulty?

As you begin with the first clues to unlock your relationship mystery, write them down and then make them headings to expand in your journal. Visualize a setting in which individual truths are played out. Pay attention to your emotions. This is the arena of emotional truth—you're finally where answers are possible!

The Technique of Sentence Completion

Sentence completion is a powerful way of exploring such truths. Identify a relational difficulty and then try the following sentence completion: It's necessary for me to have this problem for the following reason ...

> *Bruce* tried this after a session in which his wife complained about his chronic lateness from work. He said, "I must be late because I don't want to face Sally. I'm too passive to ask for what I want in this relationship, so it's best for me to withdraw, no matter how much unhappiness it causes. This is my only way to protest and express my unhappiness!"

This technique can be done with any of the areas that comprise emotional truth (listed above). You can also try viewing your difficulty from a vantage point from which the problem has completely disappeared.

> *Sally* thought about how she would feel if Bruce came home on time, like clockwork: "Yes, I can see him coming through the front door every night at 6 p.m. At first, it seems like a relief, but then I feel myself becoming uneasy. It's too regular, it's boring. Maybe I want the uncertainty of not knowing when he'll come in the door. Actually, I need something to blame him about to justify my despair about remaining in this marriage."

In this way, Sally and Bruce found that they both "needed" the problematic behavior. It served different unconscious agendas that stabilized their relationship but were equally very unsatisfactory. But now, with this new understanding, both could begin to address the real issues in their relationship. As a first step, it's important to realize that "There's a part of me that's not on board with making the changes I think I want to make in this relationship."

Reflect: When you begin to explore the hidden meanings, you may encounter a wall of resistance. This is a good indication of meaning that exists outside of your awareness. Think of it like you're in a boat wanting to go forward, but something lies beneath the water that blocks your way. It's time to acknowledge and explore what's in your way.

Think about the mismatch of what you discover. Exaggerate the differences, use vivid language, express your emotions!

To do: Once you identify a difficulty in your relationship, can you and your partner or spouse each try the following? *If* we didn't have this problem, *then* (this would happen), *so I'm staying in my attitude* (or behavior, or responses to you) *even though we're both miserable.* This will vividly express why you need, as a couple, to be stuck. Both write out your reasons to be stuck in this way. Don't try to solve it yet, but live with the dilemma for a week or so and then try to talk with all the cards on the table.

Examples of Emotional Learning

The following are examples of using sentence completion to dig for the gold of emotional learning.

Mike, a young Christian adult, is frustrated that he hasn't found a wife through the youth group at church. He's somewhat passive, waiting for God to provide, as it were. His therapist helped him write his assumption in this sentence: "I'm waiting for God to change his mind." His schemas seemed to be in the area of Emotional Deprivation and Failure, but that called for a working assumption about God.

Matilda, a very successful young doctor, had been frustrated in a romantic relationship. She felt that she was unable to commit, though she felt she loved him. Eventually they separated. She used the sentence, "I need my space because ..." This was completed as "I would feel valued but restricted," giving some focus beyond her presenting Entitlement-Grandiosity schema.

Simon, a 49-year-old man who had been robbed at gunpoint, had many trauma symptoms. He also found his life terribly restricted by his constant surveillance of the environment for any possible threat. He had a long-standing Vulnerability schema, aggravated by the traumatic experience. The sentence completion: "If I didn't keep watch ... I would no longer be safe. I wasn't safe in childhood, with violence between my parents. I have to do everything possible; it's my responsibility."

Henry was nearly 50 when he was charged with the sexual assault of one of his nephews. He was a Buddhist and his meditation group was gracious enough to support him through the trial and his pending incarceration. His schemas were Emotional Inhibition, Unrelenting Standards, and Subjugation. Henry had himself been sexually abused as a young child, and gave a number of sentence completions to "I have needed this addiction [to sexual acting out] to (1) cope with pain, (2) express rebellion, (3) suppress my emotions, (4) escape. His therapist thought that rebellion felt most emotionally charged. This became the sentence: "I need to rebel because a trusted authority figure changed who I was. I want control of that back!"

We have worked with people who discovered emotional learning in the messages of parents and discovered what they believed about themselves. A young man with chronic depression struggled with "I cannot allow myself to be happy because ..." A woman seriously abusing alcohol: "I need to sabotage myself because ..." A very unassertive woman: "It's unsafe for me to express any personal needs because ..." A frustrated academic with schemas of Failure, Unrelenting Standards, and Emotional Inhibition: "I avoid completing big tasks because ... I cannot achieve perfection." A middle-aged woman who had entered a series of disastrous relationships came to realize that her programming was "For me not to feel alone ... I have to fix the distress of others."

To Address Emotional Learning

It isn't easy to bridge the two realms: one obvious on front stage and one hidden backstage. That's the purpose of engaging you in a number of exercises designed to "turn the light on" and guide you in a process of discovery. This is necessary because we have no idea what you might find behind your relationship difficulties, what childhood events were important, what emotional learning you carry through life. So at this point there are no easy self-help answers, just a self-help process that you can apply.

To do: Try the following with a single schema domain. What schema worries you the most? It may be, say, Abandonment. First try a more generalized statement about your sense of need. This can be done with a sentence completion: "I need emotional support because ..." Keep finishing this sentence until something clicks strongly for you. Then work on the sentence until it fully resonates with what you believe about yourself.

Once you have a sentence, write it on a card and say it aloud once a day for a week. You may find yourself challenging the "truth" of your emotional learning. This will happen because you learned that truth as a young child, but have also had a lifetime of different learning. We often neglect other life truths in order to hold on to our early emotional learning.

These two will naturally clash. After two weeks, do a dialogue in your journal between the position of believing the sentence and the anti-position of challenging it. Track how true it feels to you now.

Exercise: You might try this cognitive exercise, which leads to a juxtaposition of a belief with the opposite.

Imagine a situation that annoys you. You have a belief that you were treated badly. Rate that belief according to how strongly you believe it to be true (out of 100%). Then write the negation or opposite of the belief. Then list all the reasons or proof that supports the negation. Then rate how you feel and what actions might be appropriate. Finally, rate how strongly you believe the original belief to be (out of 100%).

Gary was annoyed at a decision his supervisor made. He felt that he had been neglected in the process and his boss should have consulted with him. He expressed the belief: "My boss should have talked to me and made a better decision." He rated this at 90%. He then wrote the negation of this: "My boss didn't have to consult with me and made a wise decision." He then listed the reasons why this might be true: (a) It's his responsibility to make such decisions; (b) he might have consulted widely but not included me; (c) he may know some things about which I haven't been informed and see it from a different perspective; (d) and so on. Gary found himself feeling differently about the situation. He now rated his original belief to be 30% "and dropping" (adapted from Bernstein, 2010).

Reflect: Staying with the idea of an emotional learning statement is remaining cognitive to allow greater specificity. The sentence completion task allows this to happen. Once you arrive at your statement, you have a target to hit with the experiential exercises.

The juxtaposition of two opposites can help to resolve the original attitude, which can represent the pro-symptom position. This can lead to a reappraisal of the emotional learning. The idea of juxtaposition has been linked to neuroscience research in memory reconsolidation, which is outlined in Ecker's later work. There seems to be solid evidence that a deeply help emotional truth can be unlocked and rewritten by using juxtaposition experiences. This is illustrated in the following example.

Extended Case Example

The following case is used with permission.

Sally is a senior military officer. She's highly respected in her field and had responsibility for hundreds of soldiers in a training camp. She thought that her life was going well. "I had what I thought was a loving husband, two teenage children, and some very close friends. I also had a range of people I knew through a family movie club I attended with my children."

In a few months, things turned. Her husband announced he was leaving her. He had been having an affair, which shocked her, and he went to live with his new partner. Sally survived all this, but about six months later her three closest friends, for a variety of reasons, ended their friendships with her. One started to gossip about her at church, another moved to another city to pursue graduate studies, and the last became overinvolved in a romantic relationship. The new relationship took precedence and the girlfriend objected to his friendship with Sally.

All this devastated Sally. She became acutely suicidal and had to be admitted to a psychiatric facility. She was seeing a counselor, who did some good work on Sally's grief, but became worried about the suicidal crisis. I (Bruce) saw Sally at that point and worked closely with her family doctor and a psychiatrist, who prescribed an antidepressant medication.

Over the next year, I saw Sally more or less weekly. Some of my graduate students were also involved in counseling support. She made great progress. She was able to return to her military duties through a variety of psychological interventions, including exposure therapy. She seemed like she was almost fully recovered, and we were thinking about completing therapy. But then I thought about how intensely suicidal she had been. It was as if she held her life lightly, almost with no value. I worried that a similar crisis might occur in the future and then she would be highly at risk of suicide. It had been a close thing.

So I used sentence completion about why she felt she had to kill herself. I gave her the sentence completion "I need to kill myself because ..." The result was very surprising:

> "I am of value only to the degree I am helpful to others. If I need others, I become a burden. My overall worth is the balance; if it's negative, then I should kill myself to restore the balance to zero."

I wrote this on a card and she said that every word resonated as true for her. She was asked to read the card once a day for the next week. When I next saw her, she reported a huge shift. She said that the first sentence ("I'm of value only to the degree I'm helpful to others") felt about 40% true, but that the rest were not at all true (0%). She saw that previously her sense of self-worth was extrinsic and was now shifting to be intrinsic, and she felt freer. She revised her emotional learning to "I'm a valuable person because I have my own values, which I can satisfy without needing affirmation from others. I can make a valuable contribution without needing it recognized."

I had Sally visualize saying this to a crowd that included her ex-husband, children, parents, and siblings. She had made some new supportive relationships, and they were included as well. I asked if anyone was missing and she said, "I want to see me there, too." She added, "I need to hear myself say it." I could see a profound shift and I was finally satisfied that the risk of suicide was in the past. Her recovery, as far as I could tell, was complete.

To do: Ecker has written that the ultimate stage of separating from your family of origin emotionally is to hold to a different reality when in their presence. Can you articulate a different truth you have come to in your life? Can you imagine yourself seeing them at a future family gathering and saying that truth clearly?

> *Brian* was able to say to his father and stepmother, "I have felt put down by your comments over the years, and I came to believe it. But now I know I have value and that is recognized by others whose opinion I value."

Rehearse your statement in your mind and then see if you can say it. If you have a highly disconfirming family, it would be best to prepare for the family event with a therapist.

Applying such techniques will help you to have greater freedom in your intimate relationship.

It's All in Your Hand: Counting Down Numbers

To support your Healthy Adult in maintaining change processes, we offer you a simple tool that's always available: your hand, which probably has five fingers. Each finger represents one step to take from the pro-symptom position and the old maladaptive coping mode to a contra-symptom position and adaptive coping. The steps are as follows:

1. *Realize* you're in an emotionally activated state. What front stage coping mode does your automatic pilot suggest?
2. *Explore* the backstage motives. What emotional wounds or child modes and presuppositions and beliefs (or parent mode voices) are activated in the background?
3. *Try changing* into a Healthy Adult mode by taking an internal observer's stance. Stop for reappraisal. Distance yourself from your emotions, thoughts, and action impulses. Get in touch with your basic emotions, your needs, and the underlying activated systems. What do you really need? What are your long-term goals? What first steps point in the right direction?
4. *Breathe out* and let the old coping mode go.
5. *Talk to yourself*, supporting the right steps to take, like a good parent talks to a child, and do what has to be done to take the new road. Later, take a look at how your experiment worked.

Each time you find yourself at a crossroad with a juxtaposition of two opposite options, use your hand. Try to take the new road, even if the old one seems more familiar, broader, and easier. The new road takes you to higher ground. Just give it a try!

Conclusion

In this final chapter, we've gone as deep as we can go. We've encouraged you to explore the basic truths of your emotional learning and suggested many exercises to aid you in your discovery. Once you discover the dysfunctional aspects of such learning, you can see them clearly and address them. One way to do that is to set up juxtaposition experiences that you can use to rewrite previous emotional learning, an application of the idea of memory reconsolidation.

Lay new tracks in your brain! Understand what's there and you'll have solid ground for lasting, loving relationships.

To Read Further

- Cognitive exercises: Bernstein (2010)
- Emotional learning: Stevens (2016)
- Emotional learning and coherence therapy: Ecker and Hulley (1996), Ecker, Ticic, and Hulley (2013)
- Brain pathways: LeDoux (1996).

References

Bernstein, A. (2010). *The myth of stress: Where stress really comes from and how to live a happier, healthier life*. London, UK: Piaktus.

Ecker, B., & Hulley, L. (1996). *Depth oriented brief therapy: How to be brief when you were trained to be deep—and vice versa*. San Francisco, CA: Jossey-Bass.

Ecker, B., Ticic, R., & Hulley, L. (2013). *Unlocking the emotional brain: Eliminating symptoms at their roots using memory reconsolidation*. New York, NY: Routledge.

LeDoux, J. (1996). *The emotional brain: The mysterious underpinnings of emotional life*. New York, NY: Simon & Schuster.

Stevens, B. (2016). *Emotional learning: The way we are wired for intimacy*. Available as Kindle through Amazon.com or http://www.vividpublishing.com.au/emotionallearning/

Epilogue

This book has outlined a unified vision of relationships. This has been informed by a number of therapeutic approaches, including schema and coherence therapy. How does all this tie together?

It All Comes Together

We now have the main components for a model that ties together schemas, coping styles, and modes. This will also include Healthy Adult and emotional learning. Think about the interactions shown in Figure below.

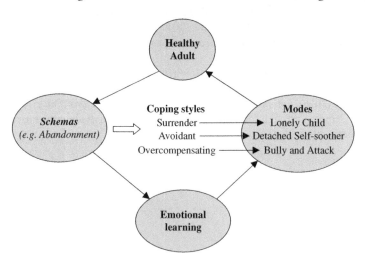

Breaking Negative Relationship Patterns: A Schema Therapy Self-help and Support Book,
First Edition. Bruce A. Stevens and Eckhard Roediger.
© 2017 John Wiley & Sons, Ltd. Published 2017 by John Wiley & Sons, Ltd.

The Healthy Adult mode is overall—it has an executive capacity to integrate and meet the needs of child modes. The schemas have developmental origins in childhood, in formative experiences, that shape our later emotional reactions. But schemas are not just vulnerabilities, or traits—they pass through coping styles and eventuate as activated schemas or mode states. You can think of this as a dynamic process shifting back and forth between the two poles of schemas and modes but through coping styles. You can begin with either schemas or modes and trace the steps. But deeper than this dynamic movement is the emotional learning that underlies it. This is a nuanced explanatory model bringing together both schema and coherence therapy.

And Finally

Your relationship can be enhanced on a number of fronts: building friendship, transforming maladaptive schemas into their positive, adaptive counterparts, recognizing modes and patterns of clashing, strengthening Healthy Adult, having fun with Happy Child (including through rituals), and relapse prevention.

By reading this book, you've gained a range of resources. You may have the support and wise guidance of a schema therapist to help you with your relationship, or not.

There's a sense in which this is all clay in your hands: You and your partner are the potters. What will you make of your relationship?

Index

Breaking Negative Relationship Patterns: A Schema Therapy Self-help and Support Book,
First Edition. Bruce A. Stevens and Eckhard Roediger.
© 2017 John Wiley & Sons, Ltd. Published 2017 by John Wiley & Sons, Ltd.

Printed and bound by CPI Group (UK) Ltd, Croydon, CR0 4YY

25/03/2025

14647327-0003